# Peter Maxwell Davies Studies

2009 marks the 75th birthday of Sir Peter Maxwell Davies, an occasion that presents an opportunity for reflection upon, and appreciation of, a period of compositional achievement that extends from the 1950s to the present. This book forms part of that reflection through a statement of the current condition of research on Davies's music. Detailed analytical discussions of individual works, such as the opera *Taverner* and the First Symphony, coexist with broader issues and perspectives; these include Davies's own writings about music, his engagement with sonata form, the compositional sources, problems of text, and the situating of this music within and in relation to 'modern times'. The book describes selected works from all periods of Davies's rich and diverse career, resulting in a portrait of the music that, while it may be incomplete, reveals the essence of this remarkable composer and his music.

KENNETH GLOAG is Senior Lecturer in Music at Cardiff University. His publications include books on Tippett's *A Child of Our Time* (Cambridge, 1999) and Maw's *Odyssey* (2008). He is co-author of *Musicology: The Key Concepts* (2005), and is currently reviews editor of the journal *twentieth-century music*.

NICHOLAS JONES is Lecturer in Music at the Centre for Lifelong Learning, Cardiff University. He has a specialist interest in contemporary British music and has written a number of articles on the music of Peter Maxwell Davies for *Music & Letters, Tempo* and the *Musical Times*.

# Peter Maxwell Davies Studies

EDITED BY

**Kenneth Gloag**

AND

**Nicholas Jones**

CAMBRIDGE
UNIVERSITY PRESS

CAMBRIDGE UNIVERSITY PRESS
Cambridge, New York, Melbourne, Madrid, Cape Town, Singapore, São Paulo, Delhi

Cambridge University Press
The Edinburgh Building, Cambridge CB2 8RU, UK

Published in the United States of America by Cambridge University Press, New York

www.cambridge.org
Information on this title: www.cambridge.org/9780521886581

First published 2009

Printed in the United Kingdom at the University Press, Cambridge

*A catalogue record for this publication is available from the British Library*

ISBN 978-0-521-88658-1 hardback

*In memory of John Warnaby (1942–2007)*

# Contents

# *Contributors*

## Editors

KENNETH GLOAG, Cardiff University

NICHOLAS JONES, Cardiff University

## Other contributors

DAVID BEARD, Cardiff University

PHILIP GRANGE, University of Manchester

GRENVILLE HANCOX, Canterbury Christ Church University

RODNEY LISTER, Boston University and New England Conservatory

RICHARD McGREGOR, University of Cumbria

PETER OWENS, Trinity Laban Conservatoire of Music and Dance, London

PHILIP RUPPRECHT, Duke University

ARNOLD WHITTALL, King's College, London (Emeritus)

# Preface

2009 marks the 75th birthday of Sir Peter Maxwell Davies, an occasion that presents an opportunity for reflection upon, and appreciation of, a period of compositional achievement that extends from the 1950s to the present and during which Davies has been at the forefront of musical life in Britain and beyond. The status of Davies as one of the leading international composers of the present is now generally accepted, with numerous recordings and a seemingly endless succession of high-profile commissions reflecting this status. Yet, while attention is drawn to some seminal studies of this music, such as David Roberts's thesis on Davies's compositional techniques, completed in 1985,[1] which is referred to throughout this book, and articles from Peter Owens, Arnold Whittall, Richard McGregor, Nicholas Jones, and John Warnaby, among others, there is still a notable shortage of extensive, informed studies of this music, with the collection of essays edited by Richard McGregor, published in 2000, still appearing as a somewhat isolated example.[2] Paul Griffiths's short book, an invaluable source, was published in 1982 and obviously does not reflect the composer's development after this point,[3] while Mike Seabrook's book is essentially biography and therefore cannot do justice to the musical detail.[4] While *Peter Maxwell Davies Studies*, in itself, cannot begin to address the absence of a fully developed discourse on this music, we are confident that it will provide a meaningful reflection of the current condition of research and suggest possible directions for future investigation and interpretation.

Each chapter is effectively a self-contained study that involves an engagement with a clearly defined subject that reflects the diversity of the music in terms of periods, genres, forms, techniques and related issues through a wide range of critical, theoretical and analytical interpretations and perspectives. It is clear therefore that this book does not seek to provide a comprehensive overview; rather the works, and related issues, that are selected for discussion reflect the current interests and approaches of the individual contributors.

[1] David Roberts, 'Techniques of Composition in the Music of Peter Maxwell Davies' (PhD thesis, University of Birmingham, 1985).
[2] Richard McGregor (ed.), *Perspectives on Peter Maxwell Davies* (Aldershot: Ashgate, 2000).
[3] Paul Griffiths, *Peter Maxwell Davies* (London: Robson Books, 1982).
[4] Mike Seabrook, *Max: The Life and Music of Peter Maxwell Davies* (London: Gollancz, 1994).

While important works, such as the First Symphony and the opera *Taverner*, for example, are selected for commentary from a number of different perspectives, inevitably some important works, such as *Eight Songs for a Mad King*, are not brought into focus in the way that a comprehensive overview of Davies's music would require.

Davies emerged in the 1950s as a young composer already aware of current developments in Europe, and sceptical of the conservatism of British music of the time; at this early stage of his career he put in place the elements of a rigorous modernist musical language. Early works such as the Trumpet Sonata and the Five Pieces for Piano, both of which feature extensively in Philip Rupprecht's contribution to this book, highlight the European, modernist context of the period, but they also give an indication of Davies's emerging individuality, with Rupprecht's explication of the 'thematic drama' of these and other works providing a telling insight into this emergent individual compositional identity. The early stages of Davies's career also involved recourse to the written word as a means of articulating ideas and concerns about music; the somewhat trenchant nature of his writing from this period is captured and contextualized in Nicholas Jones's contribution. Davies's role as an essayist and polemicist has not received the attention it deserves, and we expect that the complete listing of such writing as Appendix I will help stimulate further thoughts on this body of writings and its potential connection to the music.

During the 1960s Davies defined himself as a radical voice through innovative works such as the music theatre of *Eight Songs for a Mad King*, which situated his musical language on the sharp, avant-garde edge of modernism. However, the mid-1970s saw a turn towards more explicit historical forms and genres, with the First Symphony, which both is the subject of Kenneth Gloag's chapter and is discussed as part of Rodney Lister's overview of Davies's engagement with sonata form, in retrospect being seen as the opening of a path to the long sequence of genre-based works, such as the Strathclyde Concertos and Naxos String Quartets, the project that has come to define the latest stage of Davies's musical journey.

At each moment in that journey Davies has produced music that evinces both a powerful sense of drama, regardless of the context, and an immediate means of communication. However, as much of the emerging scholarship indicates, these qualities are constructed and articulated through an often highly complex level of musical structure and compositional technique: hence the relevance of Rupprecht's definition of 'thematic drama'. Issues of compositional technique and process are highlighted in a number of the contributions to this book. For example, Richard McGregor provides a detailed account of Davies's use of plainchant as the starting point of an often labyrinthine transformational process, and Peter Owens's description of textual issues in the published scores is based upon a deep understanding of the source material. We hope that the publication of the complete listing of Davies's usages of plainchant and other musical materials as compositional sources in the form of Appendix II, compiled by Richard McGregor, will help enable and develop further work in this area. The importance of the compositional origin and source is also evident in David Beard's interpretation of *Taverner*, Davies's seminal encounter with the operatic genre and a work that is pivotal in his development as a composer through the 1960s.

Davies himself was not invited to contribute to this book, but he is of course a constant presence, and not just as its subject. Davies, more than many composers, most likely unintentionally, has done much to shape the evolving critical discourses around his own music. His written commentaries on music, which, as Nicholas Jones demonstrates in his focused survey of Davies's writings of the 1950s, first emerge in parallel with the early stages of his compositional career, provide potential insights into the composer's thought processes. However, the music-literary form of the programme note, for example, increasingly presents signposts towards interpretation. Davies's programme note for the First Symphony, which was published as a text in *Tempo* and reprinted along with other programme notes in the Griffiths book, is a good demonstration of this.[5] This text gives 'clues' to the harmonic language of the work, through factors such as Davies's written references to contextually defined 'tonics' and 'dominants' and the 'ghost of sonata form' that invite the analyst to look in certain directions, an invitation that both Gloag and Lister, in different ways, respond to.

In conjunction with the direction towards interpretation that the programme note provides, the copious amounts of sketch material – drafts, pre-compositional plans, and so on – that are available provide a rich research resource, which several contributors to this book make great use of. However, the ready availability of such materials, in conjunction with the programmatic clues and signposts, can often ground the process of interpretation at the level of intent, which is valuable and insightful, but perhaps a future study of this music will start to go beyond this framework into new critical terrain through the cultivation of theoretical models and analytical strategies that are positioned at some distance from what the composer has to tell us about his work, and the documents that tell us how it might have been composed, and begins to explicate the music in and for itself. Of course, the possibility of music 'in itself' has, in recent years, become increasingly problematic, and either in dialogue with, or in contrast to, other approaches,

---

[5] Peter Maxwell Davies, 'Symphony', *Tempo*, 124 (1978), 2–5, reprinted in Paul Griffiths, *Peter Maxwell Davies*, 157–62.

we may begin to bear witness to an engaged, hermeneutic response to this music.

Such a response may start from the wide perspective of Arnold Whittall's contribution to this book, within which Davies's music is presented through an apposite comparison with Mahler and Berg, and refracted through the reference to Adorno. Even the most passing of references to the critical theory of Adorno may still stand as exceptional within the evolving study of Davies's music, but Whittall suggests the need to understand modernism as both a context and a concept in order to effectively situate this music; it is at this level of conceptual engagement that we anticipate new, critical responses may begin to be positioned. Scope for further approaches to this music may also be embedded in the sensitive interplay between source and interpretation that David Beard employs in relation to *Taverner*. Beard's chapter may come to provide a point of departure for studies that use the pre-compositional materials as part of a dialogue with the completed work within wider interpretative frameworks, with Beard's references to a draft of the libretto, which leads towards Jung, acting as a reminder of the multiple nature of what may actually constitute a source.

Other chapters in this book highlight the fact that Davies is not only a composer but also, as indicated above, a commentator on music, including his own. He is also a performer, directing performances and recordings of his own music, activities that are effectively summarized by Grenville Hancox. Teaching has also been important to Davies throughout his career, from working with schoolchildren at Cirencester to the development of young composers as part of the Dartington summer school and beyond, and the context of the Dartington experience is reflected in this book in the composer Philip Grange's personal recollection of, and reflection upon, that experience. The consideration of these activities helps provide other perspectives on the role of the composer as defined by Davies.

The various contributions to this book provide telling insights into the selected works and related issues, presenting a statement of current research and indications of future directions for the study of Davies's music. We hope it will be received as a healthy mix of differing responses to a wide range of music from one of the most fascinating composers of our time.

KENNETH GLOAG
NICHOLAS JONES

# *Acknowledgements*

We would like to express our gratitude to Victoria Cooper, without whom this volume would not have been possible, and the staff at Cambridge University Press, especially Rebecca Jones whose help and assistance have been invaluable. We also record our thanks to Nicolas Bell at the British Library, and to David Wyn Jones for his advice and helpful comments on this project. Finally, Nicholas Jones wishes to thank his wife and children for their patience and understanding, and his parents for their unfailing support of him and his work over the years.

All examples of Peter Maxwell Davies's published music are reproduced by kind permission of Boosey & Hawkes Publishers Ltd., Chester Music Ltd., and Schott & Co. Ltd., as follows:

*St Michael Sonata* © Copyright 1963 by Schott & Co. Ltd., London. Reproduced by permission. All rights reserved.

*Alma Redemptoris Mater* © Copyright 1965 by Schott & Co. Ltd., London. Reproduced by permission. All rights reserved.

*Leopardi Fragments* © Copyright 1965 by Schott & Co. Ltd., London. Reproduced by permission. All rights reserved.

*First Fantasia on an 'In Nomine' of John Taverner* © Copyright 1966 by Schott & Co. Ltd., London. Reproduced by permission. All rights reserved.

*Second Fantasia on John Taverner's 'In Nomine'* © Copyright 1968 by Boosey & Hawkes Music Publishers Ltd.

Sonata for Trumpet and Piano © Copyright 1969 by Schott Music Ltd., London. Copyright renewed 1997. Reproduced by permission. All rights reserved.

*Revelation and Fall* © Copyright 1971 by Boosey & Hawkes Music Publishers Ltd.

*Taverner* © Copyright 1972 by Boosey & Hawkes Music Publishers Ltd.

*Ecce Manus Tradentis* © Copyright 1978 by Boosey & Hawkes Music Publishers Ltd.

*Stone Litany* © Copyright 1975 by Boosey & Hawkes Music Publishers Ltd.

Symphony No. 1 © Copyright 1978 by Boosey & Hawkes Music Publishers Ltd.

*Hymn to St Magnus* © Copyright 1978 by Boosey & Hawkes Music Publishers Ltd.

Sonata for Piano Music by Peter Maxwell Davies © Copyright 1980 Chester Music Ltd. All rights reserved. International copyright secured. Reprinted by permission.

*Job* Music by Peter Maxwell Davies. Words from the Book of Job translated by Stephen Mitchell © Copyright 1998 Chester Music Ltd. All rights reserved. International copyright secured. Reprinted by permission.

*Veni Creator Spiritus* [for flute and bass clarinet] Music by Peter Maxwell Davies © Copyright 2003 Chester Music Ltd. All rights reserved. International copyright secured. Reprinted by permission.

Naxos Quartet No. 1 Music by Peter Maxwell Davies © Copyright 2004 Chester Music Ltd. All rights reserved. International copyright secured. Reprinted by permission.

Naxos Quartet No. 3 Music by Peter Maxwell Davies © Copyright 2005 Chester Music Ltd. All rights reserved. International copyright secured. Reprinted by permission.

Extracts from Davies's sketch material appear by kind permission of the composer. Exx. 3.11 and 8.17 are reproduced from Davies's sketches by permission of the British Library Board. Ex. 7.1 (a) is reproduced by kind permission of Harvard University Press from *The Historical Anthology of Music – Volume 1: Oriental, Medieval and Renaissance Music*, edited by Willi Apel and Archibald T. Davison, 2nd rev. edn (Cambridge, Mass.: Harvard University Press, 1949), No. 65: *Alma Redemptoris Mater* by Guillaume Dufay (primary source: *Denkmäler der Tonkunst in Oesterreich* (83 vols., 1894–1938), XXVII.I, p. 19).

Nicholas Jones would like to thank Francesca Kemp (BBC), Lee Taylor (British Library), Anthony Powers, Charles Wilson, Gill Jones, Judith Hurford (Cardiff University) and Judith Agus (Royal Welsh College of Music and Drama) for their help in preparing Appendix I.

# *References to* MaxOpus

In this volume, references to Peter Maxwell Davies's official website, *MaxOpus*, are given in the following format: www.maxopus.com. At the time of writing, however, *MaxOpus* is temporarily unavailable and undergoing reconstruction. As a result, many of the links cited in this book may be unavailable. However, an instance of the website (from 1 October 2006, when it was last updated) is available through the UK Web Archive. To access *MaxOpus* material through the Archive, the original URL needs to be prefixed with 'http://www.webarchive.org.uk/wayback/archive/20070131163627'. For example, www.maxopus.com/works/symph_1.htm thus becomes http://www.webarchive.org.uk/wayback/archive/20070131163627/www.maxopus.com/works/symph_1.htm.

# 1 'A dark voice from within': Peter Maxwell Davies and modern times

*Arnold Whittall*

## Aspiring, despairing?

The first part of my title, a quotation from Georg Trakl's *Offenbarung und Untergang* [Revelation and Fall] indicates a desire to pin down something fundamental in the aesthetic and cultural practice of Peter Maxwell Davies.[1] All artists for whom the societies and cultures of modern times are very far from ideal might be expected to make darkness a dominant image in their work. But dominant images do not operate by totally excluding alternatives, and the whole point of modernism, in art, is that tensions and dialogues between opposites are fundamental to both form and expression: tensions that may never fully resolve, dialogues that may never result in harmonious synthesis. In other words, darkness implies the coexistent presence of light – in a subordinate capacity, perhaps, but helping to support the claim that no significant work of art can (or should) leave an entirely negative impression.[2]

The phase of musical modernism that has unfolded since 1945 can be seen in terms of dialogues between many such opposites: the within and the without, the stable and the unstable, and so on. But no cultural commentator today can be content with such straightforward binary oppositions: the reductiveness of exclusive alternatives has been displaced by the network, the interactive continuum, with different shades of emphasis and degrees of intersection between contrasting elements. For a hint of what this can mean, we need look no further than Davies's note for the Fourth Naxos String Quartet (2004), and his comment that 'adult motives and implications, concerning aggression and war' impinge on the 'innocent childhood fantasy'

[1] This is a revised version of a paper given at the 'Peter Maxwell Davies at 70' study day held at Canterbury Christ Church College on 16 October 2004.

[2] Raymond Geuss, in his consideration of the relationship between Berg and Adorno, states that 'art by its very nature is affirmative. The very fact that an internally coherent, aesthetically satisfying work has been produced tends to promote reconciliation with the world' (Geuss, 'Berg and Adorno', in *The Cambridge Companion to Berg*, ed. Anthony Pople (Cambridge University Press, 1997), 43). Geuss has useful things to say about Adorno's problems with the 'nature' of art in this sense.

of the games depicted in the Breughel painting – *Children's Games* – that forms part of the composer's background to this work.[3]

A large number of interpretative networks will be brought into play in this chapter, and the first moves between the national and the international. After 1945, there was a common perception that nationalism was not only politically perverse but culturally regressive. Yet, as several significant commentators have argued, it was an important feature of such 'Year Zero' enterprises as Book 1 of Boulez's *Structures* for two pianos that extreme textural fragmentation could be heard as acknowledging, if not actually representing, utopian social and political ideals.[4] Many composers emerging during the early decades after the Second World War shared the aspiration to be both progressive and idealistic, and it is easy to detect an irony here, with brave talk of a new, genuinely anti-nationalist common-practice requiring the suppression of any suggestion that the essence of that style might be more Austro-German than truly supra-national.

In the 1950s it seemed easier for composers to distance themselves from Austro-German nationalism if the primary stimulus for progressiveness was Webern's post-expressionistic serialism rather than Mahler's late-romantic chromaticism. Yet Mahler proved to be as vital a source as Webern for late-modernist compositional initiatives after 1950: and that could well be because the presence of the unrefined vernacular alongside the elevated sophistication thought proper to high art was a fundamental feature of that Mahlerian fracturing of late-romantic organicism that had been central to musical modernism since early in the twentieth century.[5] It is therefore not surprising that two British composers who owe much to Mahler – Britten and Davies – should have demonstrated such resourcefulness in exploring another important twentieth-century stylistic continuum, the high (or cultivated) and the low (or popular): both composers also embraced the culturally functional – especially in music for young people and amateurs – while playing off the international against the local.

## Mahler, Berg, Adorno

In referring to stylistic as well as formal connections between Davies and Mahler, I am acknowledging a tradition in critical commentary that goes back

[3] Peter Maxwell Davies, liner notes to Naxos String Quartet No. 4 (CD, Naxos, 8. 557397, 2005).

[4] For example, see Mark Carroll, *Music and Ideology in Cold War Europe* (Cambridge University Press, 2003); Ben Parsons, 'Sets and the City: Serial Analysis, Parisian Reception, and Pierre Boulez's *Structures Ia*', *Current Musicology*, 76 (2003), 53–79 and 'Arresting Boulez: Post-War Modernism in Context', *Journal of the Royal Musical Association*, 129/1 (2004), 161–76.

[5] See T. W. Adorno, *Mahler: A Musical Physiognomy*, trans. Edmund Jephcott (Chicago University Press, 1992).

at least as far as 1965, when Stephen Pruslin claimed that 'the relationship between the musical thinking of Gustav Mahler and Peter Maxwell Davies becomes ever more apparent'.[6] This 'relationship' has been detected as early as the *Five Klee Pictures* originally written for Cirencester in 1960, and it was surely a factor in the composer's turning away from the kind of integrated, avant-garde progressiveness that his pre-Cirencester works display. One can well understand the appeal of Mahlerian polarities to a composer fascinated by the challenge of bringing the modality, flowing rhythms and conjunct voice-leading of plainchant and medieval music into meaningful confrontation with their post-tonal, fractured, expressionistic opposites. The result, as in the *Leopardi Fragments* (1961), is rather closer to the contemporary Italian lyricism of Dallapiccola's *Canti di liberazione* or Nono's *Ha venido* than to the more determinedly centrifugal textures of Boulez or Stockhausen. Pruslin saw the appeal of Mahler for Davies in the mix of cultural and musical factors; and (as Pruslin put it) a common concern with 'irony – not in its modern misuse as "cynicism" but in its original meaning of a sense of contradiction which is implicitly tragic'[7] – promoted the kind of allusions to Mahlerian materials and moods that Pruslin was the first to illustrate in detail. These allusions took on 'a crucial importance' in the *Second Fantasia on John Taverner's 'In Nomine'* (1964): although, in 1965, Pruslin considered the final climax of the *Second Fantasia* more in relation to Beethoven than to Mahler, he later referred to the *Second Fantasia*'s last section as a 'luminous Mahlerian adagio'.[8]

The Mahler association is important, and also long-lasting. For example, Roderic Dunnett, reviewing Davies's Seventh Symphony in 2000, claims that it 'contains as bewitching a Mahlerian adagio as any Davies has composed since the *Second Taverner Fantasia*';[9] the composer himself has noted that 'a passage in the development of the first movement of Mahler's 3rd Symphony' has left traces on the structure, if not the style, of the Fourth Naxos String Quartet.[10] But for me what helps to make the dark quality of the Mahler/Davies association as potent as its luminosity, at least in the works of the 1960s, is the way it suggests allusion to a further association, between Mahler and Berg. It is appropriate, then, that the version of Mahler proposed by Berg's pupil Adorno seems especially relevant to a consideration of this aspect of the Davies aesthetic.

[6] Stephen Pruslin, 'Second Taverner Fantasia', in *Peter Maxwell Davies: Studies from Two Decades*, ed. Pruslin (Boosey & Hawkes, 1979), 26.

[7] Ibid., 27.

[8] Stephen Pruslin, 'Nel mezzo del cammin – In Mid Flight', in *Peter Maxwell Davies*, ed. Pruslin, 4.

[9] Roderic Dunnett, Review of St Magnus Festival, *The Independent*, 21 June 2000, 12.

[10] Davies, liner notes to Naxos String Quartet No. 4.

As always, Adorno underlines the link between compositional technique and political ideology: Leon Botstein claims that Adorno recognized in Mahler 'the power of instrumental music to advance through its own material the cause of resistance to oppression: … Mahler realized this power by foregrounding radical discontinuities, aborted expectations, and formal innovations'.[11] As Peter Franklin has understood, an even more basic aspect of that emphasis on discontinuity is pinned down in Adorno's perception that Mahler's 'relentless quest after some sort of grounded certainty runs up against the spectre of its own wilfulness, its potential untruth. This results in a music that quite literally questions its own artfulness and thus progressively, modernistically presages its emancipation from myth and ideology'.[12] It is a music in which 'joy remains unattainable, and no transcendence is left but that of yearning'.[13] In such phrases, I think, it is possible to feel that Adorno might just as well have been writing about Berg, and I will return to the topic of Adorno on Berg later. First, however, I will discuss some of the potential relationships between Mahler, Berg and Davies's opera *Taverner*.

## Mahler, Berg, Davies, *Taverner*

A capsule representation of the chain of affinity between Mahler (Symphony No. 10), Berg (*Lulu*) and Davies (*Taverner*; 1962–8, partly reconstructed 1970) is shown in Exx. 1.1–1.4. In all three works, shown here in fairly drastic reduction, there is an anguished, aspiring melodic line, which rises rapidly through wide intervals without seeking to evade the basic metre. But there are differences as well as similarities. Mahler does not lose contact with tonality, and the thematic elements of his Adagio, however chromatic, remain within the voice-leading constraints of a musical world in which dissonance resolves onto consonance, and the melodic outlining of triadic intervals – not least the octave – is formally as well as expressively primary (Ex. 1.1).

Berg and Davies cross the great divide that separates Mahler's essentially traditional voice-leading from motivic processes stemming from the full emancipation of the dissonance. I am not claiming that there is conscious, intentional allusion to specific passages in Mahler by Berg, or to specific passages in Berg or Mahler by Davies: and there are many other aspects to the dialogue between convergence and divergence in these examples which

[11] Leon Botstein, 'Whose Gustav Mahler? Reception, Interpretation, and History', in *Mahler and His World*, ed. Botstein (Princeton University Press, 2002), 24.
[12] Peter Franklin, '"… his fractures are the script of truth" – Adorno's Mahler', in *Mahler Studies*, ed. Stephen Hefling (Cambridge University Press, 1997), 278.
[13] Ibid., 284. The reference is to Adorno, *Mahler*, 57.

Ex. 1.1  Mahler, Symphony No. 10, first movement, bars 16–23 (woodwind parts omitted)

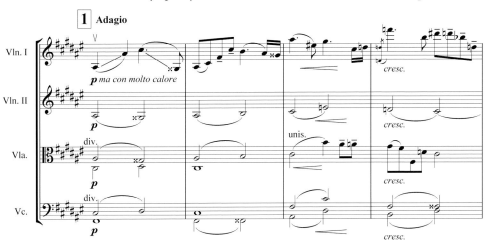

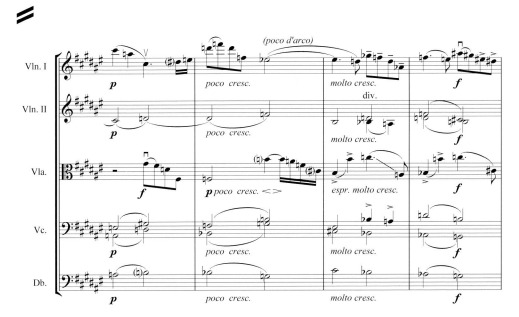

would need to be addressed in a full exposition of the subject. Nevertheless, I believe that this kind of stylistic affinity helps to create a special sense of affective affinity between Berg and Davies. Moreover, this affect, or mood, intensifies – and perhaps also distorts – the Mahlerian spirit. In both Berg and Davies, that Mahlerian spirit is loaded with additional irony and tension, in ways that are worth considering in a little more detail.

The Berg material (Ex. 1.2) is first heard in Act I, Scene 2 of *Lulu*. This traces the battle of wills between Lulu herself and Dr Schön, with the result that Schön's initial intention to end their relationship is overturned. The contest is played out against the musical background of a sonata-form

**Ex. 1.2**  Berg, *Lulu*, Act I, Scene 2, bars 622–6

Lulu:  Do you think I can forget it?
        Who except you in the whole world
        has ever paid me real attention?

Schön:  Leave me out of this!
         If you feel obliged to me, then ...

Ex. 1.3 Davies, *Second Taverner Fantasia*, bars 1089–98

structure, and the passage in question provides what Berg calls the 'coda to the exposition', running into the sonata's reprise shown at bar 625. Dramatically, the music accompanies the moment where Lulu's strategy of forcing Schön to change his mind begins to take effect. In relatively rapid speech, as if impersonating a dedicated and submissive fiancée, Lulu explains exactly what she owes to Schön, implying that he alone has 'paid real attention' to her, and treated her with genuine affection.

**Ex. 1.4**  Davies, *Taverner*, Act 2, Scene 4, bars 168–75

Berg's music for this passage does not preclude an interpretation that takes it at face value: as Douglas Jarman has written, 'above the intense and poignant Mahlerian Lento theme of the Sonata Coda … Lulu voices her indebtedness to Schön'.[14] But Jarman also notes that, 'on its reappearances during the course of the opera, the Coda theme will gradually acquire powerful, and … disturbing associations': and what seems especially 'disturbing' is the sound of its poignancy and intensity at moments that are sordid and horrific, such as Lulu's fatal transaction with Jack the Ripper. For Jarman, Berg's strategy is aimed at making audiences 'feel pity for and identify not only with Lulu and Geschwitz … but with all the characters helplessly trapped in this grotesque *Totentanz*'; 'the return of Schön's Sonata Coda theme … as an accompaniment to the … transaction between Lulu and Jack' underlines 'the difference between the luxuriant, elegiac music and the events on stage', producing 'an emotional disorientation that is deeply disturbing'.[15]

[14] Douglas Jarman, *Alban Berg: Lulu* (Cambridge University Press, 1991), 27–8.

[15] Ibid., 98.

Nevertheless, Jarman believes, 'it can also, if we respond to the music and are prepared to give these characters the understanding and compassion that the humanity of Berg's score demands, be humanly restorative'.[16]

In another commentary on the *Lulu* Coda music, Judy Lochhead gets closer to the Mahlerian features of technique and style that underpin this dark, disorientating conjunction of the sordid and the elegiac. Lochhead notes Berg's use of 'triadic sonorities that have tonal associations, and appoggiatura-like melodic figures',[17] and she concludes that 'the sound of the Freedom and Coda musics *parodies* a Mahlerian emotional content and undercuts any sense of an emotional authenticity that might attach to the dramatic situation'.[18] In this rather extreme way, if we follow Lochhead, Berg's subversive music enhances what Pruslin (with reference to the *Second Taverner Fantasia*) defined as that 'sense of contradiction which is implicitly tragic'.[19]

Exx. 1.3 and 1.4 show parallel passages from the *Second Taverner Fantasia* and the climactic stages of *Taverner* itself, where the *Second Taverner Fantasia*'s Lento molto is overlaid with the White Abbot's tormented but not unstoical valediction. Here we might also detect the conjunction of tragedy and irony, since the Abbot accepts his fate from within the distinctive musical context of the composer Taverner's own powerful conflictedness. And just as, in *Lulu*, the sense of unease and disturbance depends on aware-ness of parodied Mahler, so, with *Taverner*, we can feel a very palpable sense of distaste at the way the Abbot's fate has come about. Luxuriant, elegiac music seduces the listener, and it also, if Jarman's Berg model applies, inculcates a sense of moral responsibility: a kind of ethical awareness in face of such pressing contemporary problems as religious fanaticism and intolerance.

## Modernism: ethics and aesthetics

No commentator on *Taverner* has made this last point more eloquently than Mike Seabrook: describing the ending as 'deeply tragic, filled with pity, fear and lamentation', he sees the opera as asking the question: 'religious faith does this to people. Why?'[20] On the one hand, we might feel 'disgust at the spiritual repression at the heart of all religions made by men': on the other hand, we might feel that – as at the end of *Worldes Blis*, as Seabrook hears it – 'the violence and fury are always suffused and eased by a very Mahlerian

---

[16] Ibid., 100–1.

[17] Judy Lochhead, 'Lulu's Feminine Performance', in *The Cambridge Companion to Berg*, ed. Anthony Pople (Cambridge University Press, 1997), 235–6.

[18] Ibid., 237.

[19] Pruslin, 'Second Taverner Fantasia', 26.

[20] Mike Seabrook, *Max: The Life and Music of Peter Maxwell Davies* (London: Gollancz, 1994), 139–40.

compassion'.[21] My own view is that hearing Berg as well as Mahler at the end of *Taverner* gives the compassion embodied in the voice of the orchestra a darker, more ambivalent tone than it would otherwise possess: this darkness and ambivalence could seem even more salient if we believe that a musical style able to evoke love, sexual obsession, and all the complex resonances of personal feeling, is being used in a situation where feelings are primarily driven by matters of religion and politics.

Perhaps there is some common ground between *Lulu* and *Taverner* in the topics of courage and cowardice, the role of acts of betrayal and resistance in cultures that are in essence decadent. But however we hear it, the ending of *Taverner* seems to go farther than anything of Berg's – even the Violin Concerto – in underlining, rather than attempting to integrate or resolve, its disparate musical sources. What follows the Abbot's valediction embodies a shattering collision of styles and genres: the Lento's atonal expressionism, the chorus's modal chromaticism, and Taverner's own sixteenth-century modality are all involved, and the effect is rather like that described by Adorno in Schoenberg's String Trio, where 'a fully-constructed totality overlaps with the opposing impulse'.[22]

Obviously enough, the question of whether the various significations we can infer in Mahler, Berg and Davies are plausibly conformant is complex and open-ended. But I feel there is a strong case for tracing that particular high/low, ancient/modern network of genres and styles through into the theatre pieces of the 1960s and early 1970s, with their confrontations between expressionistic lyricism and avant-garde fracturing. Then, in the later 1970s, and after, it is possible to sense a shift away from the expressionist Mahler/Berg continuum to a modern-classic Mahler/Sibelius continuum, as the impact of things Northern grows stronger, and the Antichrist is masked by Saint Magnus. But to do justice to this dangerously reductive notion, we need to step back and consider what that perception of a shift of direction has to do with modern times – with modernism.

Studies of the modern in contemporary culture often ground themselves in Nietzsche, who foresaw so much of what is essential to a proper understanding of art and life in our own time – and not least in relation to time-honoured questions about the relative roles of the transcendent and the everyday. According to a recent commentary by Matthew Rampley, Nietzsche believed that, although 'art raises its head where religion recedes', modern art in *his* time was 'corrupted by the dominance of

[21] Ibid., 115.
[22] T. W. Adorno, 'Vers une musique informelle', in *Quasi una fantasia: Essays on Modern Music*, trans. Rodney Livingstone (London: Verso, 1992), 279.

metaphysics'.[23] Nietzsche was undoubtedly idealistic – even extremist – in arguing that art should turn its back on metaphysics, and seek to solve 'the problem of transcendence' by abandoning certainty for ambiguity. In this way the emphasis on ambiguity or multivalence in modernist art connects with the problematization of the transcendent, suggesting that while such art might not literally be able to redeem, it can certainly console. From this perspective, Wagner is the crucial musical precursor, and in 2004 the philosopher Roger Scruton penned a hymn of praise to *Tristan und Isolde*, precisely on the grounds that Wagner managed to redefine the sacred, the numinous, in ways appropriate to a world without God.[24]

This Wagnerian quality of folding the transcendent into the ambiguous is also, I would suggest, at the heart of Davies's later music: there could even be some connection with the Wagnerian adaptation of Schopenhauer's ideas about renunciation as a post-Christian form of redemption, in which the striving for transcendence is overlaid by a stoic sense of how humanity can find a degree of uneasy fulfilment in the world of nature. Just as Wagner was, for Nietzsche, 'the tragic poet of the end of all religion',[25] so Davies seems to engage very directly with the issues that arise when matters of religious and political beliefs – especially those concerning culture and the environment – come into alignment, and conflict, with modern-day aesthetic imperatives.

## The road to modern classicism

This sense of engagement is especially acute in those Davies works where we can detect a plurality of musical voices, some darkly anxious, others more aspiringly affirmative: as, for example, when the apparent certainties and confidence deriving from medieval, Renaissance and Baroque styles and techniques are subverted by an aura of late-Romantic or expressionist introspection. In one sense, this process of darkening embraces the 'spirit of negation' of that mythic Antichrist who 'is barely distinguishable from the real Christ and yet who embodies a total reversal of Christian precepts'.[26] The very harshness of the distortions that go with the depiction of the Antichrist can conjure up a music from the opposite extreme, of a deep, sorrowing, humanity. And yet – to restore the Nietzschean categories – a modernist art

[23] Matthew Rampley, *Nietzsche, Aesthetics and Modernity* (Cambridge University Press, 2000), 122.

[24] Roger Scruton, *Death-devoted Heart: Sex and the Sacred in Wagner's Tristan and Isolde* (Oxford University Press, 2004).

[25] Georges Liébert, *Nietzsche and Music*, trans. David Pellauer and Graham Parkes (Chicago University Press, 2004), 120, quoting a posthumously published fragment taken from Nietzsche's *Sämtliche Werke: Kritische Studienausgabe*, ed. G. Colli and M. Montinari (Munich: Deutscher Taschenbuch, 1980), Vol. 9, 591.

[26] Paul Griffiths, *Peter Maxwell Davies* (London: Robson Books, 1982), 55.

that remains 'ensnared within the trap of metaphysics' can still gain legitimacy from infusions of the 'biting coldness' of uncertainty and sorrow.[27] It is the search for 'biting coldness' in music that suggests Sibelius (or Sibelius interacting with Mahler) as one possible model: this shift towards a more Classical, less expressionistic containment might be further reinforced by the associations Davies has suggested between certain later works of his and the music of Bach and Haydn.

The bracing, centred austerity and sense of sceptical, Classical restraint that it is possible to find in Sibelius is not, I would suggest, completely absent from Davies's pre-Orkney music. For example, in the carols of *O Magnum Mysterium* (1960) a more contained idiom, conjunct melodically but still emancipatedly dissonant harmonically, offers a glimpse of the musical world that emerges more fully later on. In fact, *O Magnum Mysterium* as a whole could be the first work to embody the full range of features that established the composer's personal modernism. Most obviously, there is a contrast between the socially aware practicality of the carols and instrumental sonatas and the tough virtuosity of the concluding organ fantasia. Then there is a further polarity, between the modal vocal movements and the two instrumental sonatas. The first sonata has a lyricism of the kind that can be found in post-1945 Italian music – Dallapiccola, Nono – with a strong humanitarian quality. The second is more expressionistic, with its prominent percussion tattoos, while what the composer describes as 'a simple and graphic representation of the spread and intensification of the light of the Nativity' already has more than a shade of the complementary darkness that the concluding organ fantasia brings into the foreground.[28]

## Questioning the transcendent

In these ways *O Magnum Mysterium* aligns the lyric and the expressionist, and its allusion to sacred materials, in ways that lay bare the extremes of style that can coexist coherently, remains a fundamental factor thereafter. It is even possible to trace a path of affinity between the conjunct, chant-like modal melodies of *O Magnum Mysterium* and the thematic materials of much later works, including *Job* (1997) and the Mass (2002), and to align those materials with representations of pathos and melancholy in certain other composers. But the relation between social, cultural institutions and musical practices can never be straightforward. So it is especially fitting, in the era of late

---

[27] Rampley, *Nietzsche, Aesthetics and Modernity*, 127.

[28] Davies, programme note for *O Magnum Mysterium*, in Griffiths, *Peter Maxwell Davies*, 137.

modernism, that the questioning of tonality's identity and durability should proceed alongside a questioning of transcendence, the sacred, the conventions of religion. Just as Wagner, in Scruton's view, developed a notion of the sacred, the redemptive, to fit the human aspirations appropriate for a world without God, so Davies has annexed the words, images and musical materials originally associated with Christianity. He has used them, not to depict humans reaching out for salvation in Christ (along the lines of John Tavener's 'holy' minimalism), but to show – sometimes with scepticism – the human striving for personal fulfilment in the here and now: or, failing that, to suggest the human striving for at least a degree of that relative tranquillity that comes from finding an effective way of expressing one's sense of what humanity is worth, in a world where both God and nature can exercise a grandly malign authority. So, the 'intense musical and spiritual experience'[29] that the non-Catholic Davies hopes that people will get from his Mass could legitimately relate to aesthetic sensibility – to finer human feelings – rather than to spirituality in the specific religious sense of acknowledging, worshipping, the great mystery of a supreme being.

Despite the Mass's avoidance of stylistic strategies that turn plainchant towards the absolute opposite of fractured expressionism, an echo of the post-Mahlerian dialogue of aspiration and anxiety survives in its tonally unstable cadences. These use the familiar tensions between hierarchy and symmetry in ways that seem even more strikingly pointed than they often do in the composer's more abstract and expansive symphonic music. But it is a slightly earlier texted work which I will discuss in a little more detail, with reference to Exx. 1.5 and 1.6. Towards the end of *Job* the chastened protagonist, having been confronted with the vehement grandeur of God, poignantly expresses his reconciliation with mortality, in words that are transferred from the solo baritone to the chorus, as if humanity as a whole is echoing the conclusions of that single individual. The solo and choral passages are separated by an orchestral episode (between Figs. 37 and 39; see Ex. 1.5) in which what is textlessly expressed is, of course, ambiguous. In notes issued with the work's recording, David Nice argues that Job has been 'dazzled by his glimpse of the infinite', and that the 'rich orchestral postlude … reaches out again to that infinite'.[30] In this reading, then, the orchestral voice fills out Job's perception of the transcendent, reaching beyond his words into a visionary realm of pure sound.

Alternatively, the episode can be heard as a first-person comment from the composer that responds to the paradox of Job's last words – 'therefore I will be quiet, comforted that I am dust' – by not suppressing those elemental tritonal

[29] Davies, in Roderic Dunnett, liner notes to Mass (CD, Hyperion, CDA67454, 2004).

[30] David Nice, liner notes to *Job* (CD, Collins, 15162, 1997).

**Ex. 1.5**  Davies, *Job*, Figs. 36–39

Ex. 1.6 *Job*, concluding bars

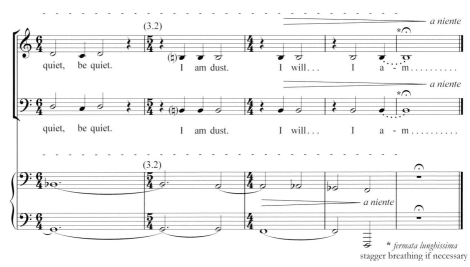

\* *fermata lunghissima*
stagger breathing if necessary

perspectives that could even imply that the sheer abjectness of Job's avowal of inadequacy is, from a modernist perspective, truly 'diabolical'. The music evolves from contained eloquence which stresses an initial B♭/E♮ polarity (at Fig. 37: see Ex. 1.5), to fiercely assertive dissonance around an F/B polarity (four bars after Fig. 38): and the music seems to suggest that consolation, the 'comfort' of an individual reconciled to his human fate, cannot completely suppress the impulse to resist, to rail against that fate. The final, choral setting of Job's words, which dies out with the words 'I will … I am' – B against F (Ex. 1.6) – reinforces the sense that even if active, violent resistance to the discomforts of humanity is no longer possible, the mind can still register both doubt and determination. This is certainly not an ecstatic, Isolde-like embrace of extinction, but a lament that compassionately turns away from the very transcendence that religion always claims to be on offer, accepting the dark voice from within as a permanent presence that can no longer be resisted.

## The consolations of nature

A fuller analysis of *Job*'s final orchestral interlude would show how its material evolves from the root stock of the initial choral chant, its voice-leading more conjunct and flowing than fractured and expressionist. The kind of orchestral song being sung here can certainly be paralleled in many other later Davies works, and these parallels are important, because they relate to two central topics of the Orkney years, which are to find consolation as well as challenge in nature; and to refuse to abandon all hope in forms of social progress while nevertheless turning away from utopian ideals and their unreal obsessions with perfection. You could even argue that, in *Job*, 'God' is more a force of nature than a divine being with human attributes.

As I have written elsewhere,[31] these ideas suggest certain parallels with the apprehensive yet stoical spirit we can find in the Sibelius of the Fourth and Sixth Symphonies and *Tapiola* – without, of course, the music sounding exactly like Sibelius. On the intertextual level, there is a similarity here to the situation in the first movement of the First Naxos String Quartet: when the composer says that 'Haydn looms large',[32] he is alluding to formal, generic affiliations rather than the kind of motivic, affective associations we can sense in saying that Mahler – and Berg – loom large in the final scene of *Taverner*.

Similarly, I think there is an important difference between the stylistic kind of associations between Mahler and Davies we can hear in the music of the 1960s and those more structural links with Mahler, and Schoenberg, that extend right through to the Naxos String Quartets. Still with reference to the ending of *Job*, we might feel that the composer's description of how the Fourth Naxos String Quartet ends applies here too: there is a sense of real if temporary resolution, and that element of the provisional, the unstable, seems to parallel the uneasy balance in the world between man and nature. Nature has not yet succumbed to man-made destructiveness, any more than, in music, tonality can be said, once and for all, to have died out. Hence the importance of place, as something sacred in the sense that it can offer the salvation of belonging, though not of course for an 'eternity'. But even when an optimistic vision of 'nature reborn' is proposed, as in the final chorus of

[31] Arnold Whittall, *Exploring Twentieth-century Music* (Cambridge University Press, 2003), 8–14.

[32] Davies, liner notes to Naxos String Quartet No. 1 (CD, Naxos, 8. 567396, 2004).

*The Turn of the Tide* (1992), the actual musical ending suggests that the dark voice of doubt cannot be completely silenced. As *The Beltane Fire* (1995), *The Doctor of Myddfai* (1996) and several other works indicate, the collective, social choice between survival or disintegration is still (just) open – but we also need to accept what with reference to *Tapiola* I have called the 'sublime indifference' of nature.[33] That nightmare – embodied by Davies most forcefully, perhaps, in the surreal climax of *Resurrection* (1987) – is never that far away.

In this context, it is useful to remember Adorno's characterization of Berg as a composer whose attitude was one of 'passive, melancholy resignation', reflecting 'the transitoriness and frailty of a world in which all structures crumble under their own weight'.[34] In Raymond Geuss's formulation, challenging Adorno, 'the basic sadness of his [Berg's] music shows that he is not "reconciled"; his "resignation" is that of a person who makes utopian demands on life and sees them eternally unsatisfied, but does not give them up'.[35] At the same time, however, as was noted early in this chapter, art is 'by its very nature … affirmative. The very fact that an internally coherent, aesthetically satisfying work has been produced tends to promote reconciliation with the world' – at least for a time.[36] Davies is certainly not a composer for whom legitimacy in art means being 'non-affirmative'. But his Classical and Romantic heritage, even when underpinned by still more stable qualities derived from medieval and Baroque models, ensures that any affirmation is as quizzical as it is intense. His relative closeness to the rhetoric as well as to the technical and generic aspects of earlier music makes his implied critique of those traditions the more telling.

This perspective reinforces the special individuality of his earlier style, and also highlights its later evolution in directions which are usually less expressionistic, with a strong sense of the local with which to contextualize, and problematize, those elements of the international (or non-national) that persist. Similarly, his continued concern with music as functional, accessible to amateur performers, interacts – often with a positive sense of unease – with the aspirational individuality and virtuoso demands of an unapologetic modernist. Perhaps there is a reflection here of that most powerful of all Mahlerian characteristics, in which the psychologically motivated striving for transcendence dissolves into contemplation of the beauty of nature, of the world here and now. All the same, I do not think we can expect a composer with present-day environmental concerns to match the most potent Mahlerian paradox: the suggestion, at the end of *Das Lied von der Erde*,

[33] See Whittall, *Exploring Twentieth-century Music*, 9.
[34] Geuss, 'Berg and Adorno', 47.
[35] Ibid.
[36] Ibid., 43.

that the ephemeral world is so beautiful that something eternal must lie beyond it. The most the present-day environmentalist can allow is the claim that if 'the warning is heeded' then nature can – might – still be 'reborn'.

In a characteristically sweeping comment on the difference between Tchaikovsky's representation of pathos in his Sixth Symphony and Mahler's in his Tenth, Timothy L. Jackson argues that the latter transfigures the nihilism of the former.[37] This kind of distinction may be hard to take, especially when placed in the often lurid psycho-sexual context preferred by Jackson; moreover, any attempt to extend the comparison from Tchaikovsky and Mahler on to Davies risks becoming laboured, if not ludicrous. Nevertheless, comparison can involve both similarity and difference, and the main difference between Davies and those earlier composers is in the way he sees and hears the concept of tonality. Even with the more conjunct melodic style and more explicitly centred harmony of the later works, Jackson-style extremes of nihilism or transfiguration are less fitting for Davies than the kind of ambivalent scenario that hears the dark inner voice of unease and menace behind the stoical, accepting pathos – rather as if the *Dies Irae* is underpinning a chant that hymns the Nativity or Pentecost.

## The classical and the modern

I am reminded here of Helmut Lachenmann's tribute to Luigi Nono, where he talks of the Italian composer's adoption and preservation, in the 1950s, of 'the traditional "big" expressive tone, the gesture full of pathos, lyricism, drama and emotion such as had been handed down from Monteverdi, Beethoven or Schoenberg'.[38] Lachenmann underlines the Schoenbergian aspect of structuralism serving expression, and he concludes that, 'at a time when false pathos is cheaply available, and we suffer from an excess of this and other empty forms of emotion – it is this very structuralist mutation which charges Nono's pathos with a mysterious power, a stringency which to this day forces the listener out of his indifference'.[39]

As with Nono, so with Davies: I believe that the power and stringency of what in *Job*, for example, I have defined as pathos is due to the particular interaction between a structuralism deriving from 'classic' serial practice and the composer's own personal perceptions about culture and society. And since these perceptions are inevitably about modern times, I would like to use

---

[37] Timothy L. Jackson, *Tchaikovsky: Symphony No. 6* (Cambridge University Press, 1999), 96.

[38] Helmut Lachenmann, 'Touched by Nono', *Contemporary Music Review*, 18/1 (1999), 20.
[39] Ibid., 20–1.

as my final context Julian Johnson's subtle and impassioned defence of the role of classical music in the modern world.

In *Who Needs Classical Music?* Johnson writes that

> art claims to fulfil what religious icons and the doctrine of transubstantiation once claimed: that a material object becomes more than the sum of its material parts, that it projects a spiritual energy. In this way, high art realizes, in secular form, what was once the domain of religion … [Art] does not necessarily deliver an experience most people would call religious, but art, even when it is most obviously concerned with the secular, implies something beyond itself, and in this sense it is metaphysical.[40]

It is important to Johnson's argument that this metaphysical dimension is not seen as somehow dehumanizing, a prelude to abstraction. Nor is commitment to religion a necessary condition for apprehending a metaphysical element: 'whether religious or not, we oscillate between the particularity of our lives and a larger, more universal whole … The capacity to exceed our limits is a basic condition of both art and humanity. It is for this reason that art is profoundly humane.' Moreover, Johnson's preferred context for the nature of art seems to turn from the metaphysical to the ethical and the utopian.[41] Near the end of his book he writes that art is utopian in the sense 'that it leaves us altered, tinged with a memory that things might be different or that things once were different'.[42] Yet Johnson also shows at least an inkling of the special qualities of post-tonal modernism when he acknowledges that 'classical music rarely offers a literal representation of a utopian, harmonious, and reconciled society': rather, it 'often presents a *metaphor* of reconciliation, one that expresses the complex competing voices of the self and society'.[43] And one of Johnson's boldest declarations is that 'art music of the last two centuries takes on the dissonance of the real world and transforms it. In that way it has a redemptive function.'[44]

Something of that essential idealism about art can be found in the views of Davies – for example, his claim that for a composer to succumb to commercialism is an act of betrayal; this suggests that it is not acceptable to speak (as some still do) of post-tonal music as a betrayal of the ideals of tonal classicism. Rather, what is involved is a notion of discipleship comparable to Schoenberg's, in which admission of debt is complemented by distance of style. If we apply the Schoenberg formula to Davies, we can trace a progression from a situation in many of his earlier works, where debt involves both style and structure, to one in the later music where other composers' styles are as distant as the styles of Brahms and Wagner are from the later Schoenberg.

---

[40] Julian Johnson, *Who Needs Classical Music?* (Oxford and New York: Oxford University Press, 2002), 87.
[41] Ibid., 116.
[42] Ibid., 127.
[43] Ibid.
[44] Ibid., 107.

In this respect, it might be argued that the space between Mahler and Sibelius (unlike that between Mahler and Berg) is a kind of stylistic no-man's-land, a space where a free-floating, chant-derived lyricism and a personal angle on modern classicism can come into their own. As the Naxos String Quartets confirm, the stormy and turbulent have not been eliminated from Davies's later music, but their energy is more contained, not least rhythmically, compared to the eruptions and explosions of the earlier scores. This modern classicism is therefore no betrayal of earlier classicism, but a continuation which learns from it: it is a demonstration of discipleship as a state in which the disciple can find the perfect freedom to underpin utopianism with dark, stoical realism. Contemplating the special strengths and challenges of this discipleship provides us with just one reason among many for celebrating the power, stringency and modernity of Davies's music.

## 2 The writings of a young British composer: Peter Maxwell Davies in the 1950s

*Nicholas Jones*

For over fifty years, the written word has been the medium through which Peter Maxwell Davies has articulated his views and concerns on a variety of subjects. These subjects have ranged widely from specific compositional matters to commentaries that reveal the composer's interest in, among other topics, music education, religion, the environment, and politics. Reflecting this diversity of subject matter, the writings themselves have appeared in a variety of different contexts and formats: journal and newspaper articles and letters, lectures and speeches, programme notes, libretti and texts, and broadcast talks.[1] Close scrutiny of these writings helps shed much light on the composer's main preoccupations and can generously reward those who wish to engage with a lively, intelligent, thought-provoking and, on occasion, provocative commentator.

This chapter focuses on Davies's writings of the 1950s. This was a crucially significant decade for the composer: it was the period when he established the fundamental elements of his technique; the decade in which he composed his first acknowledged works; and a time, coinciding with his emergence as a composer of substance, when he broke free from the confines of provincial Manchester and travelled to the Continent – to Darmstadt, the spiritual home of the post-1945 avant-garde, Paris and Rome. However, although our understanding of Davies's published musical works from this early period has benefited from close examination,[2] it is perhaps surprising, given the significance of this decade, that his written works have received relatively little scholarly attention.

This present discussion, which divides into two parts, aims to help rectify this situation by viewing this formative period through the prism of Davies's own writings. The first part chiefly reflects on Davies's articles, both published and unpublished, but also considers the composer's programme notes. Although I am occasionally content to leave Davies's words to speak for themselves (partly on the basis that they are not generally permitted such a

---

[1] For a complete listing of these writings, see Appendix I.
[2] See David Roberts, 'Techniques of Composition in the Music of Peter Maxwell Davies' (PhD thesis, Birmingham University, 1985) and Richard McGregor, 'Peter Maxwell Davies: The Early Works', *Tempo*, 160 (1987), 2–7.

luxury, and partly because they are quite simply interesting), my overriding concern – influenced by Alexander Goehr's belief that reading composers' writings requires a special sort of engagement[3] – involves asking pertinent, critical questions of them. The second part focuses on Davies's undergraduate thesis on Indian classical music, a very different type of text from those encountered in part one, but equally important. It is a text that is subject to critical commentary for the first time. This part of the chapter has a different perspective to that of the first in that it brings Davies's interest in Indian music into dialogue with his own music, in this instance the original version of *Stedman Doubles* (1955) – a strategy that can be seen as an oblique yet constructive response to another of Goehr's observations: 'Composers … do their real work with notes, and their writings have a point only insofar as they illuminate the notes.'[4]

## 'Looking the problems of composition in the face'

In the introductory note to his 1963 interview with Davies, Murray Schafer comments on how impressed he was with the composer's humanity, 'an unexpected quality in view of the pugilism of his public articles and talks on contemporary music'.[5] Indeed, Davies's early articles are notable for their potent immediacy. 'The Young British Composer', Davies's first published article, written when he was still a student at Manchester,[6] is entirely characteristic of his direct and 'pugilistic' writing style: punchy and intense, biting and sardonic. Davies's impassioned entreaty, 'Surely there are some young composers who are capable of looking the problems of composition in the face?',[7] is indicative of the article's pugnacious tone. But, in common with his writings in general, the article is also highly articulate and exceptionally persuasive, qualities that lend it a great deal of substance and credibility. Davies was motivated to write the piece as a response to Ernest Gold's article 'The New Challenge',[8] and Davies opens his article by directly addressing the main arguments put forward by Gold:

> Mr Gold is justified in acknowledging, in his article, the enormous difficulties facing anyone wishing to write good music today, but he blames the 'scientific approach' to composition for the dearth of convincing new music. Perhaps this does not take us to

---

[3] '[T]he writings of Schoenberg, Hindemith, Tippett and Boulez [should be regarded] as a separate genre of writing about music that is by its very nature different from professional critical or scholarly enterprises' (Alexander Goehr, 'Preface', in *Finding the Key: Selected Writings of Alexander Goehr*, ed. Derrick Puffett (London: Faber and Faber, 1998), vii).

[4] Ibid.

[5] Murray Schafer, *British Composers in Interview* (London: Faber and Faber, 1963), 173.

[6] Peter Maxwell Davies, 'The Young British Composer', *The Score*, 15 (1956), 84–5.

[7] Ibid., 85.

[8] *The Score*, 14 (1955), 36–40.

the heart of the matter. At least one reader suspects Mr Gold of finding a convenient scapegoat for a diverse host of evils – particularly as his suggestions for remedying these evils are somewhat unconstructive and negative.[9]

Going on to highlight this 'diverse host of evils', Davies sternly admonishes 'certain institutions' for inadequately equipping music students with an understanding of 'musical construction':

> One sees and hears so many conductors, performers, and, worst of all, composers, who obviously have no clue as to the construction of music, that one wonders just what they did in their colleges … If only they had had impressed upon them that they knew next to nothing, they might not be so keen to treat us to their appalling performances or their inane compositions, or to inflict their paltry knowledge on defenceless children in schools. As it is, the possession of a diploma is regarded as the license for all musical iniquities, and one is always mildly surprised upon meeting a knowledgeable musician who has one.[10]

Davies's views on music education, especially at primary and secondary school levels, are now of course well known and have recurred frequently in his writings and public lectures throughout his career.[11] Nevertheless, one would be hard pressed to find in any of his subsequent writings a passage to match the ferocity of his parting shot – a damning indictment of music education in mid-1950s Britain:

> There is really no 'New Challenge'. The challenge to the young British composer is the same as it always has been since Handel. He must study music, and treat it seriously. This is difficult in a country where almost nobody has the courage to face up to the fundamental problems involved in musical composition, or, to put it really bluntly, where music, with depressingly little exception, is composed, taught and practised in an amateur, and not in a professional manner.
>
>  The young composer must overcome these difficulties by himself. Only then can he possibly start to *compose*, with all the original wealth of meaning implied in that much abused word.[12]

Another key theme that becomes somewhat of an *idée fixe* in Davies's writings of the 1960s,[13] and one that is given its first public airing in this 1956 article, concerns compositional technique:

[9] Davies, 'The Young British Composer', 84.
[10] Ibid.
[11] See, for instance, 'In Classes Where They Sing and Play', *Times Educational Supplement*, 10 February 1961, 245; 'Music Composition by Children', in *Music in Education*, ed. Willis Grant (London: Butterworths, 1963), 108–24; and 'Music in Schools', Presidential Address to the Schools Music Association's North of England Education Conference, January 1985,

transcript available on *MaxOpus*, www. maxopus.com/essays/north.htm.
[12] Davies, 'The Young British Composer', 85 (original emphasis).
[13] See especially 'A Letter', *Composer*, 15 (April 1965), 22–3; 'The Young Composer in America', *Tempo*, 72 (1965), 2–6; 'Where Our Colleges Fail', *Times Educational Supplement*, 10 February 1967, 463; and 'Sets or Series', *The Listener*, 79 (22 February 1968), 250.

> Any composer worthy of the name can afford to take for granted the fact that he is expressing a 'fundamental human experience', and set about finding for himself the most suitable and convincing way of doing it. If he has any doubts about this, he should either stop composing, or convince himself, once and for all, otherwise he is guilty of fraudulent imposition on his fellows. If he cannot believe in himself, he should never try to persuade others to do so. His technique should come from exhaustive analysis of the music of not only the greatest composers, but as many of the others as he can manage. Most young composers are familiar with at least the most superficial aspects of Schoenberg, Bartók, Stravinsky, etc., – perhaps even of Messiaen or Stockhausen – but they know surprisingly little about more ancient composers – their training has led them to take for granted that they know all there is to know about them.[14]

The reference to 'ancient composers' here is obviously important, particularly when one bears in mind that certain aspects of his own compositional technique were – precisely at this time – being shaped and influenced by early music, an attitude that set him apart even from his Manchester contemporaries.[15] Yet Davies also mentions here that 'technique should come from exhaustive analysis of the music of not only the greatest composers, but as many of the others as he can manage' – a sentiment flexible enough to allow him not only to mention the names of more modern composers but also to nod reverently early on in the article to Bach, Mozart and Beethoven.[16]

Some of the themes expressed by Davies in 'The Young British Composer' are further developed in his next article, 'Problems of a British Composer Today'.[17] There is, for instance, a strong insistence on analysis and compositional technique, and, in a subsection titled 'Lack of Competent Composition Teachers', Davies asserts that 'Much of our so-called teaching of musical composition today is an accumulation of interest on vested ignorance' (564) – a position that, as will be explored in the next section of this chapter, was very much coloured by his own personal experience of composition tuition at Manchester University. However, Davies opens the article with an anecdote that paints a rather grim picture of concert life at the time. He explains that at a recent public performance in London of Schoenberg's Five Orchestral

---

[14] Davies, 'The Young British Composer', 85.

[15] As Davies recalls in interview with Richard Bolley: 'I remember even my colleagues, Birtwistle, Goehr and Ogdon being very suspicious of my liking for [early] music. And Sandy Goehr accused me of trying to escape from the realities of music (that was the kind of remark he used to make to provoke you!). But I think he was quite serious, because as far as he was concerned the real living tradition started with Bach' ('Ancient and Modern 3', *Early Music*, 8/4 (1980), 3). Richard McGregor discusses the influence of medieval music on Davies's works of the 1950s in 'The Early Works'.

[16] Davies argues, for instance, that the 'recently introduced "techniques of composition"' are 'ultimately much simpler than the technique of, say, Mozart, who is usually held up before us as the model of simplicity' ('The Young British Composer', 84). In his undergraduate thesis (discussed in the next section of this chapter), Davies treats the reader to some idiosyncratic commentaries on various aspects of Western music.

[17] Peter Maxwell Davies, 'Problems of a British Composer Today', *The Listener*, 62 (8 October 1959), 563–4. Further references to page numbers appear in the main text.

Pieces a large section of the audience 'simply found the music funny'. 'If an audience laughs at early Schönberg, how can it face the music of today?' Davies asks. By way of reply, he points out that very few audiences have been invited to listen to new music, and he concludes by suggesting that 'the English [i.e. British – he uses the terms interchangeably] have been living in a fool's paradise, in complete ignorance of recent and even distant musical developments' (563).

It will be worth pausing at this point to highlight a couple of contextual-biographical facts. Firstly, the reception of Davies's music in Britain up to this point had been, on the whole, rather less than favourable.[18] Thus Davies's markedly sour attitude is perfectly in tune with the given circumstances. Secondly, if one takes into account the cutting-edge musical experiences that trips to Darmstadt, Paris and Rome had afforded him,[19] Davies is evidently, and quite reasonably, reacting to what he considered to be the established insular and conservative musical tastes and expectations of British audiences, concert organizers, and critics.[20] So it is perhaps inevitable that in the article this attitude extends to British composers, some of whom, Davies argues, even deny that 'the old laws of tonality are dead'. He goes on to claim that British music has confined itself 'to repeating the gestures of nineteenth-century composers on the Continent, with a few superficial knobs from Stravinsky, Bartók, or jazz for good measure':

> I do not advocate, instead, an imitation of the gestures of the new 'Holy Trinity' of European music: Stockhausen, Boulez, Nono. But if we must not imitate, neither must we ignore the music of the young composers in Rome, Paris, or Cologne. Turning one's back on a crisis does not solve it.
>
> The lessons of Schönberg and Berg – in many instances of Bartók and Stravinsky – have not yet been learned in our country; but without taking the work of these masters into account, one cannot write music of any value today … The English, moreover, with their love of moderation and of the amateur, often prefer a dilettantish compromise to a deep but uncomfortable original work. As the music created by 'real' composers will gradually become better known, so the amateur works will disappear – to university music department shelves, there to moulder with the scores of Stanford, Parry and Bantock. (563)

---

[18] See, for instance, 'Workshop for Music: New Pieces by Young Composers', *The Times*, 6 March 1957, 3, and 'Two Works of Misguided Aim', *The Times*, 14 July 1959, 8; both authors are anonymous.

[19] In 1957 Davies won an Italian government scholarship and went to Rome to study with Goffredo Petrassi for eighteen months (see Davies, 'News and Comments: Italy', *The Score*, 22 (1958), 65 and 'Studying with Petrassi', *Tempo*, 225 (2003), 7–8). His time in Paris is discussed in the next section of this chapter.

[20] It is worth noting that this was at a time when, according to Paul Griffiths, 'new music' in Britain 'meant the later symphonies of Vaughan Williams or the operas of Britten, not *Le marteau sans maître* or *Zeitmasse*' (*Peter Maxwell Davies* (London: Robson Books, 1982), 15).

It is evident, then, that Davies has a certain amount of antipathy towards the composers of the so-called English Musical Renaissance, although he qualifies this by stating that the 'faltering steps' of Stanford and Parry are 'laudable, inspiring even, in view of the disastrous musical ignorance then prevailing in this country' (ibid.). However, Davies makes it very clear that there is no longer any place for nationalism in music – 'our problems are fundamental, general, international' – and urges composers instead to 'study Continental thought, understand it, absorb its principles, criticize them constructively, and, in the light of the experience of the music of the past, take the next step forward' (ibid.).

The central sections of the article – where Davies writes lucidly and authoritatively on Schoenberg, Berg, Webern, and total serialism – are most interesting because not only do they offer the reader Davies's current thoughts on such matters, they also bring to the fore Davies the educator (unsurprising, perhaps, given his appointment in January 1959 to the post of music master at Cirencester Grammar School). It is as if, aware of the paucity of information available for these composers, and possibly irritated by what he saw as an inadequate understanding of their compositional techniques, he takes it upon himself to provide what amounts to a lesson in recent musical history. Most interesting of all, though, is the critical stance taken against certain 'advanced styles of composition', particularly the most recent pieces of the post-war avant-garde:

> [T]he defects of total serialism are now realized by the initiators of the method themselves, who have in fact developed beyond that stage. The limitations of this kind of music are easy to hear. The extreme diversity of successive sounds dulls the ear's response, and in the end the effect is just the opposite of the intended extreme variety; it is monotony. (564)

Taking heed of his own advice, however, Davies's criticism proves to be essentially constructive. In the final section of the article – 'A Necessary Step' – he argues that there is something to be learned from total serialism: 'that rhythmic and dynamic serialism, applied to short note-rows, can be used to build up large musical structures whose relationships are clear to the ear. But there seems to be no more reason for using all the twelve notes' (ibid.).

Comments like these offer invaluable insights into Davies's own technical preoccupations at the time and have been used to help form a discourse around his music. Another rich source for scholars over the years has been the composer's programme notes, a practice that began in the 1950s. One of the most interesting notes from this decade is that written for *St Michael*, the sonata for 17 wind instruments composed in 1957, which received its first performance at the Cheltenham Town Hall on 13 July 1959. The programme note is lengthy and detailed and discloses much information, mainly concerning Davies's compositional technique, as this extract shows:

The orchestration is inspired directly by Gabrieli, but much of the technique of composition has earlier sources – in isorhythmic techniques, hocket, in the treatment of plainchant, etc. Various sections of the Requiem are used as cantus firmus throughout, although these are so absorbed in the texture and general style that they are seldom audible as such, except the Dies Irae in the second movement, and the Sanctus in the third.[21]

Davies then proceeds to make reference to a broad range of historical and technical terms. David Roberts has usefully grouped these references under five headings: terms associated with music of the eighteenth and nineteenth centuries (counterpoint, fugue, sonata, rondo, variation, allegro, moderato); terms associated with the music of the sixteenth and seventeenth centuries (madrigal, echo madrigal, verse anthem, reference to Gabrieli); terms associated with the music of the middle ages (plainchant, cantus firmus, isorhythm, hocket, mensural canon); terms associated with the serialist avant-garde (pantonality, series, note row, twelve-tone practice, montage); and references to extra-musical matters (Feast of the Consecration of the Church of St Michael, the Castell S. Angelo).[22] As Roberts rightly observes: 'In its density and wide range of references to musical history, it is an extreme case among Davies's programme notes; yet its strategy of casting a wide net of associations is typical of many of his other notes.'[23]

It comes as something of a surprise then, in 'Problems of a British Composer Today', not to find any mention of these historical and technical references, save those of the serialist avant-garde highlighted above. Indeed, one might have thought that Davies would make at least some reference to his interest in early music, as he had done in his 1956 article. Instead, he is content to focus entirely on more recent music, highlighting the various ways in which the young British composer can learn from it. It is perhaps not too difficult to understand why he chooses to adopt this strategy: he is obviously keen to offer his own perspective on the current domestic situation as a British composer who has first-hand experience of 'Continental thought' in a variety of contexts. Yet, as I have already noted above, he is certainly not unwilling to criticize some of this new music, and, moreover, seems happy to distance himself from it. As Davies's music of this period was at the time closely associated with Webern and the post-1945 avant-garde,[24] this position may at

---

[21] The programme note first appeared in the programme book for the 1959 Cheltenham Festival; it is reproduced in full in David Roberts, 'Techniques of Composition', 235–6.
[22] Roberts, 'Techniques of Composition', 237–8.
[23] Ibid., 236. Peter Owens has also noted that: 'With greater feeling for the function of such introductions to the general listening public, Davies has since reduced their analytical

content in favour of more approachable – though rather less specific – references to largescale form and extramusical imagery' ('Revelation and Fallacy: Observations on Compositional Technique in the Music of Peter Maxwell Davies', *Music Analysis*, 13/2–3 (1994), 162).
[24] This association was most strongly articulated in reviews, as in the following examples: 'From last night's programme of

first seem somewhat paradoxical. However, discussing his experiences at Darmstadt, Davies has recently explained that:

> Being interested in William Byrd and John Dunstable, and Mozart, Haydn and Beethoven, gave me a huge advantage over these people [at Darmstadt] because they had severed all of their roots, apart from Webern. I thought: yes, wonderful, I can learn a great deal from this, but underneath there is no root going into the ground, and any plant that doesn't have a root, with a bit of fertilizer, can flourish for so many hours or days, but then that's the end of it … But I tried to make something constructive out of it – learn what I possibly could, particularly from Stockhausen – and Luigi Nono, and Bruno Maderna, and Luciano Berio became very good close friends. But I still had this attitude of: yes, learn what you can, but beware.[25]

However, the assumed close association with the avant-garde most probably accounts for Davies's detachment in the 1959 article. Indeed, it may be argued that the overtly 'constructivist' tone of the programme note for *St Michael* – a note which undoubtedly (but inadvertently) further strengthened this association – impelled Davies in the article to clarify his position *vis-à-vis* modern serial thought: hence the key references to taking 'the next step forward' and there being 'no more reason for using all the twelve notes'. These key references are further explored in 'Formal Principles in "Prolation" for Orchestra', an unpublished article originally intended for inclusion in the music magazine *The Score*.[26] Here, Davies explains that:

> I find the twelve note series too difficult to work with, and at the same time be fully aware of all that is going on. Harmony is the main difficulty – there [are] too many notes to be clear-headed. As I can never hear a 12-tone series as such anyway, but only as a resultant melody, shape, harmony, etc., I see no objection to using another number of notes to the series, or to repeating any note, provided this is characteristic for the piece, and related to the basic idea and to all resultant ideas.

As one would expect from the title, the article offers detailed insights into the formal construction of *Prolation* (including the appropriation of the architectural

---

four works it was evident that not composition but construction is occupying composers' attention, and the works they bring forward are not even carpentry but bits of Meccano … Five piano pieces by Peter Maxwell Davies … made no sense. The medieval equivalents, hocket and isorhythm, were more efficient for formal organization than are these modern serial techniques' (Anon., 'Workshop for Music'); 'Peter Maxwell Davies's *St Michael Sonata* … was purely cerebral music. It employed devices from the Renaissance and the manner of Webern, eye music not conceived for the ear' (Anon., 'Two Works of Misguided Aim'); 'it was extremely difficult to make head or tail of this abstruse music [*St Michael*], which gave the impression of having been constructed with the aid of a slide-rule and tabulator' (Dyneley Hussey, 'The Cheltenham Festival', *Musical Times*, 100 (September 1959), 472).
[25] Davies in conversation with the author, London, 21 January 2008.
[26] The article 'Formal Principles in "Prolation" for Orchestra' is in Add. Ms. 71311, fols. 17–23, together with a draft of Davies's analytical programme note for the first British performance of *Prolation* (24 October 1960). *The Score*, founded and edited by William Glock, was published quarterly from 1949 to 1961.

principle of *Übergreifende Form*),[27] but the opening paragraphs also provide further thoughts on some of the topics that evidently preoccupied him through-out the decade – the importance of analysis, the significance of 'Webern's miniatures', and the problems that faced the contemporary British composer.

Another significant topic, but one that is absent from all the writings discussed so far, is that of Indian classical music. As it transpired, Davies would not publicly declare his interest in this music until the late 1960s:

> While a student at Manchester University, I wrote a thesis for my bachelor's degree on Indian music. Despite its title, borrowed from campanology, the influence of Indian music is very clear in my *Stedman Doubles* written at that time – 1955.[28]

In spite of this statement, however, no serious work has been carried out on Davies's study of Indian music and its impact on his own music. In fact, what little comment there has been has tended to underplay its significance. For instance, Roderic Dunnett has recently written that:

> Although its idioms have not significantly impinged on Max's [Davies's] music (in the way that certain works by Britten or Messiaen were directly influenced by Balinese gamelan music), Indian music did play a minor part in one or two very early works, notably the *Stedman Doubles*. It is possible that the expressive linear role of the sitar in Indian ragas, and the tabla's accompanying commentary of shifting rhythms, fused with Max's deep interest in medieval polyphony so as to exercise some *indirect* influence on the music Max was to compose years later, and in particular on the methodical patterns which have always been central to his music.[29]

Although the essence of this verdict is certainly reasonable, I would argue that Davies's study of Indian music in the 1950s had a much more profound effect on him and his music than this would seem to suggest; indeed, it crucially enabled him to bring new perspectives and methods to his own developing compositional technique, and these have stayed with him throughout his career. To understand such concerns, it is necessary in the first instance to examine carefully Davies's 1956 undergraduate thesis, 'An Introduction to Indian Music'. And so it is to this important text that the discussion will now turn.

## A 'midnight' *rāga*

'An Introduction to Indian Music' is a remarkable achievement for an under-graduate student. Being in the region of 28,000 words, and supported by

---

[27] For a detailed discussion of this principle at work in Davies's Third Symphony, see Nicholas Jones, 'Peter Maxwell Davies's "Submerged Cathedral": Architectural Principles in the Third Symphony', *Music & Letters*, 81/3 (2000), 402–32.

[28] 'Peter Maxwell Davies on Some of His Recent Work', *The Listener*, 81 (23 January 1969), 121.
[29] Robert Dunnett, 'Maxwell Davies: A Portrait', booklet notes to *Peter Maxwell Davies: A Portrait: His Works, His Life, His Words* (CD, Naxos, 8.558191–92, 2006), 27.

forty-three pages of musical examples, it is by far the longest and most substantial single written text that Davies has ever produced. It is appropriately scholarly in tone, methodically researched, and meticulous in its detail.[30] As the work has not hitherto been subjected to in-depth discussion in the published literature, a brief overview of its structure and contents would be useful at this point.

Volume I of the thesis is divided into three parts. Part I consists of three chapters: 'Preliminary', 'Legend and History' and 'The Theoretical Scale'. Part II, by far the most substantial component (*c.* 21,000 words), has separate chapters for 'Rāgă', 'Tālă',[31] 'Ornamentation', 'Musical Instruments', as well as a brief chapter titled 'Notes on Three Individual Composers'. Part III consists of a 'Conclusion' and two appendices – the first, to support and illustrate the third chapter in Part I, outlines several Indian legends; the second, to be discussed shortly, briefly considers Messiaen's interest in Indian rhythm. Volume I concludes with a bibliography which lists twenty books, including two classic examples of comparative musicology: A. H. Fox Strangways's *The Music of Hindostan* and Alain Daniélou's *Northern Indian Music*.[32] Volume II consists of the supporting music examples, of which there are thirty-seven.

Before I start to examine the importance of this thesis in relation to Davies's development as a composer and, more specifically, in relation to the music he wrote as a result of this study, it is certainly worth considering the reasons why he chose Indian music for the topic of his thesis. Davies's choice of topic may at first seem highly unusual; more appropriate and obvious topics immediately suggest themselves, such as medieval or Renaissance music, or the music of Schoenberg or Bartók. It seems, though, that the decision to choose Indian music was prompted by an unexpected source: Humphrey Procter-Gregg, Davies's composition teacher at Manchester University. Procter-Gregg cultivated rather conservative musical tastes: he actively

---

[30] Davies, 'An Introduction to Indian Music', 2 vols. (Mus.Bac. thesis, University of Manchester, 1956). It is even more remarkable when one discovers that Davies had no supervisor – the research and writing up of the thesis was carried out entirely on his own (Davies in conversation with the author, London, 21 January 2008).

[31] In writing Indian words in Latin script, Davies indicates the lengths of certain vowels: 'long syllables are marked with a stroke ( ¯ ) placed over the vowel, and vowels marked with a ˘ sign are hardly pronounced at all' (Vol. I, Part I, 6). When quoting passages from the thesis I preserve Davies's practice, but Indian words in my own text appear italicized and,

when necessary, with macron marks, as in *rāga* and *tāla*.

[32] A. H. Fox Strangways, *The Music of Hindostan* (Oxford: Clarendon Press, 1914); Alain Daniélou, *Northern Indian Music*, Vol. I: *Theory and Technique* (London: Christopher Johnson; Calcutta: Visva Bharati, 1949) and Vol. II: *The Main Ragas* (London: Halcyon Press, 1954). The authority and scholarly integrity of these books have, in recent years, been brought into question, so Davies's reliance on these texts (Daniélou especially) has to be treated with caution. I am deeply indebted to John Morgan O'Connell for discussing a number of issues pertaining to Davies's thesis and its relation to the field of ethnomusicology.

advised his students to avoid listening to any music written before 1550, and considered all music written after Delius as 'not worth bothering about'.[33] In an interview with Roderic Dunnett in 2006, Davies sketches a rather acrimonious student–teacher relationship:

> I was very soon thrown off the composition course because I was far too interested in 'dangerous composers' as he [Procter-Gregg] would term them, like Stravinsky and Bartók, Vaughan Williams and Benjamin Britten – not to mention Schoenberg, Webern and Berg: I didn't dare mention those people to him! … So I had to do a piano recital and write a thesis for my honours degree … [Indian music] interested me, but I think the main point was that it was something that Professor Humphrey Procter-Gregg knew nothing about, and I had to persuade him that this was his idea that I should do this thing and eventually he suggested it to me after being fed various information and I readily accepted that this was something that I would do for my thesis.[34]

Davies's decision to study Indian music was, then, a rather astute rejoinder to Procter-Gregg's highly difficult character and entrenched musical conservatism. But, as the above quote suggests, this decision was no knee-jerk reaction on Davies's part: the comment that Procter-Gregg 'eventually … suggested it to me after being fed various information' implies that the whole process was a relatively protracted affair. But it was the acquisition of several 78r.p.m. recordings of Indian music and 'the "Hindu" influence of Messiaen' that proved to be the main impetus behind his decision to choose the subject.[35]

By 1955, Davies had become very well acquainted with the music and compositional technique of Messiaen. He had closely studied (and played through on the piano) most of the scores that were then available, including Messiaen's music from the 1930s, the *Vingt regards sur l'enfant Jésus*, and the *Turangalîla-Symphonie* (a score of which was lent to him by Alexander Goehr). In April 1954, he heard on the Third Programme a performance, conducted by Walter Goehr, of the *Turangalîla-Symphonie*, and during the academic year 1955–6, Davies made several visits to Paris to stay with Alexander Goehr (who was then a registered member of Messiaen's class at

[33] See Mike Seabrook, *Max: The Life and Music of Peter Maxwell Davies* (London: Victor Gollancz, 1994), 36. In 'The Young British Composer' (85), Davies was to criticize unreservedly this style of approach: 'Perhaps even more insidious … is the reactionary [composer], who rejects all recent developments, and produces music which is often a pale imitation of some revered idol. This mentality still flourishes in Britain, and is largely responsible for the teaching of composition. It would not be so terrible if these teachers knew something about older music, but almost invariably they know no more than the most commonplace superficialities.' Although Procter-Gregg is of course not named, the subject of Davies's vitriol is somewhat obvious.

[34] 'Max Speaks: A Recorded Interview', *Peter Maxwell Davies, A Portrait: His Works, His Life, His Words* (Naxos, 8.558191–92), CD2. Procter-Gregg (1895–1980) was Professor of Music at Manchester University from 1954 to 1962.

[35] The source for this information is my conversation with Davies, London, 21 January 2008; Davies's Messiaen quote is taken from 'Recent Work', 121.

the Paris Conservatoire), and sat in on several of Messiaen's classes as an *auditeur*.[36] In the bibliography for the thesis, Davies lists Messiaen's influential *Technique de mon langage musical*, a treatise that includes a chapter on 'Hindu Rhythm' and a brief section on 'Hindu Ragas'. And in the second appendix of the thesis, Davies briefly offers examples of Messiaen's application of Indian rhythm in the *Quatuor pour la fin du temps*. He also makes reference to part of an article by David Drew that appeared in the December 1955 issue of *The Score*[37] that highlights another typical example – in Davies's words – 'of the composer's original (if un-Indian!) application of Indian rhythm' in the first movement of the *Turangalîla-Symphonie*. Davies goes on to suggest that what Drew draws attention to is a procedure that 'is a very far cry from the tālă which is at its root', and concludes by suggesting that 'Perhaps it is a little unfortunate that the tālă chosen is obsolete, and is probably incorrectly "realised" in our European note-values!' – this latter point being substantiated by Davies in a detailed footnote.

As already noted, Davies's sardonic tone is typical of his writings of this period, but its (mild) use here is highly revealing: it is clear that he is somewhat disapproving of Messiaen's 'inauthentic' approach to Indian music. In the 2006 interview with Dunnett,[38] Davies expands on this belief commenting that, at a time when he was getting to know for the first time the music of Messiaen and his interest in Indian music, he found it 'very constructive – instructive – to compare *his* way of thinking and *my* way of thinking about Indian music and being influenced in a totally different way'. According to Davies, Messiaen's approach was 'very theoretical' and 'very stylized' because he took his experience of Indian music 'entirely from books';[39] Messiaen also 'misunderstood certain basic techniques of Indian music, particularly to do with rhythm'. By contrast, Davies points out that he himself 'was in touch with people [at Manchester] who did play *rāgas* or sing or did play *tablā*, and they knew what they were about … my attitude had to be different'.

[36] A registration list of Messiaen's classes from 1941 to 1978 can be found in Jean Boivin, *La Classe de Messiaen* (Paris: Christian Bourgois, 1995), 409–32. Davies's entry is on page 418, but the date given, '1954–5', is incorrect. I am very grateful to Davies for confirming the correct date as 1955–6.
[37] 'Messiaen: A Provisional Study (III)', 41–61. Parts I and II of this substantial and detailed analytical article appeared in the December 1954 and September 1955 issues of *The Score*.
[38] 'Max Speaks: A Recorded Interview'.
[39] This view is supported by a number of sources. For instance, in his *New Grove II* article on Messiaen, Paul Griffiths states that 'central to [Messiaen] was Indian music, as mediated by the Lavignac encyclopedia. There he discovered the *jātis* and *deçi-tâlas* (melodic shapes and rhythmic formulae) catalogued in Sanskrit treatises, and these he used in most of his works, beginning with *La Nativité* (1935)' (Griffiths, 'Messiaen, Olivier', *New Grove Dictionary of Music and Musician*s, 2nd edn., ed. Stanley Sadie and John Tyrrell (London: Macmillan, 2001), 16, 495). However, John Morgan O'Connell and Nigel Simeone have pointed out to me that Messiaen and Daniélou knew each other, so their association (especially the extent of Daniélou's influence on Messiaen, if any) would need to be carefully examined.

Experiencing Indian music and engaging with it in a live and interactive context is wholly characteristic of Davies's restless, enquiring and practical mind. Indeed, there were many occasions during the 1950s when he went out of his way to experience the live performance of music, be it Renaissance music at the Cathedral and the Church of the Holy Name in Manchester, the Byzantine liturgy at the Grottaferrata Monastery, or plainchant in various Benedictine monasteries in and around Rome.[40] And so it comes as no surprise to discover that music example 35 in Volume II of the thesis is a transcription of a song that Davies himself dictated from an Indian student at Manchester University. One feels that by employing a pragmatic approach, Davies is in some way imbuing his whole enterprise with a sense of 'authenticity' – that he is being more 'sincere' to the music by experiencing it in its rightful performing and listening environment. Such an approach seems remarkable for the time, but equally one must be circumspect – Davies's notion of authenticity, specifically in relation to Indian music, is in itself questionable on several levels. But it seems that Davies was well aware of this, and in the thesis he is careful to qualify his approach with a caveat:

> Such a study as this cannot hope to be more than an introduction. To equip oneself to write an exhaustive book on Indian music, one would have to go to India and study music at first hand. In England, the best one can do is to hear gramophone and radio performances, and sometimes performances by Indian students studying in this country. One can also, of course, study the books available on the subject.[41]

Davies's interest in this obscure and intricately complex topic was highly unusual for the time, predating by a decade the public appetite for such music. This inevitably leads one to question Davies's role in the whole process: to put it frankly, what was in it for him? The following statement – made just before the caveat – seems to hold the key: 'The purpose of such a study is not only to examine an alien culture … but to *provoke thought*, in the light of what we find, pertaining to music in general, and to our own music in particular' (Vol. I, Part I, 3; original emphasis). This observation indeed seems to be the crux of the matter. It is as if he is saying: 'What musical elements from Indian music can we bring to bear on contemporary Western classical music?' Or, put another way: 'The purpose of such a study is to *provoke thought* pertaining to my own music.' And provoke thought it certainly did: whilst at university, Davies composed several pieces that were consciously influenced by his close study of Indian music. Although some of these pieces were

---

[40] See Davies's interview with Richard Bolley, 'Ancient and Modern 3', 3 and 5. In 'Problems of a British Composer Today' (563), Davies also advocates this approach to contemporary music, arguing that in Britain 'even people who pretend to a musical education often know nothing about [contemporary musical] developments beyond a few abstract generalizations which are not backed up by any real experience in sound'.

[41] Vol. I, Part I, 3. Further page references will be made in the main text.

destroyed by the composer when the Society for the Promotion of New Music rejected them,[42] several have survived, including *Stedman Doubles*, the piece that most vividly displays the influence of Indian music.

The original version of *Stedman Doubles* – the version on which the following discussion is based – was completed in February 1955. Scored for clarinet and three percussion players, this two-movement work was composed for fellow students at the Royal Manchester College of Music (now the Royal Northern College of Music); it was considered unplayable, however, and 'had to languish for more than a decade, when it was drastically revised [in 1968] for the Pierrot Players … and performed in a much slimmed-down version, for clarinet and one percussionist'.[43] The original score was rediscovered by Davies in the early 1990s when he was preparing sketches and scores to be sent for permanent housing at the British Library; subsequently the score was 'reconstructed' for its first performance, at the Royal Northern College of Music, in November 1995.[44] Lack of space precludes a comprehensive investigation of this work; therefore the following discussion will focus on the first movement, reasons for which will become clear in due course. But before I come to this, it is first necessary to outline the four main elements of Indian music that were to impact most significantly on Davies's own music, both at the time and subsequently.

Firstly, he was attracted to the form of the *rāga*.[45] The following, as discussed in the thesis (Vol. I, Part II, 15–17), outlines Davies's own understanding of the form:

> A performance of a rāgă traditionally takes the form of a series of improvisations on a preconceived plan. These improvisations are a series of free variations on the basic melodic shapes associated with the rāgă selected. Before the performance proper, there is a long prelude, usually called 'ālāp', in which the player or singer, unaccompanied save for the drone [usually the *tambūrā*], prepares his listeners for the experience which will follow. The tempo is slow …

He continues to explain that the entrance of a simple rhythmic pattern on the drums signifies the end of the *ālāp* and the start of the performance

---

[42] See Davies, 'Recent Work', 121.

[43] Quoted from Davies's programme note for the original version of *Stedman Doubles*, written for the premiere recording of the work by Psappha in 1997 (*Fantastic Islands*, CD, British Music Label BML 026).

[44] The original version remains unpublished. The British Library catalogue call numbers for the sketches and ink score for this version are Add. Ms. 71373 and 71374. The revised 1968 version was published by Boosey & Hawkes in 1978. In effect, then, the piece exists in three versions: the original

1955 and revised 1968 versions, and the 1995 reconstructed version, the second movement of which is a conflation of the two earlier versions.

[45] In the thesis, Davies explains that 'Indians use the word "rāgă" to mean two distinct things. First, it can signify all the notes employed in a composition arranged consecutively in the form of a scale … The second meaning is … difficult to define, but may be described roughly as the "mood" of the rāgă – the word originally meant "passion" or "mood"' (Vol. I, Part II, 2).

proper. At this point the soloist states a two-part theme, the first part of which is called *astaī* or *sthāyī* (Sanskrit words for 'at home'); the second part is called *antarā* (in this context meaning 'change of register'). The *sancāhrī* or *caranum* follows the statement of the theme. Davies explains that 'Both these terms mean literally "moving about", but in this context they are best translated as "development", although nothing like the development of a sonata is implied.' He continues: 'The pace of the music becomes faster and faster, the rhythm becomes ever increasingly complex, and the melodic ornamentation ever more profuse and fanciful.' The final section, known as the *ābhog* ('coda'), 'is simply a method of "putting a full stop" at the end of the piece, of indicating that it is finished'.

Secondly, he was drawn to the intervallic relationships that exist in the *rāga* scale, namely between the tonic (which is not only 'felt' throughout the *rāga*, but also sounded throughout on the drone) and its two predominant notes, the *vādī* (the note most used when playing, heard most prominently in the *astaī*), and the *samvādī* (the note a fourth or fifth above the *vādī*), heard most noticeably in the *antarā*). The idea of having a tonic and 'companion' notes (which are not necessarily a fourth or fifth away from the tonic) is indeed interesting, particularly when one relates this to Davies's singular understanding of 'tonics' and 'dominants' as employed in his own music. It is, of course, well beyond the scope of this present discussion to explain Davies's notion of 'tonality' *in toto*; in any case, I have discussed this in detail elsewhere.[46] It will be sufficient to mention here that, in the programme note for the First Symphony (1973–6), Davies states that the idea is fundamentally related 'to medieval techniques, where a modal "dominant" is not necessarily a fourth or fifth away from the "tonic"'; later, in a note for the Second Symphony (1980), he describes the system as a 'basic unifying hypothesis' – the symmetrical partitioning of a tonal procedure into minor thirds and tritones.[47] It is indeed tempting, then, to understand his concept of tonality as a synthesis of Indian, medieval and nineteenth-century techniques. But such a proposition is clearly provisional and will of course require further, detailed investigation.[48]

Thirdly, he was very interested in the manner in which Indian music has the ability to manipulate time. In his 1969 *Listener* article, Davies explains that by studying Indian music in the mid-1950s, he realized that:

---

[46] See Nicholas Jones, 'Dominant Logic: Peter Maxwell Davies's basic unifying hypothesis', *Musical Times*, 143 (Spring 2002), 37–45, and 'Playing the "Great Game"? Peter Maxwell Davies, Sonata Form, and the *Naxos* Quartet No. 1', *Musical Times*, 146 (Autumn 2005), 71–81.

[47] Both programme notes are reproduced in Paul Griffiths, *Peter Maxwell Davies* (London: Robson Books, 1982), 157–62 and 171–4.

[48] It is, however, worth pointing out here that Davies himself accepts this synthesis proposition, as long as it is understood that it exists in productive tension with the concept of the tonic–dominant relationship in common-practice tonality (Davies in conversation with the author, London, 21 January 2008).

the rate of the unfolding of events, and the whole concept of form in Indian music, is not a sequence of closed – or enclosed – events or periods, but that the forms, on both small and large time-scales, are open, defining themselves as they unfold in a way that not only, particularly in slow alaps, concentrates one's attention on each individual pitch and rhythm relationship with maximum intensity and tension, but also bends, or even suspends, perception of the 'passing' of time, so that the formal terms 'too slow' or 'too long', which in western music can be used so often with complete justification, can have no application to such music.[49]

Finally, and arguably most important, he was fascinated by the absolute concentration in Indian music on melody and rhythm. As he states in the thesis:

> It will be readily appreciated that, to compensate for the lack of harmony, with its features of varied spacing of chords, modulation, harmonic rhythm, etc., melody itself has had to develop to a degree amazing to us. The melody and rhythm must be as potent as the harmony of western music …                    (Vol. I, Part II, 3)

This interest in the centrality of melody and rhythm in Indian music connects logically and meaningfully with Davies's other interests at the time: the use of *color* and *talea* in medieval music; Messiaen's use of artificial modes and rhythmic experimentation; the serial organization of note rows and rhythm; and plainchant, especially 'the whole concept of how [it is] transformed and decorated'.[50] This latter point is of some significance. In the thesis, Davies argues that an intimate connection exists between the way in which plainchant is constructed and the manner in which melody is constructed in the *ālāp* section of a *rāga*. The following passage, which concludes a lengthy and detailed analysis by Davies of a specific *ālāp* melody, clarifies this relationship:

> This melody is in certain respects quite remarkable. It gives an impression of very free construction, of being composed as it unfolds. Despite this, it follows laws of construction which give it perfect balance, with no note out of place, and the way in which it builds up a powerful climax is perhaps surprising to us, both in its effectiveness and its extreme simplicity. In European music, the nearest approach to this style is plainchant, or sixteenth century church music, which, polyphonic though it is, often shows similar methods of melodic construction.     (Vol. I, Part II, 24)

One can readily appreciate that the notion of a melody that 'gives an impression of very free construction' but in fact 'follows laws of construction' is one that would have greatly appealed to a serial composer like Davies; it is a notion that can be extended to embrace further parameters, to the extent that much of his music from this decade and beyond gives the impression that it is freely constructed but is in fact rigorously planned and internally coherent.[51]

---

[49] 'Recent Work', 121.
[50] Davies, in conversation with Richard Bolley, 'Ancient and Modern 3', 3.
[51] This sentiment is also confirmed by McGregor: 'it is interesting to note that the set-progression [in the first movement of the Trumpet Sonata] is palindromic (as is the second of the Five Piano Pieces, op. 2). Here we glimpse the essence of Davies's compositional ethos – apparent freedom in a rigid technique' ('Early Works', 3).

Equally fascinating and revealing, however, is the painstaking analytical detail that Davies wrings from the *ālāp* melody itself. It will be remembered from the discussion in the first section of this chapter that in the articles from the 1950s Davies emphasizes the central importance of music analysis when training composers. It is also worth noting that analysis was a much underrated activity in British musical education in that decade. Yet, going against the grain, Davies's thesis is notable for its many instances of analyses of early and classical Western music, in addition, naturally, to Indian music. To offer an example of the latter, this discussion will now spotlight Davies's analysis of the *ālāp* melody mentioned above; I will then use this discussion as a springboard to explore the extent to which the formal concept of the *ālāp* is projected onto the opening section of *Stedman Doubles*. Davies's analysis is too long to be reproduced here in full, but the following extract – besides offering a typical example of Davies's analytical style – demonstrates the deep regard he had for this music and the fascination it held for him:

[Ex. 2.1(a)] shows the scale of rāgă Bihāgă, according to Daniélou.[52] [It] … is considered one of the most moving of all rāgăs. It is played at midnight.[53]

[Ex. 2.1(b)] is an ālāp from *50* [recte *30*] *Songs from* [the] *Panjab and Kashmir* of Ratan Devi.[54] An ālāp, it will be remembered, is the slow unmeasured prelude to the performance of a rāgă. This example illustrates admirably the way in which this is normally composed, making every interval 'tell' – so perhaps a fairly detailed analysis is not out of place. This ālāp was vocalized to vowels, very slowly, the dashes in [Ex. 2.1(b)] marking the pauses for breath.

The first part of the melody, up to the double bar, has an exploratory character – one feels each new note in the descent to the low F marks a major event, an achievement. One feels too that the music literally grows – first there is a long held C [the tonic], then another note, B, is added. This step, C–B, is repeated, with an ornament on the C. With the repeat of this ornament, the music gathers momentum, and pushes down to low F, emphasizing the step A–G on the way with a mordent on A. The lead from the B to F is repeated, with a more elaborate ornament on the A. Here, across the end of one phrase and the beginning of the next, occurs the characteristic feature, mentioned by Daniélou, of a second, F–G, followed by a major third, G–B, said to express longing.[55] This occurs several times in the ālāp, always across the phrase in this manner. The figure which leads the music from low G (fig. I) back to C, marked with a bracket, is important, becoming a sort of 'refrain' throughout the rest of the ālāp.

---

[52] Davies is making reference here to Vol. II of Daniélou's *Northern Indian Music*.
[53] Several draft pages of Davies's thesis can be found in British Library Add. Ms. 71443, fols. 42–5. *Rāga Bihāga* is described on fol. 44v as 'a midnight rāgă' – hence the origin of the title of this subsection.

[54] Trans. Ananda K. Coomaraswamy, foreword Rabindranath Tagore (London: Old Bourne Press, 1913).
[55] According to Daniélou (*Northern Indian Music*, Vol. I), many phrases and intervals in Indian music correspond to an 'index' of expressive qualities. For instance, in ascent, C–D is said to be 'confident, brilliant', C–F♯ conveys 'desire', and so on.

**Ex. 2.1**  Davies, 'An Introduction to Indian Music', Vol. II, Ex. 11

[♯ above note = microtonal inflection upwards by 1/8 tone]

… At fig. VII a repeat of the refrain would have been possible; perhaps it is even half-expected. However, tension is immediately increased by a repeat of the high B [in fig. VI], approached not as before, very carefully by step, but directly, with the leap of a seventh from the tonic C. It is a characteristic of Indian melody that leaps like this occur only after the interval has been taken by step. The climax of the ālāp is on the two high Cs, or perhaps more accurately, on the second high C, which is trilled. There is a sensation of great achievement upon arriving at this point, on the upper tonic – the whole piece, from fig. II, has been climbing towards it.

The descent to F following the trilled C recalls the first line of the piece, and is followed by a varied repeat of the refrain, transposed up an octave (fig. VIII). The final C of this figure is now reduced to a crotchet, and the refrain forms only the first half of an arc, which ends at fig. IX.

The final phrase, consisting of a slowly descending scale, uses the B♭ discussed above,[56] with telling effect. As the ālāp would normally be followed immediately by the astaī, it need not necessarily close with a tonic. This example closes with an echo of its opening, the fall from C–B.                                    (Vol. I, Part II, 20–4)

If one compares the observations made here (and earlier) with the opening section of *Stedman Doubles* (Ex. 2.2), then some notable correspondences start to emerge. To begin with, many of Davies's comments – such as 'making every interval "tell"' and 'has an exploratory character' – can be similarly applied to this 10-bar opening. The tempo is slow and the section has an unmeasured quality to it, being devoid of a well-defined pulse – the combined result of which (to recall Davies's own words) helps to bend, or even suspend, the listener's perception of the 'passing' of time. The clarinet line 'grows', note by note, interval by interval, from the dark richness of the instrument's chalumeau register (where minor seconds and thirds lend the line a smooth contour) to the more uneasy, disjunct character of bars 9–10 (where sevenths are prominent). Far from the line being 'free in construction', its durational organization and twelve-note serial structure ensure that it follows 'laws of construction'. The basic twelve-note set $(P_0)$[57] and successive set-statements $(P_1$ and $R_4)$ can be traced through this opening section (see Ex. 2.2). It can also be observed from Ex. 2.2 that the pitch class D functions as a sort of 'tonal anchor', for not only is it the first note in the set, it also appears markedly *before* the statements of both $P_1$ and $R_4$ in bars 5 and 8 respectively. (This D tonic in fact can be 'felt' throughout the work, especially towards the end of the second movement.)

Durational working pervades the piece, including, as one would expect, the compositional device used by Davies in all of his serial works: the incremental progression of a given durational unit. An example of this can be seen in

---

[56] Davies states that the *rāga Bihāga* occasionally uses B♭ in descent (Vol. I, Part II, 21).
[57] The first four notes of this set, as the sketches indicate, are derived appropriately from the chromatic *rāga Pilū* (see Add. Ms. 71343, fol. 83r). The same sketch also informs us that notes 5–8 are notes 1–4 in 'backwards inversion'.

**Ex. 2.2** Davies, *Stedman Doubles* (1955 version), first movement, bars 1–10

bars 2 and 3 (Ex. 2.3) where the durational unit of a semiquaver increases from 1 to 5. One can also see in Ex. 2.3 that other durational manipulation occurs in these opening bars: the first tetrachord of $P_0$ has the durational proportions of 3(if one includes the rest):1:3:2:1 (the repeated note); this is reproduced, in the final three notes of $P_0$ and the first of $P_1$, in retrograde (dovetailing with the end of the incremental durational progression to account for the repeated note) by the proportions 1:2:3:1:3. In the sketches,[58] Davies's rhythmic workings suggest that this rhythm is based on the Indian 10-*mātrā* ('count') rhythmic cycle of *Jhapatāla* (see Ex. 2.3).

Closely related to the incremental durational method already described is the procedure found in bar 6 (see Ex. 2.2): here, the semiquaver unit grows throughout the bar (from 1 to 4), with Davies adding one semiquaver at the appearance of each new note in the set-statement. However, this procedure (like that described at the end of the previous paragraph) seems more likely to be connected to Davies's interest in Indian rhythmic processes, an interest that is explicitly reflected in the work's subtitle, 'Two Rhythmic Studies for

[58] Add. Ms. 71373, fol. 83r.

**Ex. 2.3** *Stedman Doubles* (1955 version), first movement, bars 1–4, clarinet part: durational working

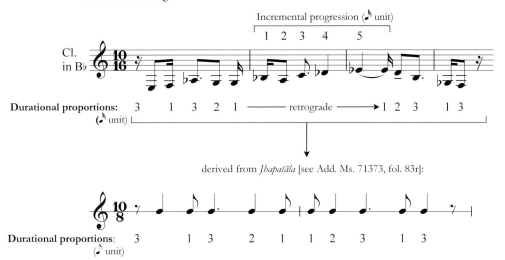

**Ex. 2.4** *Stedman Doubles* (1955 version), first movement, bars 42–9, percussion only

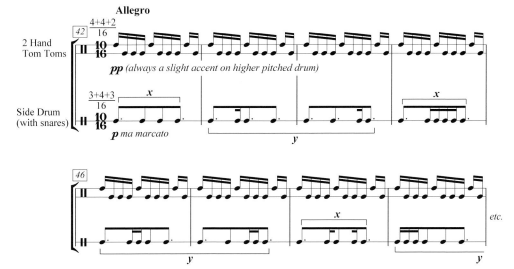

Clarinet and Percussion', written on the title page of the original ink score.[59] One can gain a good idea of Davies's interest in this area by reading the chapter on *tāla* in the thesis. He seems to have been especially interested in *tālas* whose unit – a quaver in this example – 'grows throughout the bar, adding one quaver at each appearance' (Vol. I, Part II, 53). Davies's own adaptation of this can be seen in the procedure found in bar 6 and in numerous examples elsewhere. There is also evidence in this movement of a more 'conventional' use of *tāla*. At the start of the Allegro section (Ex. 2.4),

[59] Add. Ms. 71374, fol. 52r.

**Table 2.1** *Stedman Doubles* (1955 version), first movement: *rāga* structure

| Rāga sections | ālāp | astaī | antarā | sancāhrī | ābhog |
|---|---|---|---|---|---|
| Bar numbers | 1–10 | 11–29 | 30–41 | 42–99 | 100–03 |
| Tempo | Adagio non troppo | | | Allegro | Lento molto |

for instance, Davies introduces on hand tomtoms a rhythmic cycle consisting of a fixed number of *mātrās*: a 10-*mātrā tāla*, subdivided 4+4+2 (bars 42–55 and 93–99), 3+4+3 (56–69), and 5+5 (70–92). One can also see in the side drum part in Ex. 2.4 rhythmic experimentation *à la* Messiaen, with the alternation of non-retrogradable rhythmic cells (*x* and *y*). The time signature for this movement – 10/16 – is also worthy of consideration. In the thesis, Davies states that 'Indian music often baffles western listeners by its complex rhythms, especially those of 5, 7, 10, 11 or even more units to the bar. Indian musicians have a great fondness for rhythms which cannot be arranged into symmetrical divisions of 2 or 3' (Vol. I, Part II, 38). There are plenty of examples in the work as a whole to suggest that Davies was reflecting this sentiment by the composition of intricate rhythmic patterns and cross-rhythmic effects.

The influence of Indian music can also be seen to affect the work's overall formal organization. Indeed, the factors already highlighted serve as potent indicators to suggest persuasively that the first movement's opening 10-bar section should be understood as Davies's own interpretation of an *ālāp* – a 'translation' from the original Indian context into a new and unique Daviesian context. It will be remembered from Davies's own outline of a *rāga* performance that the entrance of a simple rhythmic pattern on the drums signifies the end of the *ālāp*. The entrance of the drums in Davies's piece occurs at the end of bar 10 (see Ex. 2.2) – further evidence to suggest that he considered this gesture as signalling the end of his *ālāp* section (he even uses a double bar line). If one continues to map the formal landmarks of the *rāga* (as outlined by Davies in his thesis) onto the first movement of *Stedman Doubles*, then the overall structure – the sections of which are not of course 'improvisations' in the normal sense of the word – may be interpreted as that set out in Table 2.1.

There is abundant evidence in this movement, then, to support Davies's claim – quoted above – that 'the influence of Indian music is very clear in my *Stedman Doubles*'.[60] However, although there is a vague timbral evocation of the 'exotic' in the piece, it needs to be understood that Davies was not interested in merely replicating the distinctive soundworld of Indian classical music: the clarinet is not an instrument used in Indian music; neither is there any use of Indian percussion instruments in this original version (although

---

[60] 'Recent Work', 121.

*tablā* and *mridangam* are used in the revised version). Instead, as this discussion has attempted to make clear, he was much more concerned with how the processes of Indian music – like those he discovered in medieval music and later in aboriginal music[61] – had some practical application in his own music.

Davies's close study of Indian music, as so impressively demonstrated in his innovative thesis, left an indelible mark on his own music and compositional technique. As Davies himself explains:

> I wrote a String Quartet [in 1952], which has now gone, but a fragment of it still survives [Quartet Movement] – it was reconstructed from some sketches and is still played. This is *so* influenced by Indian music – it sounds like a Europeanized kind of Indian music. But I think it [the influence of Indian music] has permeated deeper than that; it's just there, through everything.[62]

The implications of this comment are profound. It strongly implies that any serious investigation into the works composed in close proximity to the Quartet Movement and *Stedman Doubles* – especially the Sonata for Trumpet and Piano, Five Pieces for Piano, and *Burchiello* (the unpublished three-movement piece for 16 percussion instruments, composed in August–September 1955) – and some of those composed in the next decade – such as *Hymnos* (1967) and *Worldes Blis* (1966–9),[63] pieces written around the time of Davies's revision of *Stedman Doubles* – would need to take into account the influence of Indian music if all the technical and aural nuances of this music are to be appreciated and understood in their entirety.

## *Ābhog*

The writings of Peter Maxwell Davies clearly hold much significance and interest for a number of reasons. The first part of this chapter reflected on the articles and programme notes of the 1950s and revealed the many ways in which these texts can shed light on both the composer's main preoccupations during this decade and the general musical climate in which Davies lived and worked. The second part took a different angle and used one of Davies's texts as a way into the music itself. The very nature of this chapter has meant that my discussion of *Stedman Doubles* has been relatively brief,

[61] See Davies, 'Influence of Aboriginal Music', *MaxOpus*, www.maxopus.com/essays/aborig.htm.
[62] Davies in conversation with the author, London, 21 January 2008.
[63] The opening twenty-minute section of *Worldes Blis* has something of the *ālāp* about it. With regard to *Hymnos*, Davies is explicit: 'The writing for clarinet and piano is extremely virtuoso, not only in the obvious sense but also in the matter of exact timings of long paragraphs precisely related by complex proportions, as sometimes occurs spontaneously in Indian classical music' (programme note for *Hymnos*, *MaxOpus*, www.maxopus.com/works/hymnos.htm).

my exploration of Davies's own understanding of Indian music knowingly provisional – there is much work still to be done in this area. However, the overall strategy employed in this chapter has demonstrated that there is much to be gained from close engagement with Davies's writings, particularly given the fact that the ideas and concerns expressed in them share powerful common ground with the ideas and concerns articulated through his music.

# 3    Thematic drama in early Peter Maxwell Davies: from Op. 1 to the *First Taverner Fantasia*

*Philip Rupprecht*

The play of musical themes has always been central to Peter Maxwell Davies's music. Sharply profiled thematic ideas inhabit the landscape, one in which vivid contrasts of line, shape and mood drive the argument forward, even when textures are densely contrapuntal. As early as 1956, reviewers were noting that the Op. 1 Trumpet Sonata's 'strict and complex system of interchangeability of melodic and rhythmic shapes ... managed to suggest burning impulse and spontaneity', and the score was praised, accurately enough, for being 'assertive and exuberant'.[1] Such comments identify the kind of interactions among characters and contrasts of mood one might properly consider 'dramatic' in instrumental music, and Davies himself has often asserted the central role of both theme and drama in his scores. In the later 1950s, he publicly criticized the fragmentary gestural effect of works by the European avant-garde, noting how 'extreme diversity of successive sounds dulls the ear's response'.[2] Observing that 'counterpoint and melody, as distinct dimensions, had largely disappeared in Webern', Davies urges a rejection of fully chromatic serial schemes; simpler pitch groupings, he asserts, can enhance musical 'interest and even drama'.[3] In a 1967 radio discussion, Davies told Alexander Goehr, 'I don't think my musical material is ... all that far removed from Mozart', a point he substantiated with analytic comments on phrase-rhythm in the first movement of the late G minor Symphony.[4] His ideas about drama (in both stage and concert works) relate, moreover, to a conception of themes as agents of musical 'development', understood in its familiar sense to denote an unfolding process of thematic transformation.[5] Reviewing Roger

[1] Anon., 'New Manchester Group', *The Times*, 10 January 1956, 5; Robert L. Henderson, 'Peter Maxwell Davies', *Music in Britain* (Autumn 1963), 15.
[2] Peter Maxwell Davies, 'Problems of a British Composer Today', *The Listener*, 62 (8 October 1959), 564; Alexander Goehr published a comparable critique of post-Webernian compositional fashions soon afterwards in 'Is There Only One Way?', *The Score*, 26 (1960), reprinted in *Finding the Key: Selected Writings of Alexander Goehr*, ed.

Derrick Puffett (London: Faber and Faber, 1998), 20–4.
[3] Davies, 'Problems', 564.
[4] 'Composers Today 3', BBC Third Programme, 25 June 1967, British Library Sound Archive (hereafter BLSA), tape P210RC1.
[5] As Davies explains, 'I don't really think that operatic and symphonic development are all that different, deep down. An orchestral piece has got to have a great deal of theatre in it if it's going to grip the imagination' (cited in Paul Griffiths, *New Sounds, New Personalities: British*

Sessions's *Montezuma* in 1964, Davies drew special attention to the opera's melodies, defined closely as 'long articulations with many strands, all combining to make a total melodic impulse … a "collective" melodic gesture'[6] – a remark that seems equally apt as a description of his own music. Taking the composer at his word, it would appear that the drama of Davies's art is fundamentally one of musical themes, and that his links to traditional eighteenth- and nineteenth-century Classical–Romantic forms of utterance are stronger than critics typically acknowledge.

Davies's thematic–dramatic orientation, though, has not always been clear to all listeners; particularly in the early works, his attitude to the seminal category of theme reflects a rapidly shifting stance toward the work of European contemporaries. In a 1963 interview, Davies told Murray Schafer he had 'difficulty in coming to terms with a-thematic music', rebuffing the suggestion that his own works were 'composed of tiny cells' only, a claim he corrected with the assertion that the cells 'hang together'.[7] Schafer's question was not entirely off the mark, though. John C. G. Waterhouse in 1964 compared Davies's wind sextet *Alma Redemptoris Mater* (1957) specifically to Stockhausen's *Zeitmasse*, both for its 'interplay of long held notes and flickering melismata' and the 'spiky' quality of its scherzo lines, while noting also that in the String Quartet (1960–61) Davies had begun to resolve 'fragmented intricacies … into smoothly expanding song'.[8] Writing shortly afterwards, Roger Smalley (himself then much influenced by both Davies and Stockhausen) found in Davies's music of the mid-1960s a lengthening of melodic line and a 'rediscovery of the gesture'.[9] The point is echoed by Stephen Walsh, who remarks that Davies moved toward a simpler, clearer style after assuming his teaching appointment at Cirencester Grammar School in 1959, and by 1965 adopted a more theatrical, at times 'histrionic strain'.[10]

No single narrative adequately captures the range of thematic and dramatic effects that animate Davies's idiom; the music's palpable tensions, Arnold

*Composers of the 1980s* (London: Faber and Faber, 1985), 37). For evidence of Davies's analytic interests, see his remarks on Schenker, Ratz and Hans Keller in Richard Dufallo, *Trackings* (New York and London: Oxford University Press, 1989), 147; Schenker's analysis of Beethoven's Fifth is composed directly into the 'St Veronica' movement of *Vesalii Icones* (see Peter Owens, '*Worldes Blis* and Its Satellites', in *Perspectives on Peter Maxwell Davies*, ed. Richard McGregor (Aldershot: Ashgate, 2000), 49).

[6] Davies, 'Sessions's Opera Stirs Berliners', *New York Times*, 21 April 1964, 43.

[7] Murray Schafer, *British Composers in Interview* (London: Faber and Faber, 1963), 180.

[8] John C. G. Waterhouse, 'Towards an Opera', *Tempo*, 69 (1964), 19, and 'Peter Maxwell Davies and His Public Image', *The Listener*, 71 (7 May, 1964), 773. Both articles draw attention to Davies's work on the opera *Taverner*.

[9] Roger Smalley, 'Some Recent Works of Peter Maxwell Davies', *Tempo*, 84 (1968), 4.

[10] Stephen Walsh, 'Davies, Peter Maxwell', *New Grove Dictionary of Music and Musicians* (London: Macmillan, 1980), 5, 275. Davies's own remarks on his Cirencester works stress 'openly melodic' vocal writing and the need, in works for children, to adopt 'simpler language' (Davies, 'Composing Music for School Use', *Making Music*, 46 (Summer 1961), 8).

Whittall argues, reflect both an 'expressionistic domain of lament and protest' and recognizably 'classical' aspirations toward large-scale formal coherence.[11] Perhaps because the music *is* both emotionally and technically complex, Davies's own verbal comments have often influenced its reception. Introducing *St Michael* (1957), written in his early twenties, to a more or less admiring British public, the young composer was keen to assert technical procedures, reinforcing (perhaps unwittingly) his ties to then-current modes of serial thought. A programme note for the work's Cheltenham Festival premiere adopts a music-analytic lexicon of interval, contour, and proportion:

> A basic shape (hardly a series) consciously underlies the design … This is reducible for the whole piece however to no more than a contour, and the intervals themselves change within this basic contour, so that there is no question of a 'note-row', but a basic contour whose features change slightly …. strictly controlled by a procedure in which the two pitches of each interval are expressed in a certain rhythmic proportion, variable within recognisable limits.[12]

With this document in hand, the *Times* reviewer of the premiere lit into the score specifically for its alleged lack of rhythm and melody, 'that word of fear not to be evaded by the euphemism "contour"';[13] even a more sympathetic critic, Noël Goodwin, seems to have taken his cue from the abstraction of Davies's verbal discourse, praising *St Michael* as 'sound that is exciting of itself, even if the form of the work is by no means clear … the musical equivalent of a piece of arresting modern sculpture, imbued with a spirit of medieval beauty'.[14] What these two very different reactions share is a suspicion of the music's structural complexity, and a tendency to hear the work as entirely abstract, with little comment on its rhetorical or gestural qualities.

An underplaying of expressive gesture and thematic utterance in Davies's music is equally pronounced in music-analytic writings. Much has been made, for example, of his use of plainchant (a referent evoked in many work titles since *Alma Redemptoris Mater*) and the formal routines he devises to fashion subsequent melodic derivations from a source. Davies himself remarked in 1968 that 'I have for a few years been working with series or "sets" (not necessarily 12-tone) which are in a perpetual state of transformation',[15] and subsequent analysts have often emphasized the grid-like arrays of set-forms the composer himself employs to manipulate pitch-class

[11] Arnold Whittall, 'Peter Maxwell Davies and the Problem of Classicizing Modernism', in *Die klassizistische Moderne in der Musik des 20. Jahrhunderts*, ed. Hermann Danuser (Basel: Amadeus Verlag, 1997), 146.
[12] Davies, programme note for *St Michael*, Cheltenham Town Hall concert programme, 13 July 1959, cited in full in David Roberts, 'Techniques of Composition in the Music of Peter Maxwell Davies' (PhD thesis, Birmingham University, 1985), 235–6.
[13] Anon., 'Two Works of Misguided Aim', *The Times*, 14 July 1959, 8.
[14] Noël Goodwin, 'English Summer Festivals', *Musical Courier*, 160 (October 1959), 16.
[15] Davies, 'Sets or Series', *The Listener*, 79 (22 February 1968), 250.

materials.[16] David Roberts's seminal 1985 study demonstrates just how systematic a description of Davies's background workings could be, delineating in particular how relatively abstract melodic shapes derive via 'sieving' from some longer source melody.[17]

Davies's pitch derivation procedures vary widely, though, in their relevance to the thematic and dramatic narrative enacted on the finished gestural surface. The gradual pitch transformation process in Act I, Scene 4 of *Taverner* 'is musically an enactment of Taverner's conversion';[18] similarly, the monophonic opening of *Hymn to St Magnus* changes a five-note cell audibly into the ancient 'Hymn' itself by a sequence of pitch substitutions.[19] Elsewhere, though, Davies's intricate pitch-class choices appear distant from the resultant musical surface, in that originary chant sources are either wilfully distorted or else plain inaudible.[20] Background compositional methods, Peter Owens finds, are loose enough to allow Davies to make thematic–motivic processes 'relatively clear to the listener, or to make them extremely obscure'.[21] Few musicians would dismiss the structural aspect of Davies's art, even when its results are hidden from view, as it were, in the note-to-note flow of sounding gestures. Yet there is more to Davies's scores than their often formidable structural coherence, nor does the composer write exclusively in highly structured ways.[22] There is room, then, for an account of the work that might listen closely to relatively superficial things – subtleties of musical texture, of thematic utterance, details of timbre, dynamics, and expression. The analyses that follow certainly do acknowledge Davies's background systems, but a more deliberate concern is to catch vivid expressive effects in individual gestures. How are those gestures 'delivered' (as rhetoric has it) in a given musical environment, and to what dramatic end?

[16] Early discussions of Davies's set-transformation techniques include Michael Taylor, 'Maxwell Davies's *Vesalii Icones*', *Tempo*, 92 (1970), 22–7; Stephen Arnold, 'The Music of *Taverner*', *Tempo*, 101 (1972), 20–9; and Stephen Arnold, 'Peter Maxwell Davies', in *British Music Now*, ed. Lewis Foreman (London: Paul Elek, 1975), 71–85.
[17] See Roberts, 'Techniques', 60, and his '*Alma Redemptoris Mater*', in *Perspectives*, ed. McGregor, 1–22. Roberts eschews reference to sketch materials; sketch-based studies of Davies's transformation processes include Nicholas Jones, '"Preliminary workings": The Precompositional Process in Maxwell Davies's Third Symphony', *Tempo*, 204 (1998), 14–22, and Rodney Lister, 'Steps Through the Maze: *Image, Reflection, Shadow* and Aspects of Magic Squares in the Works of Sir Peter Maxwell Davies' (PhD thesis, Brandeis University, 2001).
[18] Arnold, 'The Music of *Taverner*', 26.

[19] See Roberts, 'Techniques', 328–9, and Peter Owens, 'Revelation and Fallacy: Observations on Compositional Technique in the Music of Peter Maxwell Davies', *Music Analysis*, 13/2–3 (1994), 171–3.
[20] Early analyses of distortion techniques in the *Second Taverner Fantasia* include Stephen Pruslin, 'Second Taverner Fantasia', *Tempo*, 73 (1965), 2–11, and Arnold Whittall, 'Post-twelve-note Analysis', *Proceedings of the Royal Musical Association*, 94 (1967), 8–12; on multiple permutation and transposition operations applied to the *Dies Irae* chant source in *Hymn to St Magnus*, see Owens, 'Revelation', 173–7.
[21] Owens, 'Revelation', 176.
[22] On Davies's apparent abandonment of set-derived materials in portions of his later music, see Richard McGregor, 'Stepping Out: Maxwell Davies's *Salome* as a Transitional Work', *Tempo*, 236 (2006), 2–12.

While the polyphonic orientation of Davies's oeuvre is obvious to most listeners, the sheer range of *textures* animating his music often eludes comment. Even within the works of the early period to be considered here (from 1955 to 1962), the many ways he finds to make contrapuntal voices interweave provide an abundance of distinctive sounding surfaces. A brief tour of those surfaces, by way of preview, may clarify what I mean here by 'texture', and its links to questions of thematic presentation and dramatic argument.

In the early Trumpet Sonata, Davies writes a moto perpetuo counterpoint of clearly etched lines, yet even amid proliferating surface detail, there is stichomythic dialogue between trumpet and piano. In the Five Pieces for Piano, Op. 2 (1955–6), extensive crossing of lines, high-to-low (in No. 2), and the freezing of pitches within fixed registers (No. 5) occasionally suggest Boulezian models,[23] but the collection also encompasses the cluster sonorities of No. 4, alternately dense or brightly chiming. *Alma Redemptoris Mater* makes the inherently dramatic contrast between a slow-moving cantus firmus voice and more rapid filigree a prominent textural concern. Here, and in *St Michael*, melodic continuity emerges from a mosaic of intervallic shards (each one a simple dyad). To listen past the surface fragmentation is to discover a shifting play of near-imitation and thematic cross-talk. The pointillist aspect of these scores, vivid on the page, is less salient in performances alive to their perspectival depth – the contrast (especially clear in *St Michael* and *Prolation*) between a timbral foreground and more muted background layers. In Davies's orchestral textures, solo/tutti oppositions function as figure and ground; by the time of the *Leopardi Fragments* (1961), still finer textural gradations within a chamber group convey the narrative viewpoint of the poetry. In the *First Taverner Fantasia* (1962), finally, textural contrasts enact a thematic drama of unprecedented directness in the early music. It is not simply that the contrapuntal weaving is more aurally distinct, the gestures more urgently rhythmic, more melodically sinuous. The *Fantasia*, in its sombre instrumental recitatives and its subtly layered developments of a guiding cantus, prefigures the rhetorical and textural brilliance of Davies's music theatre works of the later 1960s.

## Trumpet Sonata, Op. 1: form and dialogue

The Sonata for Trumpet and Piano, completed in Manchester in early 1955, was first performed at Manchester University's Worthington Hall that year by two of Davies's fellow students – Elgar Howarth (whose virtuoso playing of

[23] See Richard McGregor, 'Peter Maxwell Davies: The Early Works', *Tempo*, 160 (1986), 2–7.

Bach's *Christmas Oratorio* had prompted Davies's choice of the bright D trumpet) and John Ogdon.[24] It was a piece Davies felt satisfied enough with to revive early in 1956 for the celebrated London concert he gave with Goehr and Harrison Birtwistle as the New Music Manchester Group, and eventually to publish as his official Op. 1.[25] Davies was highly self-critical during this period, but he acknowledges his own voice in the Trumpet Sonata and in the Five Pieces for Piano, Op. 2, both in matters of compositional technique and in harmony.[26] Other features reflect the personal musical explorations of his university years. One senses in the Sonata Davies's contemporary interest in the rhythmic structures of Indian music, and it is among those few early scores in which he uses fully chromatic sets rather than the smaller pitch groupings of his later practice.

The Trumpet Sonata was a self-consciously 'modernist' work for the young Davies, a departure from the manner of other scores of his university days. The Quartet Movement (1952) is metrically inventive, its clear, modally defined tonic suggesting Bartókian models; the Octet for Woodwind (completed May 1954)[27] shows lively contrapuntal skill, within supple but more traditional rhythmic bounds. But the Octet has a parodistic edge, an early instance of Davies sending up *Ländler* topics (in the 'Alla Austriaca' movement) and even, in the fugato 'Americanismo' finale, a swaggering blues episode. In the Trumpet Sonata, by contrast, just a few months later, Davies adopts the manners of the avant-garde. The piano writing is often percussive, but there is no hint of musical irony – the tone is severe, but also exuberant and uninhibited. The Trumpet Sonata delivers a punch quickly in three compact movements, well contrasted in mood.

The Sonata's gestural language is incisive and rhythmically angular: notated bars lack time signatures, and vary widely in beat groupings. This line of thought is traceable further in Davies's near-contemporaneous rhythmic-modal experimentation before February 1955 in the score for clarinet and three percussionists revised (in 1968) as *Stedman Doubles*; and on into *Burchiello* for sixteen percussionists, never published,[28] and his 1956

[24] The ink score – British Library (hereafter BL) Add. Ms. 71374 – is dated 'January 1955'; performance details are cited in Stewart Craggs, *Peter Maxwell Davies: A Source Book* (Aldershot: Ashgate, 2002), 61; for the Bach reference, see Mike Seabrook, *Max: The Life and Music of Peter Maxwell Davies* (London: Gollancz, 1994), 40.

[25] Arts Council Drawing Room, 9 January 1956; see Donald Mitchell, 'Some First Performances', *Musical Times*, 97 (March 1956), 149–50; Goehr, 'Manchester Years' (in *Finding the Key*), 38; and Seabrook, *Max*, 41–3.

[26] See Paul Griffiths, *Peter Maxwell Davies* (London: Robson Books, 1982), 103.

[27] The Octet for Woodwind was professionally performed in London in February 1955, and survives in manuscript; Davies destroyed other scores from the period 'when the Society for the Promotion of New Music rejected them' ('Peter Maxwell Davies on Some of His Recent Work', *The Listener*, 81 (23 January 1969), 121).

[28] *Burchiello* was composed during a Rome visit in August–September 1955, but apparently was not performed (see Craggs,

undergraduate thesis, 'An Introduction to Indian Music'. As Davies himself later noted, *Stedman Doubles* bears audible links to Indian music's *tālas* or rhythmic groups: the score reflects 'the "Hindu" influence of Messiaen' and the compositional challenge of manipulating music's time-scale by adjusting the rate at which events unfold.[29] Messiaen's influence certainly antedates Davies's composition of the Sonata in 1955. At the Royal Manchester College of Music, Richard Hall's composition classes (which Goehr and Birtwistle attended) included Messiaen's treatise *Technique de mon langage musical*, among other speculative compositional theories,[30] and by the mid-1950s, Messiaen's music was suddenly being introduced to post-war British audiences. In 1954, Davies heard on the Third Programme the Royal Festival Hall performance of the *Turangalîla-Symphonie* directed by Goehr's father.[31] Davies later remembered the concert as 'one of the formative musical experiences of my life', recalling the work's 'deliriously vulgar' aspect, its liberating use of rhythmic cells, and its treatment of themes as 'signals' rather than as developmental entities.[32]

One senses all such features of Messiaen's language – and especially, the separate structuring of pitch and rhythmic ideas – in the Op. 1 Trumpet Sonata, each of whose movements explores a different structural idea. Davies's first movement at first seems like a chaotic mélange of three main pitch materials – a twelve-tone row P, a chromatic scale segment S, and the fanfare motto V – all present at the opening (Ex. 3.1). These introductory bars densely overlay the twelve-tone P theme with the chromatic S scale, while in the piano, V fanfare-shapes act as interpolating embellishments of both. Rhythmically, the trumpet's repeating C pitches (bars 4–5) signal cell-like subdivisions of the 20-semiquaver *tāla* of the very opening bars; a different 20-beat cycle begins in the piano's $S_6$ phrase.[33] The first movement's large-scale ground plan, though, far from being chaotic, looks fairly rigorous:

*Source Book*, 62); for sketches, see BL Add. Ms. 71443.

[29] Of Indian improvisational practices, he mentions specifically how the slow *ālāp* 'concentrates one's attention on each individual pitch and rhythm relationship with maximum intensity and tension' (Davies, 'Recent Work', 121).

[30] Regarding Hall's teaching of Hindemith, Messiaen and Schillinger, among others, see Goehr, 'Manchester Years', in *Finding the Key*, 27–41.

[31] Walter Goehr had performed *Turangalîla* twice in BBC radio broadcasts the previous year with the LSO (26–27 June 1953) at Maida Vale studios; see W. R. Anderson's account of 'rhythmic complications which the ear cannot pretend to gather in' ('Round about Radio', *Musical Times*, 94 (August 1953), 360). The 1954 Festival Hall performance that Messiaen attended was the London concert premiere. Goehr and Birtwistle travelled down from Manchester to attend the event in person. See the *Times* review, 13 April 1954, 6; Goehr, 'The Messiaen Class', in *Finding the Key*, 42; and Michael Hall, *Harrison Birtwistle* (London: Robson Books, 1984), 7.

[32] Davies, comment in 'Messiaen and the Music of Our Time' discussion, broadcast on the BBC Third Programme, 12 March 1968, BLSA tape NP454W.

[33] In a sketch, Davies writes out pitch rows and rhythmic *tālas* separately, the latter durations noted as '10/8 (20/16)' in the margin (see Add. Ms. 71373, fol. 2r).

**Ex. 3.1** Davies, Trumpet Sonata, first movement: pitch and rhythmic materials at the opening (trumpet part notated in C)

Fig. 3.1 displays its near-palindrome of set-forms, stating prime-aspect P row-forms and ascending S scales in the first 'half' (bars 1–39), and retrogrades of P and descending S scales (also retrograded in sequence) in the second (bars 39–73). A deep 'thud' in the piano (at bar 39) marks both the movement's durational centre and the shift from P to R rows.[34]

---

[34] The shift from P to R rows begins after 71 crotchet beats (at bar 39), 10 beats before the shift from falling to rising S statements (bar 44); the total movement duration is 143 beats. For more on the palindromic row-form scheme, see Roberts, 'Techniques', 15–25.

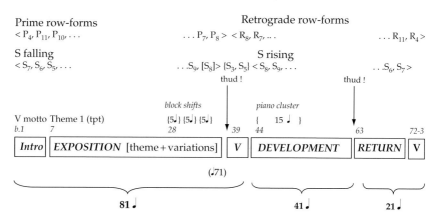

**Fig. 3.1** Trumpet Sonata, first movement: formal events and proportions

Davies is too much the dramatist to be seduced into slavish adherence to the apparent symmetries of such a scheme, nor do all 'outer-form' phrase-gestures neatly project discrete row structures. Cutting across the balanced set-form palindrome is a more asymmetric sonata design. Both 'exposition' and 'return' sections are assertively rounded out by a cadential rhythmic tattoo in the piano (marked V in Fig. 3.1). A 'development' episode leads to distinctly recapitulatory moves, announced by a second piano 'thud' (bar 63). Yet if this is sonata form, its return and coda are highly telescoped to a mere 21 crotchets, only half the length of the development.

The music alludes to a thematically defined sonata scheme by rhetorical means. The exposition emphasizes discrete melodic statements, along with the regularity of the initial *tāla* duration, which governs evenly spaced textural shifts (every five crotchets, at bars 28–36). A more elastic motivic and rhythmic discourse governs the development. After the central palindromic 'hinge' and the piano's chromatic thud (bar 39), the trumpet theme pursues a chromatic sequence on a single P fragment, slipping smoothly into an $R_1$ statement (Ex. 3.2). Framing this registrally are high piano clusters sounding a triply augmented version of the rhythmic *tāla* first heard near the opening (bars 7–10) – now stretched to 60 semiquavers – and elaborately protracted $R_9$ and $S_8/S_9$ statements in octaves.

Where the Trumpet Sonata's first-movement rhythms are motto-like in their repetition and subdivision of fixed temporal durations, the second and third movements experiment with systematic growth and decay patterns. In the slow movement, a main contrapuntal episode weaves isorhythmic patterns in the trumpet with an incremental twelve-duration growth process – 1 2 3 4 … 11 12 semiquavers, then the reverse – applied to a thirteen-unit pitch row. Similar procedures are readily audible in the finale, where the piano's bass line augments quaver durations from 1 to 8 units, while an

**Ex. 3.2**  Trumpet Sonata, first movement, bars 44–7: augmentation and fragmentation processes

upper voice does the reverse. Analysis swiftly identifies such formal regularities,[35] but for listeners a somewhat traditional thematic *dialogue* between trumpet and piano is the most salient rhetorical feature. The vivid dramatic progression of the finale, for instance, has much to do with Davies's play with dynamic contrasts, juxtaposing the trumpet's ability to crescendo

[35] Roberts, 'Techniques', 28–36, lucidly
illustrates these incremental durational patterns.

dramatically with the piano's quick alternations of extreme loud and soft attacks. In the playful central episode (bar 34 onwards), Davies overlays a lower-voice imitative duet with a Messiaenesque chordal ostinato, while the trumpet comments in loose and impulsive bursts. The sonata ends with a rhythmically direct revelation of the P row as thematic essence, *maestoso*, supported with thick piano chords. As a product of Davies's Manchester workshop, the Trumpet Sonata draws his awareness of Continental European modernism, Indian rhythmic patterns, and early English polyphony into an original synthesis. But its success has as much to do with sure instincts for dramatic pacing and compelling instrumental dialogue.

## Op. 2 and beyond: polyphonic textures

Davies published four works in the three years following Op. 1, each more ambitious than the last. The second and third of the Five Pieces for Piano, Op. 2 (1955–6) trace more extended formal designs than those in the Trumpet Sonata. In *Alma Redemptoris Mater* (1957) for wind sextet, and in the two works he wrote in Rome while studying with Goffredo Petrassi, *St Michael* for 17 wind instruments (1957), and *Prolation* for orchestra (1958), Davies pursues this fundamentally polyphonic mode of thought in increasingly elaborate textures.[36] The expressive qualities of each work would merit detailed attention, for each is highly characteristic in feeling and sound. Considering the works more synoptically as a historical sequence, attention can focus on Davies's sculpting of themes within textures. The composer's dense weaving of lines, in other words, does not preclude over-arching dramatic qualities of contrast and opposition.

Davies wrote the Five Pieces for Piano during his final college year in Manchester, for John Ogdon, who premiered them in December 1956. The published score – Davies's first to appear – was brought out by Schott in 1958. Ogdon's virtuoso technique is important here, for Davies's advanced piano idiom reflects both 1950s avant-garde concepts of the instrument and his awareness of pianistic composers such as Busoni and Sorabji (cult figures in Manchester). Davies himself recalled writing Op. 2 when 'first very much under the influence of Schoenberg', whose 'singing style' he acknowledges as a conscious model, particularly in recitative-like passages.[37] Certainly, the 'Five Pieces' genre suggests an Austro-German legacy of abstract developmental works, rather than British precursors such as Bridge, Ireland or Bax,

[36] Three other chamber works completed during this period remained unpublished or were later revised: *Stedman Doubles* (1955, rev. 1968); Sonata for Clarinet and Piano (1956, published 1989); and the Sextet (1958, rev. 1971 as Septet).

[37] Davies, spoken comments, BBC Radio 3, 21 July 1969, BLSA tape NP1465W.

who favoured colourfully titled character pieces.[38] Debts to Schoenberg at the level of genre, though, do not result in the kind of close echoes of his Three Piano Pieces, Op. 11, that one finds in a score such as the *Three Lyric Pieces* (1942) by Richard Hall.[39] The French figures that do affect Davies's piano writing are Messiaen and Boulez: he often exploits the extreme registers of the instrument, notably in the dense cluster-chords of No. 4 and in the spangled high-register trills of No. 2.

The Op. 2 pieces are no less rigorous in rhythmic and pitch construction than the Op. 1 Trumpet Sonata,[40] though their overall atmosphere is some-what different. The set encompasses extremes of violence and calm, yet there is too, as Robert Henderson observed, a 'deliberate restraint', and an 'avoid-ance of external rhetoric'.[41] All Davies's early-period works are polyphonic; in Op. 2, necessarily, the counterpoint is etched in the piano's relatively mono-chrome timbre. In No. 1, a distinction between melodic and accompanying voices is assured by carefully marked dynamic shadings and subtle variations of attack.[42] In the volatile scherzo-like second piece, the performer must clarify an interplay of three (occasionally four) voices, each of which bounds dramatically between registers, so that contrapuntal parts constantly cross one another. If this music is reticent, that impression stems perhaps from its fairly unbroken surface activity, rather than from a lack of local incident. In textures so dense, Davies articulates formal divisions by notated shifts of tempo. Even so, the most thrilling moments in Op. 2 come when he pares things down suddenly (as at the *più presto* episode in No. 2) allowing a limber melody to dance briefly as a soloist.

By title alone, *Alma Redemptoris Mater* announces an affiliation with the Marian antiphon of the same name, so introducing into Davies's music the thematic shaping force that has sustained it ever since – plainchant melody. The opening of the chant phrase provides a slow-moving oboe cantus firmus around which Davies's Andante finale revolves (Ex. 3.3). This is a strikingly direct instance of the kind of melismatic elaboration Davies favours in many subsequent works, with a foundational melody decorated by interpolating pitches. In the other two movements, though, overtly hierarchic distinction among voices is far less clear. More character-istic is the kind of intricate interplay of motivically derived fragments at the

---

[38] On the Gallic bias in early twentieth-century British piano writing, see Peter Evans, 'Instrumental Music 1', in *Blackwell History of Music in Britain*, ed. Stephen Banfield, Vol. VI (Oxford: Blackwell, 1995), 265–74.
[39] Published by Hinrichsen in 1946. Ogdon's 1965 recital LP (HMV ALP 20989/ASD 645) includes Davies's Op. 2 along with a *Suite* (1952–62) by Hall.

[40] Roberts, 'Techniques', 38–77, closely documents each piece's structural features.
[41] Henderson, 'Peter Maxwell Davies', 15.
[42] Davies's sketches for this piece show many refinements of dynamics, barring, and duration within each notated gesture, even after the basic 'notes' had been established.

**Ex. 3.3** Davies, *Alma Redemptoris Mater*, third movement, bars 9–15: chant-derived cantus firmus and melismatic interpolations

opening (Ex. 3.4). Sketches reveal Davies fashioning the music's darting weave of entrances from a simpler two-voice contrapuntal frame, itself based on a 10-pitch-class melodic set derived ultimately from the *Alma Redemptoris* melody.[43] The result has a multicursal, labyrinthine complexity, each arriving pitch suggesting many harmonic, melodic and timbral affiliations. While Davies's pitch-class choices are guided by rigorous proto-serial procedures,[44] the surface discourse is otherwise more freely shaped into playful dialogue among intervallic shards, and by frequent octave shifts within motives (the flute's first C, for example). The original chant source often recedes from the musical surface, fragmented and reshaped in ever-changing patterns. The disguise makes the finale's plain cantus firmus all the more dramatic as a melodic epiphany.

*St Michael*, Davies's 'Sonata for 17 wind instruments', follows *Alma Redemptoris Mater* in quoting plainchant fragments, though in its fuller ensemble textures, melodies are less apt to stand out aurally; nor does he distinguish them rhythmically as slow-moving cantus lines. As in *Alma Redemptoris Mater*,

[43] Ex. 3.4 summarizes features of compositional process in Davies's sketches, especially Add. Ms. 71376, fols. 1v, 3v and 4r. The plainchant source, *Alma Redemptoris Mater*, is taken from the *Liber Usualis* (Tournai, Belgium: Desclée & Co., 1953), 273. Add. Ms. 71376, fols. 56–7, contains Davies's neat transcription of the soprano and bass parts of Dunstable's *Alma Redemptoris Mater* motet, likely from the Manfred Bukofzer edition (*Musica Britannica*, Vol. VIII (London: Stainer & Bell, 1953), 106–7), though links between Davies's score and Dunstable's are less direct than prior commentators claim (see Roberts, '*Alma Redemptoris Mater*', 18–22, and Richard McGregor's chapter in this present volume). [44] Meticulously parsed in Roberts, '*Alma Redemptoris Mater*'.

Ex. 3.4 *Alma Redemptoris Mater*, first movement, bars 1–8: polyphonic elaboration of a chant-derived two-voice contrapuntal frame

Davies elaborates source harmonies in terse single-dyad gestures, with frequent changes of scoring, but in *St Michael*, the contrapuntal web is more densely woven.[45] The general shape of lines is if anything more angular than in *Alma*

[45] For rigorous parsing of the score's pitch-class and durational structures, see Roberts, 'Techniques', 198–239.

**Ex. 3.5**  Davies, *St Michael*, second movement, bars 1–6: mensural canon at the tritone on a *Dies Irae* subject, melodic intervals loosely controlled by durational proportions (other voices omitted)

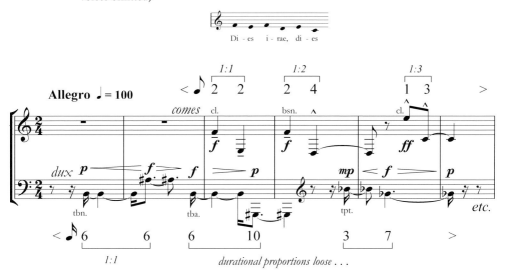

*Redemptoris Mater*, though melodies are no longer profusely decorated by grace-note accents (a mannerism the young Davies may owe to early Boulez). The recurring *Dies Irae* phrases of movement II are heavily disguised by octave shifts, and by the teeming overlay of many canonic voices sharing registral space. Ex. 3.5 shows just two of the five canonic voices that crowd in during the first few bars. The excerpt reveals the rhythmic proportions by which the mensural canon distinguishes its melodic intervals.[46] The resulting soundworld fuses fragments into an intricate whole. One critic at the premiere found it difficult to 'make head or tail of this abstruse music',[47] but a committed performance will forge from the local detail an unfolding argument of phrase motions.

Davies wrote *St Michael* upon arriving in Rome; it was a first fruit of his year of study with Goffredo Petrassi.[48] The bold contrasts suggested by a Venetian *cori spezzati* model are reimagined here using opposing choirs of nine woodwinds and eight brass, each further divided onstage into physically distinct subgroups.[49] He creates drama at the most palpable level by

---

[46] Davies employs a more consistent isorhythmic mapping of duration to pitch class in movement IV (see Roberts, 'Techniques', 203).

[47] Dyneley Hussey, 'Cheltenham Festival', *Musical Times*, 100 (September 1959), 472.

[48] It was begun on 29 September 1957, the Feast of St Michael; the completed pencil score is dated 'November 1957' (Craggs, *Source Book*, 66).

Davies in a letter from Rome reported to a friend 'producing comparatively vast amounts of music' (cited in Seabrook, *Max*, 48).

[49] The score's spatial dimension might also reflect awareness of Stockhausen's then-recent *Gesang der Jünglinge* or *Gruppen*. Davies's wide-ranging interests in new music are apparent in 'News and Comments: Italy', *The*

means of antiphonal contrasts, dialogue, and the sheer variety of mood among the five movements of the 15-minute span. The first movement, for instance, exposes a subtle interplay among onstage groups, with melodic fragments dovetailing into broader collective gestures (including high-to-low 'cascade' motions). The initially linear canon of the 'Dies Irae' movement later gives way to imposing six-part chordal clusters (bar 81). In the central Lento movement, hushed overlappings build haunting chordal sonorities of up to ten voices. A vivid acoustic perspective arises between the woodwind foreground and a ghostly background of muted brass. The scherzo-like fourth movement reduces activity to a *Klangfarbenmelodie* of woodwinds alone, maximally differentiated by constant changes of timbre. But it is in the finale that *St Michael* explores most directly the apocalyptic overtones of its title.

Davies himself in the early 1960s recalled of *St Michael* that he was 'much torn by the fundamental question of good and evil at that time'. The score was 'an attempt to come to terms with that problem'.[50] He went on to reveal a specific British inspiration, the stained-glass window at Fairford church showing St Michael weighing the souls of the dead in the Last Judgment, for the subject.[51] His title evokes the Archangel who, in the biblical narrative, with his angels expels the dragon Satan from heaven (Rev. 12: 7–9). The musical substance grows – by the composer's public admission – from several melodic phrases of the Requiem liturgy, the 'Dies Irae' sequence a famously graphic meditation on the events to come in the Day of Judgment.[52] Recalling the sonic imaginary of Revelation's Apocalypse – seven angels with seven trumpets – it is difficult not to hear in the wild D-trumpet flourishes of the final segment a conclusion more than abstractly dramatic. These startling phrases transform the soloist into a figure whose musical gestures enact a very specific narrative.

Davies's trumpet writing here follows the same distinctive thread running from the Op. 1 sonata, via the *Taverner* opera and fantasias, to *Revelation and Fall* (1965–6), a work whose narcotic text is saturated with Apocalyptic overtones ('the crystalline tears of fallen angels'). Only later in Davies's career do overtly religious artifacts (the distorted Victorian hymns in *Vesalii Icones*, for example) come to be treated allegorically as images of deception or betrayal, but one finds the roots of this move in *St Michael*. Davies's relation to the formal institutions of religion is certainly a complex one, inscribed within the

*Score*, 22 (1958), 65, where he reports hearing in Rome works by Boulez (*Structures*), Berio, Maderna and Henze.
[50] Schafer, *British Composers*, 177.
[51] Ibid. The 1959 programme note also explains the title *St Michael* as a reminder of the work's Roman origins, specifically, of the figure who surmounts the 'Castell S. Angelo,

under the shadow of which it was composed' (cited in Roberts, 'Techniques', 235).
[52] Although the published score lacks movement titles, Davies added the titles 'Dies Irae' and 'Agnus Dei – Dona Eis Requiem' to preliminary sketches for the second and fourth movements respectively (see BL Add. Ms. 71444, fols. 2r and 3r).

thematic texture of the music itself, and in techniques of musical and theatrical parody that could be taken as sacrilegious (in this his art resembles Trakl's). But in *St Michael*, as elsewhere, the question is less one of Davies's personal beliefs than of a symbolic drama played out in a score rich in allusive reference.

The largest work of Davies's Rome studies, *Prolation*, eschews the kind of plainchant derivations of *Alma Redemptoris* and *St Michael*, while building an elaborate structural ground plan inspired by medieval rhythmic practice. Picking up on the opposition between duple or triple division of a given note-value (so-called *prolatio*), Davies erects a rigorous durational scheme – in the proportion 10:4:7:6:5 – governing every level of rhythmic events, from the most fleeting local gesture, to the wider pacing of the work's five movements.[53] The five-term rhythmic schema is aligned with a five-pitch row, reflecting more than any other Davies score a 1950s avant-garde fascination with coordinating structures in various musical parameters. The work's elaborate rhythmic ground plan has attracted the most sustained commentary, yet its 'parsimonious use of material'[54] is arguably less audible to real-time listeners than are more superficial surface thematic features; my concern here is limited precisely to *Prolation* as a vivid rhetorical and dramatic trajectory.

In his unpublished draft article on *Prolation*, Davies attacks the 'muddiness of a great deal of new music'[55] – arguing that composers should create structures that are aurally direct. *Prolation* largely succeeds: for the *Times* critic, reviewing the British premiere of the work, conducted by John Carewe, its materials were 'quickly impressed on the ear'.[56] And one might add that large-scale progress is marked out in a well-judged balance between textural density and transparency. The first landmark along the way is a chaconne-like group of five pentachord verticals. It is the first of these – [F–A–D♭–G–A♭], closely voiced by treble-register woodwinds at bar 220 – that becomes the cadential goal of the entire work. By an inexorable homing-in process, drawn out in the final eight minutes, that haunting pentachord sonority is reassembled pitch by pitch in a series of long-held *crescendo* notes that punctuate the ongoing orchestral argument as hieratic signals. Over much of this expanse, the texture is a transparent scrim of solo utterances, passed

[53] The opening Vivace (bars 1–236), for example, subdivides into five segments of 160, 64, 112, 96, and 80 crotchets' duration; the 160-beat segment itself subdivides into 50:20:35:30:25-beat sections. Davies summarizes these schemes in a programme note (written for the 1960 British premiere) and in an unpublished text, 'Formal Principles in "Prolation" for Orchestra', BL Add. Ms. 71311, fols. 17–23, intended for *The Score* (which ceased publication in 1961).

[54] Roberts, 'Techniques', 78; Roberts (78–173) gives a very detailed survey of the work's pitch-class and durational structures.

[55] Davies, 'Formal Principles', fol. 17.

[56] 'Musica Viva at Liverpool', *The Times*, 25 October 1960, 14.

around the orchestra; against this chiaroscuro procession, the timbre and voicing of the 'home' chord are both static (the initial pitch G is always scored for cor anglais in its four later returns, for example).

In *Prolation*, as in *St Michael*, traditional forms of melodic continuity play a very limited role. Instead, Davies conjures a rich interplay of colours within the orchestral palette (notably in the Lento vigoroso segment, patterned among five small ensembles), and reduces instrumental utterance to terse single notes or gnomic chordal verticals. One might draw loose parallels between *Prolation* and the 1950s fascination with a post-Webernian 'discovery of the single note'[57] – as filtered through a score such as Luigi Nono's *Incontri*. But even without relying on traditional themes and with notably pared-down melodic gestures, *Prolation* shows Davies's ability to create the kinds of dramatic contrasts that can sustain arguments of increasing scope and directness.

## *Leopardi Fragments*: lyric perspectives

*Leopardi Fragments* was Davies's first work for solo voices, and his first setting of non-liturgical words – twin challenges that encouraged new lyricism in the composer's manner. The fragments of Davies's title are chosen from several of the Italian poet's *canti*, but the impression in performance is less that of discrete episodes than of one intensely felt lyric effusion, unfolding in a varied but coherent sequence of first-person utterances. Davies's work is close in genre to the chamber cantata *The Deluge* of his colleague Alexander Goehr, also for soprano–contralto duo and mixed ensemble with harp.[58] *Leopardi Fragments* was completed in 1961, and one assumes that Davies was well aware of the conscious experiment with vocal articulation of text in many then-recent avant-garde scores, notably Boulez's *Le marteau sans maître*, Nono's *Il canto sospeso*, and Berio's *Circles*.[59] Yet *Leopardi Fragments* is a relatively traditional poetic setting, its text almost never dissolved into phonetic entities – as in Nono or Berio – however elaborate the local melismatic extension of certain vowel sounds. *Leopardi Fragments* traces a more overtly dramatic arc than does Boulez's *Le marteau sans maître*, whose interlocking variation-cycles break away from 'one-way'

[57] Herbert Eimert's phrase, cited in Goehr, 'Is There Only One Way?', 20.
[58] The British contralto Rosemary Phillips sang in the premiere of both *The Deluge* and *Leopardi Fragments*.
[59] Davies may even have heard Stockhausen's 'Music and Language' lecture on the first two scores at Darmstadt on 25 July 1957, having premiered his own Clarinet Sonata there on 20 July (see *Im Zenit der Moderne: die Internationalen Ferienkurse für Neue Musik Darmstadt 1946–1966*, ed. Gianmario Borio and Hermann Danuser (Freiburg: Rombach, 1997), 3, 585). Stockhausen's essay was published in 1960.

**Table 3.1**  Davies, *Leopardi Fragments*: structural scheme

| Duet | | Soprano solo | | Duet | | Contralto solo | | Duet |
|---|---|---|---|---|---|---|---|---|
| | Interlude | | Interlude | | Interlude | | Interlude | |
| Stridore notturno | | La speme che rinasce | | Mi diedi tutto | | Campagna in gran declivio | | Ahi, tu passati |

form.[60] The nine segments of Davies's form, by contrast, run continuously, alternating five sung fragments with four instrumental interludes (Table 3.1).

Of the five fragments Davies sets, only the fourth lacks direct expression of a first-person-singular perspective. Even in the three duets, Davies's intertwining lines are the channel for twinned expression of a single consciousness (the vocal-trio utterances in Nicholas Maw's *Scenes and Arias* of 1962 create a similar effect). Responding to the ultra-subjective emotional focus of Leopardi's words, Davies's settings address listeners with intensity and near-'confessional' intimacy.[61]

Leopardi's verses themselves provide Davies no particular narrative sequence; rather, by their paucity of material detail, the poems make room for musical elaborations of emotional states evoked very directly. Davies parses the opening fragment, a couplet, into three phrases (of 13, 8 and 8 bars' duration):

> *[1]* Stridore notturno delle banderole *[2]* traendo il vento.
> *Nocturnal creaking of the weather-vanes borne on the wind*
> *[3]* Vedendo meco viaggiar la luna
> *Seeing with me the moon in its course*

The setting sustains a mood – nocturnal and sombre, but also restless – by a clear harmonic and timbral frame spanning the trombone's low E pedal points and a static pair of pitches (C, A) much higher in oboe and flute. Do these two stand, object-like, for the static image of the moon voyaging across a night sky? Perhaps; but it is more germane to listen for the way this first interlude grows from, echoes, then ultimately transforms the high dyad, which returns in the Stygian garb of harp, trombone and bassoon (bar 54) as the instruments reach a close. The vocal fragment is both complete in itself and the germ of a more elaborate and dynamic non-verbal exploration of mood, fashioned from a delicate interplay of vocal and instrumental motives.

Davies had first encountered Leopardi's poetry while a student in Rome, but the musical starting point for the *Fragments* (and for two other scores) was Monteverdi's 1610 Vespers. In his second year teaching at Cirencester, Davies arranged four movements for his pupils' choir to sing with the school

---

[60] Boulez, *Le marteau sans maître*, 'Preface' (London: Universal Edition, 1964), iv.

[61] Bayan Northcott, 'Peter Maxwell Davies', *Music and Musicians*, 17/8 (1969), 40.

**Ex. 3.6** Monteverdian gestural allusion in *Leopardi Fragments*

orchestra.[62] He has pointed to the influence of the 'Sonata sopra Sancta Maria', with its intervening cantus firmus phrases, as a specifically formal model for both the String Quartet (1961) and the third movement of the *Sinfonia* (1962). For the Leopardi cantata, Davies mentions the vocal and instrumental decorative techniques of the soli in Monteverdi's Sonata as a direct forebear, though he compares his relationship to the original with Picasso's pictures after Velázquez which he had discovered at a Tate Gallery exhibition in summer 1960.[63] Like the great cubist painter, Davies draws out motives from a historically distant style in personal and indirect ways. One senses only occasional hints of stylistic emulation. Rather, for Davies – and for Birtwistle and Goehr, who also saw the Tate show – what was 'overwhelming' in Picasso's visual studies was the idea that a distant musical past might provide answers to pressing aesthetic and technical questions.[64]

The vocal writing in *Leopardi Fragments* does contain a few gestural details that closely recall Monteverdi: pointed dissonances as a unison splits into two distinct voices; ornately repeating trills (Ex. 3.6). But even at his most allusive, Davies sounds mostly like himself: the alto's *'villani'* unfolds a whole-tone hexachord from E♭, a reflection of pitch-intervallic consistencies of the entire cycle. The opening itself (Ex. 3.7) establishes thematic and harmonic motives that endure throughout. Melodically, the leaping fifth- and ninth-arpeggiations of *Leopardi Fragments* oscillate between open-sounding diatonic fifth-cycles (B–E–F♯ in the soprano, D–G–A in the alto) and more dense whole-tone voicings. Overlapping arpeggio figures at the opening recall the contrapuntal part-crossing of earlier scores; what is new here is the

[62] 'Domine ad adjuvandum', 'Pulchra es', 'Sonata sopra Sancta Maria', and 'Ave Maris Stella', performed at Cirencester, March 1961.
[63] Griffiths, *Maxwell Davies*, 138–9. Davies mentions 'a Goya original', but it is Picasso's 44-painting sequence of studies based on Velázquez's *Las Meninas*, and one picture after Delacroix, that were at the Tate from July to September 1960 (see the catalogue, *Picasso*

(London: Arts Council of Great Britain/Lund Humphries, 1960)).
[64] 'We were all overwhelmed by the studies on works of earlier painters': Goehr, in Griffiths, *New Sounds*, 19; on Birtwistle's reaction to Picasso, and *The World Is Discovered*, subtitled 'after Heinrich Isaac', see Hall, *Birtwistle*, 23 and Jonathan Cross, *Harrison Birtwistle* (London: Faber and Faber, 2000), 163–5.

Ex. 3.7  *Leopardi Fragments*, bars 1–7: melodic arpeggios, underlying third harmonies

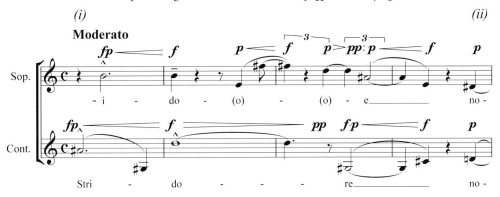

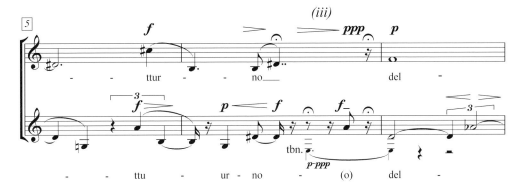

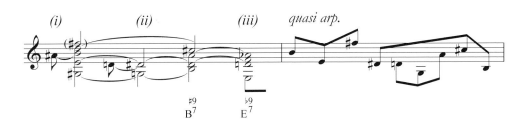

luminous, third-rich harmonic milieu. This opening is itself a form of musical cubism: the voices sketch two melodic views, as it were, of the same affect. The vertical result is a warmly major-mode assertion of Fragment 1's E tonic (marked (i) on Ex. 3.7) prolonged by an astringent D♯/D♮ dissonance (ii), resolving – or better, dissolving – smoothly over the trombone's arriving pedal tonic (iii).[65]

[65] Davies's set-form chart for *Leopardi Fragments* (BL Add. Ms. 71404, fol. 1r) divides a ten-note row symmetrically into two five-note sets, marked 'i' and 'ii'. Set i presents five pitch classes (pcs) from a fifth (ic 5) cycle; set ii, also five pcs, is whole-tone (ic 2) based, repeating three pcs from set i and adding two new pcs. The row's resultant seven-pc collection is transposed cyclically to generate twelve row-forms of distinct pc content. By this mechanism, Davies moves systematically around a pitch vocabulary that is often suggestively diatonic.

Thematic textures in *Leopardi Fragments* are generally less hectic and contrapuntally dense than in the earlier works up to *Prolation*. Particularly in the duets (Fragments 1, 3 and 5), the vocalists command centre-stage by a capella openings, and the ensemble responds either with vertical chord gestures, or with restrained imitative elaboration. In the two solo fragments, the poetic imagery finds expression in Davies's placing of the voice within the larger texture. To hear voice–ensemble interplay in these cases is to sense a musical elaboration of the viewpoint implicit in Leopardi's poems.[66] Davies's Fragment 2, for instance, uses a proto-Baroque texture of instrumental obbligati to symbolize the speaker's mental state. Leopardi's rapid poetic progression from 'grief' to 'ennui' plays out here in instrumental counter-melodies, first for piccolo–cello, then for trumpet–oboe. 'Terror', finally, engenders a filigree ensemble texture combining all four instruments (the harp, at each stage, has a continuo role). The landscape vista pictured in Fragment 4 ('*Campagna in gran declivio*': steep slope of the countryside) is sketched by the voice against the full registral expanse of the ensemble, in a backdrop of softly sustained notes. Davies's setting grows impressively here: the appearance, in the distance, of villagers prompts playful imitation of the voice's trill figurations (see Ex. 3.6), while the existential conclusion ('*altra immagine dell' infinito*': another image of Infinity) is tellingly caught with a pedal drone on B♭.

The rhetorical potential of Davies's newly direct thematic writing is equally clear in Interlude 2, the one passage in *Leopardi Fragments* where Davies builds a texture around an explicitly stated cantus firmus layer (Ex. 3.8 shows the opening). In this case, 'cantus' notes form a gradually accelerating sequence of dyads, over which are heard multiple overlapping 'decorative melismas'.[67] The dyad layer is determined intervallically as a conjunction of whole- and half-step cycles, and rhythmically as a steady durational reduction from the initial long to a single quaver. For the melismas, Davies works with by-now-familiar fifth shapes (compare these entries with the opening pitches of Ex. 3.7). What is more loosely determined is the metrical location of the melisma voices. As in the String Quartet, Davies loosens the ensemble texture to allow players to move at independent tempi.[68] In this case, the structural process of the interlude – a systematic telescoping of intervals and durations – matches the almost filmic juxtapositions of distance and proximity described in the '*Campagna*' fragment into which it flows.

---

[66] On 'voice placement' as an agent of narrative viewpoint in opera, see Philip Rupprecht, *Britten's Musical Language* (Cambridge University Press, 2001), 115–19.
[67] Davies uses these terms in his prefatory note to the score (London: Schott, 1965).

[68] 'The point of entry of each melismatic part is indicated by the spacing … the notes of each part are proportional within themselves, but not to the notes of other parts' (ibid.).

**Ex. 3.8** *Leopardi Fragments*, Interlude 2: 'cantus' and 'melisma' voices (trombone and cello parts omitted)

*cantus scheme, bb. 145-57*

*half-step cycle*

*whole-step cycle*

In the wider context of Davies's early period, *Leopardi Fragments* marks a significant stage in the development of his thematic and rhetorical techniques. It is not that he has abandoned the animated contrapuntal textures of the early works – far from it. But in *Leopardi Fragments* one senses more clearly a play of foreground and background. Pursuing the painterly metaphor, one might say that Davies's textures here acquire a new sense of perspectival depth. One hears more frequently a clear hierarchy of thematic 'actors', centre-stage, and subsidiary voices or layers providing a setting or environment (the term 'accompaniment' seems inadequate). Davies readmits traditional block-harmonic writing with telling rhetorical effect – hear how the soloists' a capella cadence in Fragment 5 is caught and re-harmonized by a delicately spaced wind chord, one with an inner life of dynamic shadings (Ex. 3.9). A sombre chorale-phrase follows, darkening to a cluster. The entire gesture leads the listener back to Davies's setting of the only word Leopardi repeats in the text – '*passati*' – now bitter with chromatic wandering and tritone emphasis. In this, the most world-weary and elegiac of the fragments – '*Ahi, tu passati eterno sospiro*' (Ah, you have left me, my eternal sighs) – Davies's textures and melodies match every subtle hue of the poetic image. In these haunting final moments the music steals one backward glance, as the soprano's '*di tutti*' (bar 262) briefly conjures pitches from the opening. Leopardi's words speak now in a past tense of 'bitter memory' ('*rimembranza*

**Ex. 3.9** *Leopardi Fragments*: vocal and instrumental interplay

*acerba*') as the two singers, against a gentle trembling sound in the harp, intone their last few hushed syllables.

## *First Taverner Fantasia*: thematic drama and textural invention

The *First Fantasia on an 'In Nomine' of John Taverner* of 1962 inaugurates a group of works deriving from Taverner's famous sixteenth-century In Nomine phrase, a melodic well from which Davies drew a remarkable flow of contrapuntal invention. With the *First Taverner Fantasia*, he returned to the full-orchestral canvas essayed in *Prolation*, though with smaller forces.[69] From thematic and dramatic perspectives, one senses both continuities with earlier scores and fresh developments in Davies's idiom. Adapting the more pronounced sense of textural hierarchy of *Leopardi Fragments* from chamber to orchestral setting, the *Fantasia* creates greater effects of textural depth.

[69] In addition to strings, *Prolation* requires 23 winds, harp, celesta, and various percussion; the *First Taverner Fantasia* requires 15 winds and handbells.

Exploring more fully the opposition between a 'cantus' and other textural strands, Davies writes a newly heterophonic counterpoint. Lines and their 'shadow' doublings form gestures that are often tautly physical in shape; equally, the interplay of parts can soften edges in a kind of sonorous scumbling. Elsewhere, the solo–tutti contrast available in an orchestra makes for very stark separation of figure and ground.

Many features of Davies's earlier contrapuntal style are transformed in the new *Fantasia*. Compared to the textures of *Prolation*, the weave of polyphonic parts is less intricate, and there is no longer a division of one melodic strand among several instruments in point-like articulations. Rhythmically, there is very little complex subdivision of individual beats (quintuplets and septuplets simultaneously, for example); continuous passages of constant tempo and metre in the *Fantasia* supersede the frequent tempo modulations and metric shifts characteristic of *Prolation*.

The reimagined thematic rhetoric of the *Fantasia* goes hand in hand with a more overtly dramatic argument than before. Where 'drama' in *Leopardi Fragments* arises by episodically arranged contrast, in the purely instrumental *First Taverner Fantasia* Davies constructs a form that is more emphatically punctuated, more goal-oriented and narrative in conception.[70] Combining a sonata allegro with two titled 'Recitative' segments, the *First Taverner Fantasia* has an obvious Beethovenian caste.[71] More will be said about form later on, but it is Davies's shaping of themes and, especially, his invention of polyphonic textures that impress the listener most in the *Fantasia*.

The choppy string counterpoint opening the work is among those passages in Davies's music that stay in one's ear. 'Rhythmic impetus'[72] is everything – the stone in the water whose energy radiates outward, even as far as the near-still coda. Davies's public remarks on transforming musical ideas that are 'in a constant state of flux' refer specifically to the *Second Taverner Fantasia* of 1964,[73] but it will be obvious by now that the procedure emerged much earlier in his oeuvre. His notion of 'musical identities' being 'gradually established and disintegrated'[74] – rather than announced by fiat, as it were – already

---

[70] One sketch leaf (Add. Ms. 71444, fol. 93v) includes a draft scenario for the work's later stages in handwritten verbal form, as for example: '*Recit* end on high org[an]/ [woodwind] chord extended down by addition to climactic *fff*. Then *bells* come in, chorale fragments getting shorter &/or slower & higher. End on highest reg[ister] *ppp*.' While the organ role was dropped in the final published work, one sees that handbells figured among Davies's early ideas for the piece.

[71] Interest in classical sonata form is evident also in the third movement of the *Sinfonia*, also completed in early 1962. For further discussion, see Nicholas Jones, 'Playing the "Great Game"? Peter Maxwell Davies, Sonata Form, and the *Naxos* Quartet No. 1', *Musical Times*, 146 (Autumn 2005), 71–2.

[72] Robert Henderson, 'Prom Novelties', *Musical Times*, 103 (November 1962), 780.

[73] Davies, programme note for the *Second Taverner Fantasia*, reprinted in Griffiths, *Peter Maxwell Davies*, 141.

[74] Davies, 'Sets or Series', 250.

**Ex. 3.10** Davies, *First Taverner Fantasia*: opening chain of thematic transformations

informs *Leopardi Fragments;* in the *First Taverner Fantasia* an unceasing aural play with evolving material is the very stuff of the work, compelling to the intellect and beguiling to the ear. A close hearing of the first two minutes – a five-part string fantasia – establishes at once Davies's ability to shift melodic shapes before one's eye, so to speak. The string fantasia has a surging trans-formative and variational energy, but it is itself prefaced by three earlier links in a chain – see Ex. 3.10 – comprising an originary plainchant fragment (played on solo oboe), Taverner's original four-voice In Nomine (woodwinds, the plainchant heard as alto cantus firmus), and a brief trumpet motto that restates Taverner's original *superius* melody with disguising octave displacements.[75]

How Davies achieves counterpoint of such supple, tumbling energy is revealed by a glimpse at his extant sketches for the work (Ex. 3.11). At the top of the page is a relatively mechanical chart of transpositions (numbered vertically 1–10 in the left-hand margin) of a ten-note melody soon to become the violin 1 part at bar 4.[76] Davies's pencil numbers below line 1 mark intervallic proportions ('3–1, 2–1', etc.), a technique familiar from Op. 2 and *St Michael*. Lower down the folio, Davies sketches variations of individual lines 2 and 10 (circled) in a sculpting process. For line 2, the top stave ('mel. 1') departs from its chart source by single-pitch shifts (G♭ to G♮ for the second note) and by introducing a triplet rhythm in its second bar. Line 2 'mel. 2' enlarges the initial A♭–G half-step to a minor third, A♭–F: versions of both line 1 and its 'mel. 2' variant become a violin duet in the opening phrase of the *Fantasia*. Inspecting that phrase in the score (see bars 4–7, Ex. 3.10 (d)) one finds Davies transfers the second half of line 1 to the viola entry, breaking up its contour by octave displacement; violin 1, meanwhile, sustains its B pitch.

Davies's choices for the actual contour of a melodic shape are not particularly systematic here. A smooth source melody quickly turns angular (as in the viola), when individual pitch classes shift octave.[77] Another freedom is Davies's filling out of the texture by echoes and blurrings of the main melodic progress (as with the violin's low B). More radical melodic transformations appear in the same sketch. While Davies's line-2 variants hew close to their source melody, the line-10 sketch (last three staves, Ex. 3.11) alters the original through interval expansion: pencil numbers ('+2 , +3 …') below the middle stave refer to distortions by half-step increments of the original line 10. This almost giddy ascending thrust becomes the concluding phrase of the initial string fantasia (bars 59–61).

[75] At the *First Taverner Fantasia*'s 1962 premiere, the Taverner original was played on the organ, but it is Davies's woodwind arrangement that appears in the published score. In the sketches, what is now the opening string fantasia was originally scored for a wind sextet (flute, oboe, two clarinets, trumpet, trombone); see Add. Ms. 71444, fols. 19r–22r. Comparable indications appear in fol. 92r, a sketch for the allegro second subject (R11 in the published score), with the eventual cello line scored for trombone, and vague indications for 'organ'.

[76] Since this melody includes internal pitch repetitions, the grid has duplicate lines (1 and 4, 2 and 9, 5 and 7), marked by Davies with a tie. This sheet is not the start of the compositional process – the melody has itself already been derived from the source tune in earlier sketches.

[77] The evolution of these decisions is clear in numerous continuity sketches (in Add. Ms. 71444) for the *First Taverner Fantasia*. The less systematic side of Davies's working methods typically gets short shrift in analytic commentary. Roberts's central concern (in 'Techniques') is with pitch-class structures, with few references to registral displacement in melodic shapes; Owens's analyses in 'Revelation and Fallacy' refer more extensively to processes of contour variation on the music's surface.

**Ex. 3.11** *First Taverner Fantasia*: transposition chart for opening string fantasia; melodic sculpting of lines 2 and 10 (British Library Add. Ms. 71444, fol. 16v)

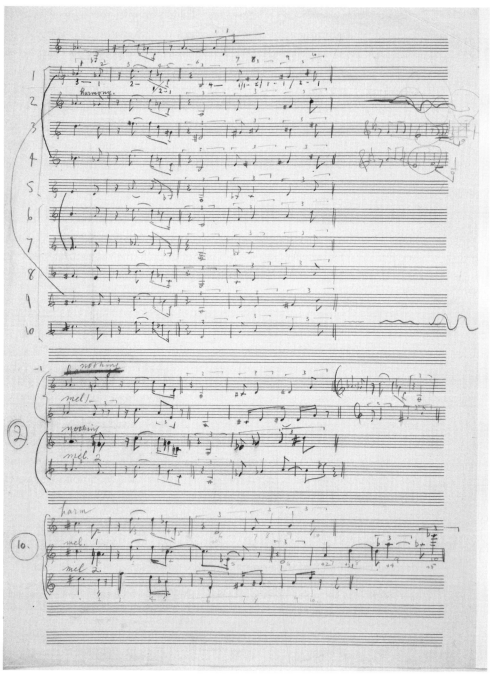

Ex. 3.12 *First Taverner Fantasia*, bars 43–8: 'line 8' varied in double values (lower strings omitted)

One last detail of Davies's sketch folio is telling: in the right-hand margin, he has jotted down a familiar tune, together with a capsule analysis. Examining his sketch process for the *First Taverner Fantasia*, with its seemingly complicated intervallic sculpting processes, we do well to remember that the composer himself had none other than Beethoven's Fifth Symphony in his ear. Apparently, Davies's own opening thoughts were informed by the motivic force of its famously direct opening gesture. In this case, the accentual weight of Beethoven's minims caught Davies's imagination: much of his own reworking of the In Nomine phrase draws out the heavy downbeat in Taverner's phrase, and the effortless floating descent that follows.

Extant sketch materials allow a glimpse of Davies's workshop, revealing a growth process informed by both systematic transformations and 'freer' composerly taste. In the finished score, a single originary pitch line may generate varied surface manifestations throughout the long-range form. A case in point appears in Ex. 3.12, which excerpts a part of the string fantasia derived from line 8 of the original chart.

This melody is initially heard as a soft inner voice (violin 2) in doubled values, shadowed canonically (viola), with a louder, more agile descant over-laid (violin 1).[78] Imitation between violin 2 and viola is audible in the head phrase, but lost when the parts cross (bar 50). Some minutes later the same pitch lines return, transformed as the second subject of the full-orchestral sonata allegro (the passage is stated twice: Ex. 3.13 shows the repeat, which

[78] Davies is strict about doubling the line 8 durations, but freely elongates rests between head and tail phrases (for example, the viola-part rests, bar 49 onwards).

**Ex. 3.13** *First Taverner Fantasia*, second subject, bars 137–45: cantus firmus, and heterophonic shadow lines (numbers mark reorderings of the 'line 8' melody)

adds a horn descant). Davies's violin melody here plays in succession the two variant forms heard before as *dux* and *comes*, inflected now by insistent dactyl rhythms from the first-subject trumpet motto. Nor does the transformation process end here – the questing cello obbligato melody, beginning E–G–F♯, is itself a more distant variant, achieved by running through three scrambled derivations of the original line 8 melody (these reorderings are marked numerically on Ex. 3.13).[79]

Discussing his experience writing for symphony orchestras, Davies drew attention to a textural issue in his music, that of a 'central tenor … in the mediaeval sense as a main part, a holding part … moving around the orchestra'.[80] This clearly stratified conception of texture is plain in the exposition and development phases of the *Fantasia*, and it is allied now to a vibrant and subtle heterophonic elaboration of musical line. The simultaneous unfolding of different versions of one melodic impulse requires that one listen closely to the textural disposition of Davies's thematic ideas.

It is hard to say 'how many' real parts are present in the texture of the Ex. 3.13 passage, so lively is the sense of decorative cross-reference among gestures. The strings present the main melodic force, a slow-moving cantus firmus (violas) surrounded by the violin theme above and cello/bass counterpoint below. Definition of this three-part texture, though, is complicated by heterophonic inflection of each voice. At the same time, Davies's precise dynamic differentiation among voices promotes the autonomy of each textural strand. The cantus voice itself is shaped by crescendos and sudden *mfp* accents; above this, the violin 1 line (*mf*) is shadowed by short thrusts (*p < ff*: violin 2) upstaging the 'host' theme and challenging the duple metre. Below in the cellos, an expressive *crescendo–diminuendo* line is 'thickened' by double-bass attacks (alternately *pizzicato* or *arco*). Meanwhile, the polyphony has two further elements: woodwind 'points' with their own dynamic profile (*f, mf*), harmonically distinct from the string music; and (in the bar 137 repeat) the horn solo, independently shaped in both dynamic profile and loping triplet pulse. The horn shadows the violas' cantus firmus (echoing the initial D tonic) before splitting on an independent melodic path. Davies once noted that intervallic and contrapuntal relations in Webern are 'thrown into relief by characteristic dynamics'.[81] His own heterophonic textures reference various 1950s sources – the Stravinsky of *Agon* and, closer to home, Britten's *Noye's Fludde* – but Davies's orchestral reimagining of cantus firmus texture sounds in the end quite distinctive.

---

[79] See also Add. Ms. 71444, fol. 92r, where Davies's sketch progression from first-order variants to second-order scrambled variants and finally to continuity sketch of the second subject is readily legible.

[80] Davies, 'The Symphony Orchestra – Has It a Future?', *Composer*, 37 (Autumn 1970), 6–8.

[81] Davies, 'Problems of a British Composer Today', 564.

Ex. 3.14 *First Taverner Fantasia:* 'plain-hunt' processes of pitch ordering
*sketch [Add. Ms. 71444, fol. 93v]*

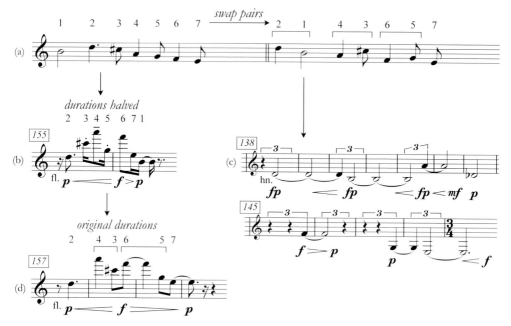

By such textural invention does the music pursue ongoing thematic transformation. Much rides on Davies's ability to build paragraphs that sustain
supple forward momentum, even a carefree bounce (see, for example, the
tumbling phrase with which the climax subsides: Ex. 3.10 (e)). The overall
form of the *First Taverner Fantasia* may be schematic in its sectional divisions, but *within* paragraphs the music flows on freely. The Davies of 1962
owes less to a Viennese-classical rhetoric of antecedent–consequent balance
than to the unbroken intensity of Taverner's early English counterpoint.

Another specifically British inspiration is apparent if one inspects the
close detail of the *First Taverner Fantasia*'s evolving themes – the change-
ringing of English churches. Davies's familiarity with this tradition may
have prompted his scrambling of pitch orderings in melodic sequences –
specifically, reversing the order of adjacent bells in a change (so-called plain-
hunting).[82] A seven-note phrase (Ex. 3.14 (a)) is easily remade by swapping
each pair, which is exactly how Davies generates both the measured horn
cantus of the exposition (Ex. 3.14 (c)) and the sprightly flute interpolations
of the development (Ex. 3.14 (b) and (d)). The original seven-note phrase is
itself rhythmically akin to Taverner's famous opening melody (Ex. 3.10 (b)).

[82] See Wilfrid G. Wilson and Steve Coleman,
'Change Ringing', *New Grove Dictionary of
Music and Musicians*, 2nd edn., ed. Stanley
Sadie and John Tyrrell (London: Macmillan,
2001), 5, 464–70. An earlier instance of Davies
swapping the internal melodic order of
discrete pitch pairs is in the fifth of the Five
Pieces for Piano, Op. 2, bars 23 and 37.

The rhythm is retained precisely for the flute melody (diminuted to half-values) but entirely abandoned in the serene horn cantus firmus. The changing-ringing process creates the flute's next phrase also (Ex. 3.14 (d)): rhythmically, this is the Taverner phrase with durations restored (i.e., twice as long as the bar before); melodically, Davies switches the order of two pitch pairs – (3, 4), (5, 6) – and drops pitch 1 altogether. Audible in both flute and horn (and throughout the *Fantasia*) is D's role as local tonic or melodic starting point.

Not every dramatic aspect of thematic utterance in the *First Taverner Fantasia* can be ascribed to Davies's fastidious shaping of note-to-note details or to niceties of polyphonic texture. The score can feel longer in performance than its twelve-minute duration, in part because the coda is protracted.[83] Another factor influencing real-time perception of the form is sheer beat speed. Davies juxtaposes faster tempi (crotchets at 104, 116, 100, 112) for the sonata sections with slower tempi (48, 40) for the two Recitatives and the Coda, accenting rhetorical contrast within the form. The opening string fantasia is only moderately fast (104), allowing for relatively intricate pulse subdivisions; the main sonata allegro, on the other hand, presses forward (at 116); the development relaxes slightly (to 100), drawing out the cantus-firmus-based section; the return (marked crotchet 112) jolts back to close to the previous faster tempo. In the *lentissimo* coda, far slower than any previous music (crotchet 40), the drama becomes intrinsically sonic as melodic outline blurs in a haze of tintinnabulating bells.

Davies took the thematic and dramatic preoccupations of the *First Taverner Fantasia* much further in the works composed around *Taverner* between 1962 and 1965 – the massive orchestral *Second Taverner Fantasia* (1964), portions of which reappear in the opera, and the more compact *Seven In Nomine* (1963–5). A fuller view of Davies's expressive and technical means during this period might say much more about thematic rhetoric in the *Second Taverner Fantasia* in particular. Where transformation begins to shade into 'distortion', as it does so emphatically in the instrumental chorale-canons of *Revelation and Fall* (1965–6), Davies reaches the brink of the harsher ironies of his later 1960s music theatre scores. The composer himself once described the works up to the *Second Taverner Fantasia* as 'apprentice pieces', in which he was consciously 'building up a solid foundation of compositional technique'.[84] If one accepts that account, one might acknowledge too that elements of what I have termed 'thematic drama' – motivic patterning of rhythm, motto-like pitch signals, the interplay of 'cantus' and 'melisma' gestures, and so on – run throughout Davies's output, beginning

---

[83] Pruslin ('Second Taverner Fantasia', 11) notes the reverse effect in the *Second Taverner Fantasia*, a relatively perfunctory Coda that distorts perception of the work's substantial duration.

[84] Cited in Griffiths, *Peter Maxwell Davies*, 109.

with Op. 1. Later phases of this interest confirm the composer's inherently dramatic view of thematic statement and re-statement. Audible transformations of plainchant melody and concluding thematic epiphanies by instrumental soloists are as central to the unfolding of the 'Motet for orchestra' *Worldes Blis* (1966–9), for instance, as to a later ensemble score such as *A Mirror of Whitening Light* (1976–7). In relation to the latter title, the composer draws attention to a 'purification or "whitening" process by which a base metal may be transformed into gold and, by extension, to the purification of the human soul'.[85] The listener is invited to experience the most elemental musical processes in terms of pronounced symbolic valence. Davies's thoughts are invariably entangled in such metaphors, and he continues to imagine a music in which themes are actions that compel our witness.

---

[85] Davies, 'Composer's Note', in the published score (London: Boosey & Hawkes, 1978).

# 4    *Taverner*: an interpretation

*David Beard*

*Taverner* (composed 1962–8; partly reconstructed in 1970), Peter Maxwell Davies's first opera, marked a watershed.[1] The source for many of the composer's varied musical concerns of the period – plainchant, medieval and Renaissance music, parody techniques and expressionist devices – the opera was profoundly significant for, on the one hand, Davies's development of music theatre, and, on the other, a symphonic style, which dates from the *Second Fantasia on John Taverner's 'In Nomine'* (1964). *Taverner* remains the most substantial and ambitious of the composer's stage works and it established dramatic themes that are consistent right through to his most recent opera *The Doctor of Myddfai* (1995). This chapter is concerned with the interest in dogma and transformation evident in *Taverner* – two clearly foregrounded themes that reappear in his later stage works – and with what has been termed the central character's 'predicament'.[2] These subjects will be examined from two new perspectives: a discussion of the opera's reception, and Davies's intentions, as far as they can be discerned from his unpublished pre-compositional materials, his documented statements, and his music.

Common to all the operas and chamber operas composed by Davies for adults are plots motivated by rigidly held convictions. These may vary in kind, from the superstitious to the puritanical, but they always result in transformations of persons or character.[3] *The Martyrdom of St Magnus* (1976) charts the transformation of Earl Magnus Erlendson from Orkney's twelfth-century ruler into a martyr and the island's patron saint. Three lighthouse keepers are transformed in *The Lighthouse* (1979) into hysterical wrecks by their growing conviction that a supernatural beast lurks beyond the lighthouse walls. Lured outside to their deaths they call upon God's help,

[1] For their generous assistance I wish to thank David Allenby and Pippa Patterson at Boosey & Hawkes, Victoria Small at Chester Music, Nicolas Bell at the British Library, Charles Wilson, and the editors of this volume.
[2] Bayan Northcott, '*Taverner*', *Music & Musicians*, 21 (September 1972), 63.
[3] For more on the notion of Davies's 'ideology of puritanism', see Arnold Whittall, '"A Dance of the Deadly Sins": *The Beltane Fire* and the Rites of Modernism', in *Perspectives on Peter Maxwell Davies*, ed. Richard McGregor (Aldershot: Ashgate, 2000), 143.

'bellowing a hymn … to defend themselves against the spirit, which they now see as the Antichrist'.[4] In *Resurrection* (1987; originally conceived in 1963), the social conditioning and physical surgery endured by a teenage boy (a silent role represented on stage by a 'larger-than-life-sized dummy') results in the boy's transformation into the Antichrist.[5] According to Davies, this represents 'a double resurrection: the surgery has produced a monster, ready to do the bidding of those who created him, but capable of turning even on them'.[6] And in *The Doctor of Myddfai*, a family doctor is transformed into a Messianic figure as a result of his crusade to overthrow the Ruler (a political despot) and the Ministry (a characterization of the European Commission). The doctor is trampled to death by a crowd of worshippers, and his rhetoric passes to his daughter who, by the end of the opera, seems likely to continue the displaced Ruler's fanatical role but unlikely to heed his warning to her father: 'You have become an idealist. Nothing is more dangerous.'

*Taverner* is the blueprint for Davies's obsession with dogma and transformation, embellished by an anti-authoritarian stance, an interest in symbolism and betrayal, and a concern with the difficulty of distinguishing truth from falsity, or the real from the unreal.[7] The opera's two acts are divided into four scenes. Both acts begin with a public court scene, in which Taverner is present, followed by two private scenes, one of which is set inside a chapel while a service is in progress and Taverner is present (in Act II the service is disrupted by the intervention of soldiers). The other private scene takes place inside the King's throne room, from which Taverner is excluded. The dialogue in this scene focuses on the concerns of the King and his Cardinal who are modelled on Henry VIII and Cardinal Wolsey (here the libretto reflects historical detail more directly than elsewhere in the opera). Each act ends with a climactic fourth scene that involves a public spectacle: in Act I, there is a mock crucifixion, modelled on the medieval Mummers' play; in Act II, an abbot is burned at the stake.

The opera opens with the eponymous sixteenth-century composer protagonist on trial for heresy. Although prosecuted by the White Abbot for his supposed involvement in Protestant conspiracies, Taverner is pardoned by the Cardinal, who values the composer's musical contribution more highly than his religious sympathies. In Act II, which parodies and inverts many of

---

[4] Peter Maxwell Davies, programme note for *The Lighthouse*, in Paul Griffiths, *Peter Maxwell Davies* (London: Robson Books, 1982), 168.

[5] Davies, 'Preface', in *Resurrection: Libretto* (London: Chester Music, n.d.), 3.

[6] Davies, 'Resurrection: A Précis', in *Resurrection: Libretto*, 8.

[7] Plans for the opera date from 1956 when Davies was a student in Manchester. The libretto was completed in 1962 while Davies was a Harkness Fellow at Princeton; the music was composed between 1962 and 1968 and partly rewritten in 1970 following a fire in the composer's Dorset home.

the events from Act I, the tables are turned and the context switches to a reformed England. An agent of Thomas Cromwell and a Protestant zealot, Taverner turns informer on Catholic sympathizers and it is he who now prosecutes the White Abbot who is then burned at the stake.[8] Other characters are also transformed: the Cardinal becomes an Anglican arch-bishop; the Jester becomes Death and then Joking Jesus who, according to Davies, 'emerges eventually as the main character: the power behind the Reformation or Revolution, the master-puppeteer for whom all the other "characters", including Taverner himself, are as marionettes'.[9]

Besides determining the concerns of Davies's librettos, both his own and that of David Pountney (for *The Doctor of Myddfai*), the dramatic themes detailed above are also revealed in Davies's compositional techniques, most obviously his method of continuous thematic transformation whereby ostensibly contrasting themes gradually mutate from one form to another to reveal different 'manifestations of the same character-principle'.[10] Davies revealed his use of such techniques in 1968 when he referred to the use of '"sets" (not necessarily 12-tone) which are in a perpetual state of trans-formation, so that given musical identities, such as "straight" or "inverted" set-forms, are only gradually established and disintegrated'.[11] Subsequent research has indicated that such techniques – what I shall refer to as 'goal-directed transformations' – occupied Davies from roughly 1965 to the mid-1970s when they partly gave way to the use of magic squares. For some writers, such as Stephen Arnold, these techniques may be considered anal-ogous to Taverner's religious conversion.[12] For others, such as David Roberts, as far as experience of the music goes, they are 'profoundly trivial': 'whatever importance they have lies in the fields of intellectual history and the psychology of creation'.[13] In light of this difference of opinion, Davies's compositional techniques will be considered here in relation to Taverner's transformation, since this is one of the most contentious issues raised by the opera's reception.

[8] Davies based his libretto on accounts of Taverner's life that have since been discredited. His initial source was E. H. Fellowes's introduction to *Tudor Church Music, I: John Taverner, c. 1495–1545*, Part I, ed. P. C. Buck *et al.* (London: Oxford University Press, 1923). Evidence suggests that the 'real' Taverner was a charitable person who tried to protect and support Catholics, the irony of which has been argued away by most commentators as irrelevant because the opera's themes are symbolic. For more on the life of Taverner see David Josephson, 'In Search of the Historical Taverner', *Tempo*, 101 (1972), 40–52.

[9] Davies, '*Taverner*: Synopsis and Documentation', *Tempo*, 101 (1972), 5.

[10] Davies, programme note for the *Second Taverner Fantasia*, in Griffiths, *Peter Maxwell Davies*, 141.

[11] Davies, 'Sets or Series', *The Listener*, 79 (22 February 1968), 250.

[12] Stephen Arnold, 'The Music of *Taverner*', *Tempo*, 101 (1972), 22.

[13] David Roberts, 'Techniques of Composition in the Music of Peter Maxwell Davies' (PhD thesis, Birmingham University, 1985), Vol. 1, 369.

## *Taverner*'s reception

> It seems clear in retrospect that he [Davies] would sooner or later write *Revelation and Fall*, [*Eight*] *Songs for a Mad King*, and *Vesalii Icones*. But in all these works the focus is on one figure only – double of the artist if you like, but of the spectator too. In the libretto of *Taverner* I think one finds the traces of the struggle to reach that degree of direct expression of the animal scream of the heart without the immediate disintegration of the music. The opera and the long years spent on it surely made the later works possible. Whether it can stand beside them only a visit to Covent Garden will reveal. But let us remember: few works could.[14]

In his preview of Davies's libretto for *Taverner*, Gabriel Josipovici sensed a tension between the composer's desire to set the action inside Taverner's mind and the presentation of episodes from English Tudor history. His unease that the result would sit awkwardly beside Davies's music theatre works was prescient: despite – or perhaps because of – a heightened sense of expectation, *Taverner* received 'a divided Press'.[15] This may seem surprising given that Davies's turn to parody originated within the opera. However, *Taverner*'s ambitious Grand Opera dimensions, its use of Latin scripture and quotations from fifteenth-century Reformation texts presented a rather learned contrast to such genre-defying stage works as Birtwistle's *Punch and Judy* and Davies's own fashionable music theatre pieces, which had so brilliantly captured the mood of the late 1960s.

Some of the reasons for the opera's divided reception were clearly beyond the composer's control. In the opinion of most reviewers, Ragnar Ulfung, who sang the title role in the Covent Garden premiere, failed to declaim or project the text sufficiently and struggled with the language.[16] The onstage period instrument ensemble, used in the two throne room scenes, was largely inaudible because the composer's instructions on where it should be situated were ignored (it was positioned too far backstage). For some critics, Michael Geliot's production erected barriers that were 'all but impossible to penetrate'.[17] Ralph Koltai's sparse, modernistic stage design consisted of a central mast 'supporting a huge balance that swoops and swivels' with platforms to

[14] Gabriel Josipovici, '*Taverner*: Thoughts on the Libretto', *Tempo*, 101 (1972), 19.
[15] Northcott, '*Taverner*', 62.
[16] Following its premiere in July 1972, *Taverner* was revived by the Royal Opera House, Covent Garden, later the same year and again in 1983. It has been performed since in Stockholm (1984) and Boston (1986). The original production was broadcast by BBC Radio 3 on 13 July 1972; the revived production was broadcast on Radio 3 on 6 July 1983; a subsequent studio recording was broadcast on Radio 3 on 2 April 1997, conducted by Oliver Knussen. At the time of writing, these recordings are not commercially available but all three are stored at the British Library Sound Archive in London (1972 broadcast: T504/5, 2009/02; 1983 broadcast: T5706–5707BW C1; 1997 broadcast: H8705/1 – this latter recording is also in the possession of Boosey & Hawkes).
[17] David Roberts, '*Taverner*', *Musical Times*, 124 (September 1983), 562–3.

carry the actors on aerial journeys.[18] While this device impressed some it confused others: 'is it meant to represent the scales of justice? a see-saw? the Cross? It does poor duty to any of these. And when it wasn't distracting attention by its sheer inscrutability it was irritating the ear with its creaking.'[19]

Other criticisms, however, were directed at the composer. For Joseph Kerman, while *Taverner* impressed in terms of ambition and scope, it failed to clarify its supposed themes owing to a 'basic confusion of ideas'.[20] Although the opera manifested dramatic powers that were 'very impressive indeed', Kerman argued, the opera's dramatic form was 'essentially static and schematic, calculated to place ideas in relief and push personalities into the background'.[21] By contrast, the White Abbot's aria before his burning at the stake, during the opera's final scene (Act II, Scene 4), was a moment of powerful subjective force: 'At last a character is allowed to develop and the static "drama of ideas" yields to drama of human personality'.[22] Taverner, Kerman argued, is given no such opportunity to come to life, despite what Kerman believed was the composer's intention to break through to the subjective by ending the opera with a quotation of Taverner's In Nomine on the *Gloria Tibi Trinitas* plainchant, which is the basis of Taverner's most celebrated festal mass.

Kerman compared this final gesture to the closing bars of the *Dr Fausti Wehe-klage*, or *Faust Cantata*, the first serial piece by the fictional composer Adrian Leverkühn in Thomas Mann's novel *Doktor Faustus*.[23] As John Harbison comments, 'The suggestion throughout the libretto that an artist may have to be in league with the Devil, Antichrist, or Death to realize new possibilities is right up his [Davies's] alley. Act II, with its shrill, compressed, rhythmically unstable parodies of material from Act I, is "of the

---

[18] Andrew Porter, 'Taverner – 2', *Financial Times*, 14 July 1972. Also, according to Porter, 'Space is further defined by an inclined circle, ringing the whole stage; in the second act it can flash many-coloured lights.'

[19] Roberts, 'Taverner', 562.

[20] Joseph Kerman, 'Popish Ditties', *Tempo*, 102 (1972), 20. This review prompted a robust defence from Hans Werner Henze who was impressed by 'the sense of a dialectic mind working in a theatre of ideas' (see Henze, 'Letters to the Editor', *Tempo*, 103 (1972), 63).

[21] Kerman, 'Popish Ditties', 21. The question of the opera's dramatic effectiveness divided opinion more than others. Kerman conceded that 'in its own terms the lay-out of the opera is ingenious and powerful' (ibid.), Andrew Porter reported that the opera's 'structure is formally strong' ('Opera on Radio', *Opera*, 48/6 (1997), 741), and Paul Griffiths argued that it

is 'a work of immense richness and vigour' ('Much Dared, Much Achieved', *The Times*, 1 July 1983). Keith Potter, on the other hand, disliked a first act that 'seemed still-born dramatically', 'cardboard characters' and a 'severely symmetrical structure' ('Taverner: Two Reactions to a Problematic Stage Work', *Classical Music* (6 August, 1983), 18), while for Andrew Clements 'the real drama' was 'going on in the orchestra' ('Sweden: Not So Memorable', *Opera*, 36/4 (1985), 442).

[22] Kerman, 'Popish Ditties', 22.

[23] To Kerman, the closing bars represent Taverner's hesitant recollection of his music and his former self but also his 'hope against hope for salvation' (ibid., 23). Kerman also likens Davies to Leverkühn because they both attempt to reconcile their modern, anti-establishment consciences with Renaissance myths and musical structures.

devil's party" and has a special power.'[24] As far as Kerman is concerned, however, Taverner's attempted breakthrough to the subjective proved hollow, and it is the White Abbot and Death who sing most eloquently.[25] Kerman was also unconvinced by Davies's notion of betrayal. Taverner abandons the Roman Catholic Church, his wife, father, and composition but unlike Leverkühn, who achieves compositional mastery, Taverner profits nothing from his pact with the Devil. His motivations are therefore unclear.

> Taverner betrays music … not for the sake of religion but for the sake of the perverse rewards of fanaticism. Even this he doesn't do for any motive that is clearly dramatized, but as the result of some sort of obscure trickery. Or brain-washing, as Davies calls it. What remains is a straw man, a caricature out of a counter-reformation tract complete down to the last scurrilous, superstitious detail.[26]

Kerman therefore concluded that Davies's use of the term 'betrayal' was misguided: 'so much is strong and impressive about *Taverner* that one regrets keenly the ultimate sense of misdirection'.[27]

Many of the aspects that Kerman criticized, however, need not be considered weaknesses. The motivations that lead a person into fanaticism may well be illogical, free of personal gain, and the result of 'some sort of trickery'. As Griffiths remarks, the Jester's role as Death in Act I, Scene 4 is crucial to Taverner's transformation, 'confusing him as to his ability to tell good from evil' because 'goodness carries with it its antithesis': '"Wherever Christ is, there are Judas, Pilate and the whole Passion".'[28] This is the symbolic purpose of the Joking Jester's mock crucifixion during the Passion play, which is staged in order to convince Taverner to take up arms against Rome. However, although the libretto clearly conveys Taverner's struggle during this scene, the question of whether the music adequately conveys his crisis is an important one to which we will return.

Kerman's belief that Taverner should sing more eloquently than the White Abbot or Death disregards Davies's intention that the opera is a projection from Taverner's mind in which the characters are 'incarnations of departments of his own mind or soul or psyche'.[29] Kerman assumes, like Josipovici,

---

[24] John Harbison, 'Peter Maxwell Davies's *Taverner*', *Perspectives of New Music*, 11/1 (1972), 240.
[25] Winton Dean also remarked of Taverner: 'He is not big enough to dominate the opera' (Dean, 'Taverner', *Musical Times*, 113 (September 1972), 879).
[26] Kerman, 'Popish Ditties', 23. He further remarks that Taverner is 'simply stunned into his "conversion", certainly *not* driven to it by the application of reason, the force of hubris, or a prudent instinct to

strike before he himself is struck again. (These are motives indicated by Davies in the libretto – and elsewhere – but never projected in dramatic terms with anything like the force of the entirely irrational joking Jesus play)' (ibid).
[27] Kerman, 'Popish Ditties', 24.
[28] Griffiths, *Peter Maxwell Davies*, 50; the last quotation is sung in Act I, Scene 4 by a monk dressed in black.
[29] See Stephen Walsh, 'Taverner', *Musical Times*, 113 (July 1972), 653.

that we need to identify with a single protagonist, but the fact that Taverner's character is no more than a cipher may be born of necessity, for he is both projected onto, and led by, those around him. The hollow-sounding In Nomine quotation at the end of the opera, played by a recorder ensemble, is surely intended to highlight Taverner's failure to attain true selfhood. But besides projecting aspects such as reason and emotion onto other figures in the opera, there is much evidence to suggest that Davies's real response to Taverner's struggle lies in the orchestra.

Davies's disclosure of the presence of transformational processes in *Taverner* resulted in a growing fascination among critics with his compositional techniques. Arguably, it also contributed to the opera's mixed reception, for listeners were led to declare that they could not hear such processes at work. With such reservations in mind, the following section seeks out a middle ground, a place where sketch study may inform an appreciation of the concepts that underpin *Taverner*, in particular its focus on dogma and individual transformation.

## Taverner's transformation

> Unlike Stravinsky and Birtwistle, he [Davies] cannot find it in him to rely on distancing conventions. His roots are deep in Romanticism and in German music, which is only another way of saying that his problem has always been to render the *cry* articulate, rather than to transmute it into a more formal scheme.[30]

Davies has commented that the characters in *Taverner* are 'either cardboard figures, in that they state the dogma of the church or represent a cut-and-dried viewpoint; or they are complicated beings who state at one time one side of the problem and at another time another side'.[31] But this glosses over two fundamental concepts associated with Taverner: gradual transformation, and a sense of internal conflict, as embodied by his line in Act I, Scene 4: 'I am but a poor, lank shadow of myself, so racked by acid doubt.'[32] This seminal line is downplayed by the music – the accompaniment is sparse while the voice, although angular, is thin and not especially tortured (Ex. 4.1).

When Taverner sings 'I am confused. What must I do to be saved?', the only audible clues to his sense of crisis are soft timpani strokes and trills that centre on B♭ and E (bars 108–15). This idea is more comprehensively developed in the central Scherzo of the *Second Taverner Fantasia* where, as Arnold Whittall has observed, there is an opposition between a 'ubiquitous

[30] Josipovici, '*Taverner*: Thoughts on the Libretto', 19.
[31] Davies, in Walsh, 'Taverner', 653.

[32] *Taverner*, full score (London: Boosey & Hawkes, 1984), 149–50.

**Ex. 4.1** *Taverner*, Act I, Scene 4, bars 130–8

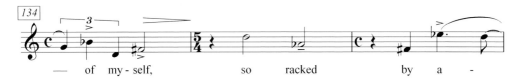

tritone E flat/A' and the 'Taverner cantus firmus' (D–F–C–G–A), a conflict that is 'normalised, not resolved'.[33] However, at least one reviewer of the opera's premiere performances – Bayan Northcott – was persuaded that the various elements of the opera do combine effectively to convey a sense of Taverner's plight:

> Death's revolution of a huge Wheel of Fortune [in Act II, Scene 1] to the terror of all on stage and accompanied by the whirling strings and quicksand bass progressions of the orchestra went straight to mind, heart and gut as an awesome symbol of Mutabilty [*sic*]. […] Once adjusted to its lack of hurry and, in the first act, its predominant sobriety, it was remarkable how, in gradually yielding a web of cross-references and an increasing sense of varied contrast, the interest of the music expanded to 'fill' the spaces and justify the pace of the drama. Similarly many of the visual and verbal references began to fall into place round the realisation that the opera presented not a moral but a predicament.[34]

A number of issues remain unclear from this reading. What precisely is Taverner's predicament, and how, if at all, are mutability and varied contrast related to this notion?

[33] Arnold Whittall, 'Post-Twelve-Note Analysis', *Proceedings of the Royal Musical Association*, 94 (1967–8), 10 and 11 respectively. The 'white-note' motif in question is formed by eliminating every note repetition of the cantus firmus in John Taverner's In Nomine, which is based on the *Gloria Tibi Trinitas* plainchant. This motif is heard in the flute at the end of the *Fantasia* (bars 1207–15), but is first presented, in a modified, seven-note version, in the oboes in bars 415–42.

[34] Northcott, '*Taverner*', 63.

Indications of Davies's own thoughts on these matters are provided by the pre-compositional materials for *Taverner*, stored in the British Library.[35] The first piece of evidence is an early draft of the libretto that most likely dates from October 1957. This reveals that in Act I, Scene 1, the relationship between Taverner and his wife, Rose Parrowe (referred to as Mrs Taverner), was to have been more fully developed than it appears in the final version.[36] The libretto is a patchwork of citations lifted from the Bible, sixteenth-century sources, Joyce's *Ulysses*, and texts by Carl Jung. This results in an oddly impersonal style which in certain instances, such as Rose's text in the court scenes, was subsequently rewritten in a more natural manner (for example, 'the whole head is sick, the heart faint' became 'My Lord, he is all my love, and I am his').[37] However, in restyling Rose's text Davies both altered its meaning and erased important symbolic associations. Originally, it was intended that Rose should be called to witness first, before Taverner's Father (it is the other way around in the opera), and Taverner would enter into dialogue with Rose (no such dialogue exists between the two at this moment in the final version). In the earliest version, Rose is even ordered by the Judge (later renamed the White Abbot) to be silent to allow Taverner to speak first (Fig. 4.1).[38]

A number of points emerge from this discarded text. In Davies's mind, Taverner's relationship with the Church is analogous to his marriage to Rose, which is in turn symbolic of Taverner's relationship to a female collective that consists of his mother, the Virgin Mary, and Wagner's Erda. This is made explicit in Act I, Scene 4, during the mock crucifixion, when Rose assumes the role of Mary. Taverner's rejection of the Catholic faith is interpreted in Jungian terms as a rejection of marriage and a consequent failure to realize 'inner integration'. Although Davies eventually opted to abandon this particular emphasis, he reintroduced Rose's warnings – that Taverner has been led to a place of darkness and bitterness – during Act I, Scene 4 (bars 398–420), and again at the very end of the opera (Act II, Scene 4, bars 273–80). Her words are the last lines addressed to Taverner in the opera.

---

[35] All manuscripts referred to in this chapter are stored at the British Library in London. Three folders were consulted. Ms. Add. 71259 consists of 90 pages, most of which relate to *Taverner*. It includes composition charts, musical sketches and drafts, source texts, and drafts of portions of the libretto. The other folders were new additions to the British Library collection at the time of writing: MS Mus. 1400 (unpaginated when consulted) consists of 120 pages and includes preliminary notes, some libretto, and an almost complete early draft of Act I; MS Mus. 1401 consists of 135 pages and is a mixture of sketches for Act II and the *Second Taverner Fantasia*.

[36] Add. Ms. 71259, fol. 64v – this is among the earliest notes and drafts of the libretto. The page also includes the draft of a letter written in Italian, with a reference to Petrassi, dated '21.10.57'.

[37] *Taverner*, full score, 23–4.

[38] All transcriptions of Davies's sketches that appear in this chapter have been carried out by the author.

JUDGE Call the first witness, the wife of the accused.

(Enter Mrs. Taverner.)

JURY                          Alma Redemptoris Ma

JUDGE (interrupting, to the Jury)
                    Pax!
                    (to Mrs. Taverner)
                    Pax tecum!

TAVERNER   My wife, through whom I lived, my image! I was unaware of
your simplicity, and knew you only as my mother, star of the sea.
[note in left margin: JUNG, MARRIAGE AS A PSYCHOLOGICAL
        RELATIONSHIP]
I buried myself in your soft, rich *earth [left margin: *ERDA], and suffocated in the cell.
My hands bled from the effort to escape; you, protective, covered the grating.
[left margin: MATTHEW XXVII v 45] There was darkness over all the land, only now
does the light glow from within, the potential light of the world.

[left margin: (REQUIEM)] JURY              Et lux perpetua luceat eis.

TAVERNER   In shutting out the light you lit me, which light shall kindle the flames
round the stake. [left margin: JUNG. DEVEL. of PERSONALITY] You, the agent of these
undergraduates, betrayed and destroyed me, who am no phoenix.

JURY (Sings the 'Alma Red. Mater'          Mrs. TAVERNER If the cell was
Throughout the next few speeches)          mine, you locked me out. I saw
'Alma Redemptoris Mater, quae pervia caeli, your pride about to destroy you,
/porta maes, Et stella maris, succurre cadenti/ who held the key to salvation.
Surgere qui curat populo: Tu quae genisti, /  You are not the elect; I took the
Natura mirante, tuum sanctum Genitorem:/   key and held you prisoner; too
Virgo prius ac posterius, Gabrielis ab ore   weak to face revelation, in
Sumens illud Ave, peccatorum misere'.      Despair I hid you from yourself; I know you
                                           wished it.

[more dialogue between the two]

MRS TAVERNER   Unmitigated evil succeeds. Your vocation is a lie, your heresy
universal death. Why should you be stricken any more? You will revolt more fiercely,
the whole head is sick, the heart faint. [left margin: ISAIAH I v 5]

(EXIT MRS. TAVERNER)

JUDGE   John Taverner, accused; in turning from disintegration, failed to realise inner integra-
tion, and destroyed his wife, immaculatum divini fontis uterum.* [left margin: *JUNG.
'MARRIAGE as a PSYCHOLOGICAL RELATIONSHIP' and 'SIGNIFICANCE of the
UNCONSCIOUS in INDIVIDUAL EDUCATION']

**Fig. 4.1**  Sketch of the libretto for Act I, Scene 1, ultimately discarded (BL Add. Ms. 71259,
fols. 66 and 68)

The implication is that Taverner's rejection of the Catholic Church is
symbolic of a deeper psychological rejection of a suffocating mother figure.
Whether this extends to unease with women in general is an interesting
question. On the one hand, Taverner's lines to Rose in Act I, Scene 4, convey
terms of affection and physical attraction that are completely absent from the
draft for the earlier scene ('My hands, my loins burn for your cool body'),[39]
and she very nearly persuades him to return to her (bars 462–6). On the other

---

[39] *Taverner*, full score, 181–2.

hand, Rose's presence in the opera is very limited, and she is the only female character in the opera.[40] The question of possible links between Taverner and Davies inevitably arise. One would expect Davies to have been entirely unsympathetic to the Judge's dogmatic verdict, but is it not also possible that his decision to present Taverner's predicament in terms of a turning away from women was informed, at least partially, by his own gay perspective – what Lloyd Whitesell, in the context of Britten's *Death in Venice*, has referred to as 'an urge to wish away the heterosexual world'?[41] Ultimately, Taverner heeds the Jester's entreaties to 'reject her' and 'abhor her seductions utterly'.

As the marginalia of the early draft for the libretto make clear, Davies's principal sources at this moment in the trial scene were several essays by Jung. One of these texts, 'The Significance of the Unconscious in Individual Education', establishes a more specific link between Church, mother figure and homosexuality. In this essay, which was the source of the Latin citation in the Judge's verdict, Jung discusses dream analysis. The dreams in question are those of a young man conflicted by his homosexuality, of whom Jung observes:

> As in nearly all cases of this kind, he had a particularly close tie with his mother … a secret, subterranean tie which expresses itself consciously, perhaps, only in the retarded [i.e. slowed down or arrested] development of character … nothing is more obstructive to development than persistence in an unconscious – one could also say, a physically embryonic, condition. For this reason instinct seizes on the first opportunity to replace the mother by another object … Hence the enthusiasm with which his childish imagination took up the idea of the Church; for the Church is, in the fullest sense, a mother. We speak not only of Mother Church, but even of the Church's womb. In the ceremony known as the *benedicto fontis*, the baptismal font is apostrophized as *immaculatis divini fontis uterus* – 'immaculate womb of the divine fount'.[42]

While any hypothetical resonance between Jung's theories and Davies's own sexual identity may remain open for interpretation, what the draft confirms is that his conception of Taverner's (and perhaps even of his own) personality was informed by Jung's association of arrested personal development with obsessive interests that stem from sexual conflict.

[40] Of relevance here is Northcott's concern that 'despite Gillian Knight's accomplished performance' of Rose's 'Muse' aria in Act I, Scene 4, it 'obstinately refuses to yield up the expressive shape and ambience the words demand' (Northcott, '*Taverner*', 64).

[41] Lloyd Whitesell, 'Britten's Dubious Trysts', *Journal of the American Musicological Association*, 56/3 (2003), 653; see also Whitesell's suggestion that artists may inflect 'the problems of the modern subject with the terms of their own private sexual subjectivity' (ibid., 641).

[42] C. G. Jung, 'The Significance of the Unconscious in Individual Education', in C. G. Jung, *The Development of Personality*, trans. R. F. C. Hull (London: Routledge & Kegan Paul, 1954), 157, n. 268 and 158, n. 270 ('n.' here does not denote footnote: it refers to the number in the margin of the main text).

## 'Strange bedfellows'

Further important clues to the nature of Taverner's predicament may be gleaned from the relationship between the opera and the *Second Taverner Fantasia* – works that Harbison refers to as 'strange bedfellows'.[43] The *Fantasia* was composed between Acts I and II of the opera, and Davies has stated that it reinterprets the first act of *Taverner* in symphonic terms, to which Griffiths has added that it was composed 'with some segments from the first act of the opera and containing others that were to serve in the second'.[44] An example of the overlap between the two works is provided by the opera's last scene, the White Abbot's execution (Act II, Scene 4, bar 95 onwards). This is accompanied by the final Adagio of the *Second Taverner Fantasia* (bars 1009–1215),[45] to which Davies simply added various new elements, such as the solo vocal lines, a chorus, and, at the end, a cello solo and the recorder ensemble quotation of the In Nomine.[46]

It is likely that the *Second Taverner Fantasia* was composed in order to cultivate the goal-directed transformational technique that, according to Stephen Arnold, was first introduced into the opera in Act I, Scene 4.[47] It was Arnold's summary of transformations of an eight-note set at the start of Act I, Scene 4, that set Roberts on his analytical quest,[48] and the systematic, at times dogmatic, nature of Davies's techniques meant that it was possible for Roberts to trace many complex procedures without access to the sketches. The sketches for the opera, which are interspersed with those for the *Second Taverner Fantasia* and the *Seven In Nomine* (1963–5),[49] demonstrate that Roberts's account of the two works is remarkably accurate. They also clarify some of the links between the opera and the *Second Taverner Fantasia*, and they explain some – but not all – of Arnold's remarks in his analysis of the opera.

Arnold identifies two primary 'themes' in the closing quotation: the treble recorder theme (D–F–E, etc., from bar 291), which he labels T1, and the *Gloria Tibi Trinitas* cantus firmus in the alto recorder (D–F–D–C–F–G–F–G–A),

---

[43] Harbison, 'Peter Maxwell Davies's *Taverner*', 235.

[44] Griffiths, *Peter Maxwell Davies*, 141 and 45 respectively. Davies has suggested that the opera was always foremost in his mind: 'For me the opera isn't the outcome: it's the first one' (see Walsh, 'Taverner', 653).

[45] All bar references are to the full score (London: Boosey & Hawkes, 1968).

[46] Stephen Arnold and Paul Griffiths report that the cello solo alludes to an Easter plainchant (*Victimae Paschali Laudes*) and

by association to a potential resurrection (see Arnold, 'The Music of *Taverner*', 29, and Griffiths, *Peter Maxwell Davies*, 53).

[47] Arnold, 'The Music of *Taverner*', 22. Roberts's discussion of transformational processes in the opera also focuses on this scene (see his 'Techniques of Composition', Vol. 1, 315–19).

[48] See Roberts, 'Techniques of Composition', Vol. 1, 418, n. 10.

[49] British Library (hereafter BL) MS Mus. 1401.

Ex. 4.2 Source sets for the *Second Taverner Fantasia* (BL MS Mus. 1401, fol. 134)

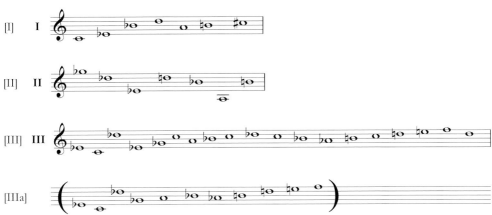

which he terms T2.[50] These, he explains, 'are the origin of two of the opera's three basic groups of "precompositional" material'.[51] In a later article, however, he refers to 'sets of eight, nineteen, eleven and seven pitches', describing the eight-note set (Gb–Eb–G–D–C♯–B–A–C) as 'the "main" set of the opera' since it appears at the beginning of the work.[52] Arnold does not explain the association between T1 and T2 and the sets, nor does he refer to the substantial overlaps between the opera and the *Second Taverner Fantasia*. As Roberts has demonstrated, part of the confusion about the number of sets used in both works arises because a basic stock of set types – approximately nine set types in the opera, most of which are obviously related to the *Gloria Tibi Trinitas* plainchant and also used in the *Fantasia* – are adapted to make smaller or larger sets (what Roberts refers to as second- and third-level sets), so that the complete number is inestimable.

Although there does not appear to be a 'source' page in the sketches for the opera, one does exist for the *Second Taverner Fantasia*, and the opera can be read more clearly through processes that crystallized in the *Fantasia*. On the page in question, four set types are written, one beneath the other: two seven-note sets, one nineteen-note set, and one eleven-note set (the latter in brackets). Of these, the first three are labelled I, II and III (Ex. 4.2).[53]

Roberts identifies the use of these numbered sets in the *Second Taverner Fantasia* and several other pieces composed at this time, including the *Seven In Nomine* and *Revelation and Fall* (1965–6), the last two being works that employ goal-directed transformations. It therefore seems likely that the labelled sets are identical to 'the three main melodic figures' that Davies

[50] Roberts labels the set formed by these pitches N ('Techniques of Composition', Vol. 2, 66, Ex. 7.32).

[51] Arnold, 'The Music of *Taverner*', 22.

[52] Stephen Arnold, 'Peter Maxwell Davies', in *British Music Now*, ed. Lewis Foreman (London: Paul Elek, 1975), 80.

[53] BL MS Mus. 1401.

**Ex. 4.3 (a)**  Sketch extract, BL MS Mus. 1401

[* = 'Death Chord']

mentions in the first section of the *Fantasia*,[54] and also the 'three basic groups of "precompositional" material' to which Arnold alludes in relation to the opera.[55] Set I is almost identical (with the exception of two interval classes) to an example that Owens suggests was produced by first-only sieving, transposition and complementation of the *Gloria Tibi Trinitas* plainchant,[56] the basis of Taverner's In Nomine.[57] Davies was clearly interested in the symmetrical properties of this set (Ex. 4.3 (a)). He rearranged the set into a series of dyads, which included the ubiquitous tritone E♭-A mentioned earlier (see dyad 2 in Ex. 4.3 (a)), and transposed these to form chords, such as the so-called 'Death Chord',[58] which also relates back to the *Gloria Tibi Trinitas* plainchant (Ex. 4.3 (b)).

The exact provenance of set II is unclear, but it shares the same pitches as I, with a single exception (G♭ instead of C), and its contour is an approximate inversion of I.[59] Set III is an expanded variation of Taverner's In Nomine

[54] Davies, programme note for the *Second Taverner Fantasia*, in Griffiths, *Peter Maxwell Davies*, 141.

[55] Arnold, 'The Music of Taverner', 22. In 'Peter Maxwell Davies', 83, Arnold refers to 'three subsidiary sets'.

[56] Sarum Antiphon: *In Festo Ss. Trinitatis*.

[57] See Peter Owens, 'Revelation and Fallacy: Observations on Compositional Technique in the Music of Peter Maxwell Davies', *Music Analysis*, 13/2–3 (1994), 179, Ex. 18, set Bc. Roberts labels this set B, but writes it with the smallest interval classes possible ('Techniques of Composition', Vol. 2, 63, Ex. 7.26).

[58] Writing about Act I, Scene 4, Stephen Arnold notes that: 'The scene introduces the one *Leitmotiv*-like idea in the opera. When Taverner realizes that he is in the presence of Death, the low brass sound the chord of superimposed major thirds based on the whole tone tetrachord [D-F♯-E-G♯] … which is henceforth associated with the idea of death, real or symbolic' ('The Music of Taverner', 26).

[59] Labelled C by Roberts, with different interval classes ('Techniques of Composition', Vol. 2, 65, Ex. 7.28).

**Table 4.1** Summary of the use of set-forms I, II and III at the opening of the *Second Taverner Fantasia* (bars 1–20), and the instrumental transition between Scenes 2 and 3 in Act I of *Taverner* (bars 147–63)

| Section | Bars | Set-forms | Realization |
|---|---|---|---|
| Introduction | 1–14 | $III^0$ | vc., vln. 1 |
| | | $I^9$ | vla. |
| | 15–20 | $I^9_R$ | vln. 1 |
| | | $II^0$ | vln. 2, vla., vc. |

**Ex. 4.3 (b)**  Sketch extract, BL Add. Ms. 71259, fol. 1

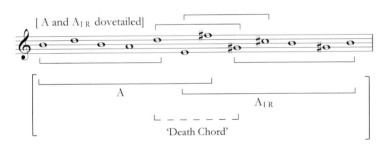

theme and is identical to another example given by Owens, who suggests that it may have been formed from transposed and inverted segments of the *Gloria Tibi Trinitas* plainchant that are concatenated (overlapped).[60] The fourth, unnumbered set – which I shall refer to as IIIa – is a variant of set III, produced by an application of the first-only sieve.[61] A summary of the way these sets are used at the very opening of the *Fantasia* is given in Table 4.1.[62] Although barred differently, the pitch content is effectively identical to the opening of the transition between Scenes 2 and 3 in Act I of the opera.

[60] Owens, 'Revelation and Fallacy', 169, Ex. 8 (b). I was unable to find any evidence in the sketches to confirm or disprove Owens's explanation for the construction of this set or the one cited earlier. Roberts labels this set $+A_0$, with different interval classes ('Techniques of Composition', Vol. 2, 62, Ex. 7.19).

[61] Roberts labels this set $-A_0$, with different interval classes (ibid., Ex. 7.20). According to Roberts, the technique of deriving a smaller set from a larger one dates back to *St Michael*, composed in 1957 ('Techniques of Composition', Vol. 1, 200).

[62] This table is based on Fig. 8.2 in Roberts, 'Techniques of Composition', Vol. I, 309. The sketch labels and those in Roberts's figure correspond as follows: I = B; II = C; III = $+A_0$.

The principle behind Davies's goal-directed transformational procedures, when they occur, is to move either from one set-form to another (for example, from $I^0_O$ to $I^0_R$) or from one set type to another (for example, from $I^0_R$ to $III^0_O$).[63] This produces sets, or subunits, that are not set-forms of the initial set or its destination. Appropriately enough, given the context of Taverner's situation, many of the transformations are 'self-transposing', that is to say, the transposition levels of each subunit are determined by the successive pitch classes of the set that is gradually altered. The result is a transposition square. This is illustrated by an early draft for the music that depicts the spinning Wheel of Fortune in Act II, Scene 1, bars 239–96 (Ex. 4.4).

In this highly symbolic scene, the fortunes of the King, and by association the Church, are depicted by a huge revolving wheel turned by the Jester, and accompanied by images of St Michael and the Serpent. This scene therefore confirms the structural importance of set-forms I–IIIa within the opera. The sketches reveal that the unison strings present self-transposing statements of $III^0$ (E♭–C–D♭–E♭–G♭ etc.) that alternate between prime and retrograde forms (E♭$_O$–C$_R$–D♭$_O$–E♭$_R$–G♭$_O$ etc.). Meanwhile, the horns move from $II^9$ to the inversion of IIIa, although the transpositions rise chromatically (Ex. 4.5). The original seven-note set ($II^0$) expands progressively to eight notes in the fifth transposition (bars 251–3), nine in the seventh transposition (bars 255–7), ten and eleven in the tenth and eleventh transpositions, respectively (bars 264–6 and 281–2), and reaches its goal (IIIa$_I$) in the thirteenth transposition, when the chorus sings: 'But who shall know St Michael, who the Serpent?'

How closely, if at all, do such goal-directed transformations relate to Taverner's predicament? To explore this question, another important piece of pre-compositional evidence should be introduced. This is the outline of a musical plot that Davies sketched, titled: 'Interrogation (obliteration of personality under pressure)'. During this scenario, a personality, 'P', is obliterated under the pressure of another melodic form, 'x'. P eventually loses its identity and assumes the form of its interrogator. Davies divided his scheme into six stages. In stage 1, P is defined by a 'complete statement of the "In nomine"'. This is inverted and retrograded before, in stage 2, x 'invades' P. During this stage, the 'superposition of motive x' results in the 'Slight Disorientation of P'. In stage 3, 'x in various transpositions jumps on & subtracts something' from five versions of P. In stage 4, P remains 'in emaciated state' and 'confused' with a 'Gradual loss of [its] melodic identities'. A retrograde transposition of P is further reduced 'by x and silences' in

**Ex. 4.4** *Taverner*: early draft for the opening of the Wheel of Fortune Section, Act II, Scene 1, bars 239–42 (BL Add. Ms. 71259, fol. 84)

The demisemiquaver running figures on strings doubled at octave or even two octaves also. 'Sanctus' on highest woodw & low brass & bsns. OR doubled by many strings at unison.

**Ex. 4.5** Goal-directed transformation in the horn, Act II, Scene I, bars 239–96
(BL Add. Ms. 71259, fols. 84–9)

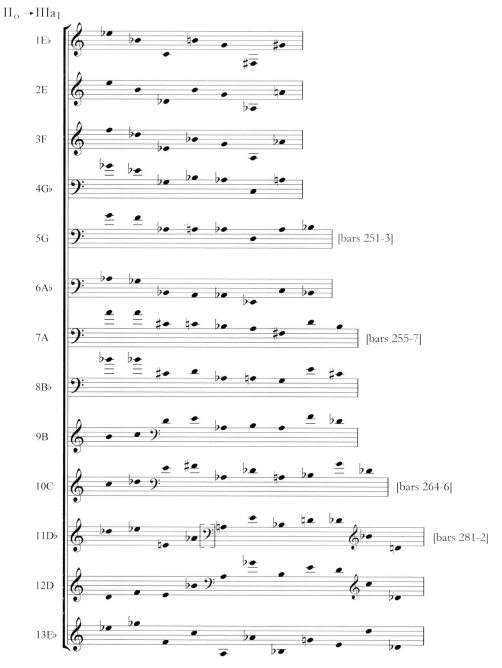

| | |
|---|---|
| Intro. | 1. Statement of tune<br>2. Amplification<br>3. Fanfare ff |
| Exp. | 1. Exposition of 3 themes [as subjects ?]<br>2. Demonstration of [inversion of …?] |
| Devel 1. | 1. Devel by transformation [to the … ?] Flute<br>[2]Fanfare (rpt by […] |
| Recap | 1. by inversion<br>2. Dim. of retro […] |
| Devel 2. | of fanfare 1 3 [of intro ?] <<<<br>2 of devel 1 |
| Climax | Statement of [March?] theme<br>[… ?] |

[… ?] of [here the 'Death Chord' is written in the bass clef] [… ?]

**Fig. 4.2** Davies's summary of the 'sonata-form movement' in the first half of the
*Second Taverner Fantasia* (BL MS Mus. 1400)

stage 5. This culminates in a 'Reduction of R [the retrograde transposition] to
x and Rock hammer rhythm' in stage 6.[64]

Since no character names are mentioned, this plot does not obviously relate
to the opera, although it may relate to the Jester's interrogation of Taverner in
Act I, Scene 4, which culminates in Taverner's conversion. However, the six-
part division of the plot may also relate to the first six sections of the *Second
Taverner Fantasia*, which, according to the composer, are combined within a
sonata-form movement.[65] For example, section 6 in Davies's summary of the
*Fantasia* (bars 539–48) features 'very prominent drum strokes' that correspond to the 'Rock hammer rhythm' to which the plot refers.[66] This section
reappears in Act II, Scene 1 of the opera (bars 287–96) where it brings the
depiction of the Wheel of Fortune and the scene as a whole to a dramatic
conclusion. By this stage in the opera it is clear that the Jester, as Death, has
transformed Taverner and that, according to stage 6 of the plot, the
'Reduction of R [the retrograde of P] to x' has been performed, which lends
support to the use of the so-called 'Death Chord' (D-F♯-E-G♯) after the first
prominent drum stroke (bar 546).

These examples suggest there was a conceptual link in the composer's
mind between the psychological profile of Taverner and an exploration
of his condition both in symphonic and serial terms. Further evidence
for this is provided by a page that was badly burned by the fire in the
composer's Dorset home, in 1970, on which it is just possible to discern
a six-part scheme, which corresponds to the *Fantasia*'s sonata-form
movement (bars 1–548; Fig. 4.2).

[64] BL Ms. Add. 71259, fol. 36.
[65] See Davies's programme note for
the *Second Taverner Fantasia*,

in Griffiths, *Peter Maxwell Davies*,
142–3.
[66] Ibid., 143.

Although this chart was superseded by the composer's programme note for the *Fantasia*, its reference to 'development by transformation' in the first development section is unique. This supports Roberts's analysis that goal-directed transformations are scarce in this sonata movement, but that they first appear in development 1, up to the return of the fanfare (bars 219–58). Roberts identified set transformations from prime sets to their inverted forms here and the reverse of this process in the recapitulation section. However, he found 'more active' transformations, from one set-form to a different set-form, in the second development section. This led him to conclude: 'there is a strong correlation between, on the one hand, non-transforming set structures and "exposition" or "recapitulation", and, on the other, transformation processes and "development"'.[67]

A closer examination of the transformational techniques used in the opera and the *Fantasia*, as they are described by Roberts and confirmed by the sketches, reveals more specific parallels with the interrogation plot. For example, the idea that P is 'invaded' is mirrored by a technique in which a 16-note set is expanded to 34 notes. This is achieved by the insertion of notes in three different parts of the original 16-note set. The pitches are distributed between various instruments in Act I, Scene 4, bars 355–466.[68] The inserted notes accumulate until they assume the form of three 7-note sets, two of which are $I^2$ and $II^7$ (Ex. 4.6).[69]

By contrast, the plot's direction that x 'jumps on & subtracts something' from P, and the 'Gradual reduction' of P 'by x and silences',[70] is paralleled by a transformation technique that reduces a 16-note set to a single pitch (Ex. 4.7).

A retrograde version of the reduction process appears in Act I, Scene 4 in the viola, bars 298–354, followed immediately by the expanding transformation. This assumes greater significance when it is considered that it underscores Rose's attempts to, in the words of the Jester, seduce Taverner (bars 298–466). While the terms of the interrogation plot may imply an analogy between the interrogator (x) and the Jester, the context (Rose's seduction) introduces a second interrogator, to which may be added Taverner's Father, also present in this scene. The process of invasion also recalls the more confrontational nature of the discarded dialogue between Taverner and Rose cited earlier. In light of the opera's source materials, Taverner's predicament appears as a double bind: either to choose between Rose and the Jester, or to reject them both.

---

[67] Roberts, 'Techniques of Composition', Vol. 1, 315.

[68] See also ibid., 316–17, and Vol. 2, 83, Ex. 8.23.

[69] Roberts reports that the third set, which he labels $E_5$, is located elsewhere in the opera and also in *Shakespeare Music* of 1964 (ibid., Vol. 1, 317).

[70] BL Ms. Add. 71259, fol. 36.

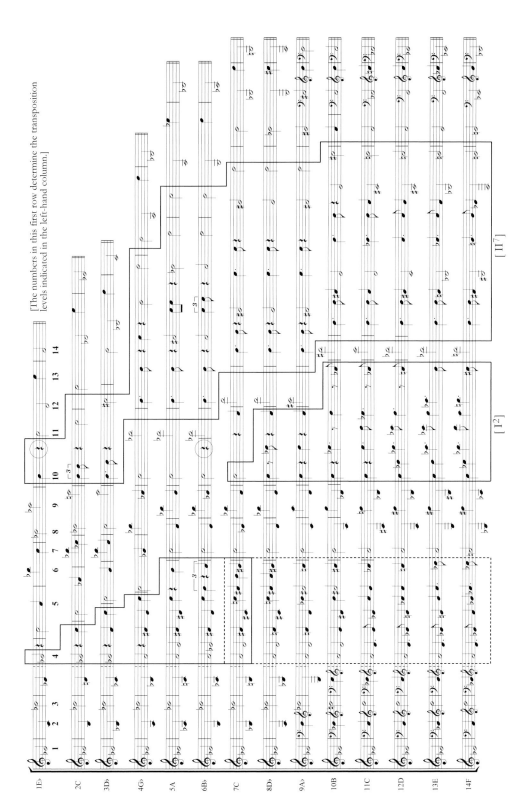

[The numbers in this first row determine the transposition levels indicated in the left-hand column.]

**Ex. 4.6** Sketch for Act I, Scene 4, bars 355–466: the invasion of a goal-directed transformation by three other goal-directed transformations (BL MS Mus. 1400)

**Ex. 4.7**  Reduction of a 16-note set to a single pitch (BL MS Mus. 1400)

The Jung essays cited in Davies's early draft of the libretto further illumi-
nate these compositional techniques. Jung's essay 'The Development of
Personality', in particular, encourages a more sophisticated interpretation of
Taverner's predicament and the role of the Jester. This essay examines what
Jung refers to as modern society's 'yearning for personality'.[71] According to
Jung, personality is unpredictable; it must be goaded by inner or outer forces
but it should proceed from free choice and moral deliberation. Yet it depends

[71] Jung, *The Development of Personality*, 168.

upon vocation – an inner voice, or calling, which acts 'like a law of God from which there is no escape', the best-known example being Faust.[72] Jung points out that the original meaning of 'to have a vocation' is 'to be addressed by a voice'. This voice is an inner daemon that brings evil before us 'in a very tempting and convincing way in order to make us succumb'. If we succumb entirely then 'catastrophe ensues', and if the voice is resisted 'no regeneration or healing can take place' either. However:

> … if we can succumb only in part, and if by self-assertion the ego can save itself from being completely swallowed, *then it can assimilate the voice*, and we realize that the evil was, after all, only a semblance of evil, but in reality a bringer of healing and illumination. In fact, the inner voice is a 'Lucifer' in the strictest and most unequivocal sense of the word, and it faces people with ultimate moral decisions without which they can never achieve full consciousness and become personalities. The highest and the lowest, the best and the vilest, the truest and the most deceptive things are often blended together in the inner voice in the most baffling way, thus opening up in us an abyss of confusion, falsehood, and despair.[73]

Jung argues that developing a personality is a dangerous gamble. However, heroes, leaders or saviours will only appear when individuals are prepared to take such risks. Hence, the 'daemon of the inner voice is at once our greatest danger and an indispensable help'.[74] What emerges from all of this, I believe, is a more detailed notion of the concepts that were behind Davies's opera and his choice of compositional techniques. For example, when viewed in relation to Jung's text, the process of expansion (Ex. 4.6) appears to assimilate the invading sets, rather than submit to them. Jung's text also draws attention to the importance of the Jester as Taverner's 'inner daemon' – which explains his lively presence, in contrast to Taverner – and it focuses attention on the interaction between coercion and choice in Taverner's life, which is clearly one of the opera's central concerns.

## Caveats and conclusions

Arnold and Roberts both give the impression that goal-directed transformation processes are not used in the opera before Act I, Scene 4. This is a convenient conclusion since it coincides with the beginning of Taverner's religious conversion. However, the sketches put a fly in the ointment for two reasons. Firstly, they indicate that goal-directed transformations of sets I–III, and other sets, are used earlier in the opera. For example, in Act I, Scene 3, the

[72] Ibid., 175, n. 300.
[73] Ibid., 185, n. 319 (italics added).
[74] Ibid., 186, n. 321.

**Ex. 4.8** Sketch for the Cardinal's vocal line in Act I, Scene 3, bar 243 (BL MS Mus. 1400)

Cardinal's soliloquy that begins 'Often I have kneeled before him the space of an hour or two' (bar 243) starts with transpositions of set type I (Ex. 4.8).

The first two subunits are $I^{11}_R$ and $I^5_O$, and these are transformed in the subsequent subunits. The numbers in the sketch ($6B_R$–$6F_O$–$5A_R$–$5E\flat_O$, etc.) also indicate that the transformation is self-transposing. Annotations in early drafts of Act I, Scene 1, both in the voices (for example, the White Abbot's opening line 'John Taverner, you are accused of possessing heretical books') and instrumental parts, suggest that goal-directed transformations were also applied to a five-note set ($G\flat$–$E\flat$–$G$–$D\flat$–$B$), which is a filtered version of the eight-note set Arnold analysed at the opening of Act I, Scene 4.[75] This provides evidence of a musical relationship between the throne room scenes and those in which Taverner is present, although it may not fully alleviate concerns that such scenes 'remain peripheral to Taverner', or that the long political exchanges between the Cardinal and the King fail to dramatize the schism between artist and state.[76]

Josipovici's comment that Davies cannot bring himself to rely on the use of distancing conventions, and that his 'problem has always been to render the *cry* articulate, rather than to transmute it into a more formal scheme' should

---

[75] The eight-note set (spelled $G\flat$–$E\flat$–$G$–$D$–$D\flat$–$B$–$A$–$C$ in the drafts) is labelled $F_0$ by Roberts

(see 'Techniques of Composition', Vol. 2, 85, Ex. 8.27).
[76] Dean, 'Taverner', 879.

also be reconsidered.[77] Davies's 'problem', I believe, was his decision to portray Taverner's suppression – the obliteration of a personality – to the practical exclusion of his 'cry' (although anguish is more clearly articulated in the expansive Mahlerian themes of the *Second Taverner Fantasia*). In the plot, P does not put up any kind of fight. It therefore does not conform to Jung's definition of personality as 'a well-rounded psychic whole that is capable of resistance and abounding in energy',[78] and Kerman's complaint that Davies pushes personality 'into the background' is neutralized.[79] P's suppression is clearly projected in the opera. For example, in the two court scenes, the rigid rhythms of the chorus, as it churns out religious dogma, form a framework – a Stravinskian distancing technique – within which Taverner's expressions are contained. Also, the Jester's line, 'But the indestructible heritage of the Church is heaped against you, Taverner' (Act I, Scene 4, bars 142–7) is supported by wild, *ritmico* figures in violins 1 and 2. These anticipate the frenzied woodwind pairings that accompany the various witnesses called upon by Taverner in the parody court scene and the swirling strings of the Wheel of Fortune. The terms of the interrogation plot are also echoed in Davies's stage directions, for example when Taverner is described as 'shrunken in on himself, dazed' (bar 559), 'somnambulistic' (bar 576) until, finally, 'he collapses' (bar 660). This situation is further mirrored by Davies's set transformations that rotate, unhindered and uninterrupted.

## Postscript: after *Taverner*

> Christianity struck at the root of pagan tolerance of illusion. In claiming that there is only one true faith, it gave truth a supreme value it had not had before. … The long-delayed consequence of Christian faith was an idolatry of truth that found its most complete expression in atheism. If we live in a world without gods, we have Christianity to thank for it.[80]

> … indeed, with the aid of a religion which has gratified and flattered the sublimest herd-animal desires, it has got to the point where we discover even in political and social institutions an increasingly evident expression of this morality: the *democratic* movement inherits the Christian.[81]

In *Taverner* the obliteration of the central character's personality is powerfully evoked and Kerman's complaint of a 'basic confusion of ideas' should be

---

[77] Josipovici, '*Taverner*: Thoughts on the Libretto', 19.
[78] Jung, *The Development of Personality*, 169, n. 286.
[79] Kerman, 'Popish Ditties', 21.

[80] John Gray, *Straw Dogs: Thoughts on Humans and Other Animals* (London: Granta Books, 2003), 127.
[81] Friedrich Nietzsche, *Beyond Good and Evil* [1887], trans. R. J. Hollingdale (London: Penguin Books, 1990), 125.

contested.[82] However, many of Jung's concepts, such as assimilation and submission, were not easy to dramatize on the opera stage, and other ideas, such as the reasons for Taverner's turn away from women, were deliberately obscured. Davies's interest in portraying Taverner's suppression also gave rise to a lack of real conflict, highlighted by the exaggerated cries of Taverner's oppressors, which at least one critic felt degenerated into 'empty grimaces'.[83] After *Taverner*, Davies clearly felt the need to explore different approaches, even though his dramatic themes remained more or less the same.

The first step in this direction was to turn away from conceptual structure towards 'perceptual structure',[84] 'austere economy of gesture' and '[s]implicity of aim and execution'.[85] Although partly a symptom of his desire to re-explore tonal forms, the intention was clearly to convey meaning more coherently than in *Taverner*.[86] Davies did not abandon the use of hysterical oppressors, and at times his subjects recede even further into the background (Magnus, for example, makes very little impact on the main drama of *The Martyrdom of St Magnus*, appearing in just four of the nine scenes).[87] However, from *The Lighthouse* onwards, Davies's stage works begin to make use of recurring devices that connote underlying tension, such as the horn line in *The Lighthouse*, or building conflict, illustrated by the recurring pop songs in *Resurrection*, and the hymn tunes in *The Doctor of Myddfai*.

One likely origin for these devices was a 'varied and cumulative rondo impulse' that Bayan Northcott observed in the opening Trial scene of *Taverner*.[88] Such recurring features in the later operas symbolize the passing of religious dogma into the social and political realms of contemporary society. But they also transform into collective forces that resist oppression and – unlike Taverner – *are* 'capable of resistance and abounding in energy'.[89] The hymn tunes in *The Doctor of Myddfai* literally burst into the Ministry, entering through a window that is suddenly blown open. John Warnaby has even argued that in *Resurrection* Davies attempted to 'turn the weapons of the culture industry against itself' through the prominent use of the opera's 'rock numbers', arguing that they 'carry the main burden of the opera's message' and 'are associated with the most important harmonic thinking in the

[82] Kerman, 'Popish Ditties', 20.
[83] Dean, 'Taverner', 879. Arnold Whittall sensed a similar problem with *The Martyrdom of St Magnus* in which, he observed, 'Magnus's persecutors are presented as mere grotesques' (Whittall, review of the score, *Music & Letters*, 69/1 (1988), 137).
[84] David Roberts, 'Maxwell Davies in Orkney: The Martyrdom of Saint Magnus', *Musical Times*, 118 (August 1977), 635.
[85] Max Loppert, 'The Martyrdom of St. Magnus', *Tempo*, 122 (1977), 30.
[86] Davies, programme note for *The Martyrdom of St Magnus*, in Griffiths, *Peter Maxwell Davies*, 163.
[87] Although in the *Martyrdom*, as Whittall points out, 'the degree of distance wavers disconcertingly' (see his review of the score, 137).
[88] Northcott, '*Taverner*', 64.
[89] Jung, *The Development of Personality*, 169, n. 286.

work'.[90] The songs are titled 'Alchemical Dances', and, like the pop group's lead singer the Cat who turns into a Dragon, they undergo a gradual process of transformation that culminates in the 'Song of the New Resurrection'. The Cat's message of obliteration ('I reflect the ways of those who have restructured me') is familiar from *Taverner* but it is conveyed by a voice as sardonic as any in punk rock.

*Resurrection* is often cited as the natural partner of *Taverner*, not least because its origins date from the early 1960s, when work on the first opera was under way. Despite its quirky humour and surreal contemporary devices – repeating television adverts and a severely dysfunctional family – the combination of short, rapidly alternating scenes and repetition results in an addictive, seamless journey towards the Song of Resurrection. However, Davies's goal-directed opera – like his set transformations in *Taverner* – masks a fundamental circularity. Quotidian lives turn to hysteria (*The Lighthouse*) and intense self-reflection leads to downfall (*Taverner* and *The Doctor of Myddfai*). One extreme will lead to another. One destination is another point of departure.

[90] John Warnaby, 'Peter Maxwell Davies's Recent Music, and Its Debt to His Earlier Scores', in *Perspectives*, ed. McGregor, 77.

**The ghost in the machine: sonata form in the music of Peter Maxwell Davies**

*Rodney Lister*

Peter Maxwell Davies, who has always been a composer with a historical awareness and a willingness to use constructive methods from former times for his own compositional purposes, has had a preoccupation with sonata form throughout most of his career. Aside from its importance in music which he has continually studied and pondered and his recognition of its power as an organizational tool, he has been both troubled and spurred on by the incongruity between the tenets of the form and his personal musical style and preoccupations, and he has exploited this tension in various ways from the early stages of his career onwards. When discussing some of his earlier works, Davies was evidently cautious to state categorically that they were in sonata form. For instance, he describes the third movement of *Sinfonia* (1962) as being 'in the manner of a classical sonata movement'; sections 1 to 6 of the *Second Fantasia on John Taverner's 'In Nomine'* (1964) as making 'roughly a sonata-form movement'; and the first movement of the First Symphony (1973–6) as having 'a ghost of a sonata form somewhere behind it'.[1] More recently, however, particularly in writing about some movements of the ten Naxos String Quartets, he simply states that certain of the movements are in sonata form.[2] His comments often raise, but less often answer, the question of exactly what it is that gives the earlier works the quality of suggesting that they are haunted by the form without actually partaking of it, and what it is about the more recent works that make them not just evocative of the form, but real examples of it. This chapter will examine these issues briefly in relation to two works by Davies, the *Second Taverner Fantasia* and the First Symphony, and in more detail in a late work, the Third Naxos String Quartet (2003) – the first movement of which Davies,

[1] Peter Maxwell Davies, programme notes for *Sinfonia*, the *Second Fantasia on John Taverner's 'In Nomine'*, and the First Symphony, in Paul Griffiths, *Peter Maxwell Davies* (London: Robson Books, 1982), 139, 141–2 and 159–60 respectively.
[2] For a discussion of the use of sonata form in the first movement of Davies's Naxos String Quartet No. 1 see Nicholas Jones, 'Playing the "Great Game"?: Maxwell Davies, Sonata Form, and the *Naxos* Quartet No. 1', *Musical Times*, 146 (Autumn 2005), 71–81. Jones also considers the composer's relationship to sonata form in more general terms by briefly looking at the form's use in a selection of works from the 1960s through to the quartet series – an approach that is expanded upon in this present discussion.

comfortable with using the terms 'exposition' and 'development', clearly considers as actually being in sonata form.[3]

Sonata form has been a mythic form for many composers over many years. It was prominent in music of the Classical tonal era and its efficiency and power as a strategy for organizing musical material into large, organic musical structures is striking and undeniable. But its fascination, which goes beyond those obvious qualities, perhaps has had as much to do with its post-Beethovenian aura of enormous prestige and seriousness. Just as composers who were intent on calling attention to their scholastic erudition and technical skill would do so by writing fugues, a composer who intended to make an imposing and important statement would do so by casting it in sonata form. The beginning of this sense that the medium itself was part of the message coincided with the moment when sonata form became less a process indigenous to the organizational thinking of composers in the course of things and more a genre, and at approximately the time when the form was given its name.

## Sonata form: a definition

As practised by Haydn and Mozart, sonata form, which was not called that at the time, was a more extended rounded binary form.[4] The first section started in the tonic and modulated to a second key (usually either the dominant or, if it was in the minor, the relative major). The second section modulated back to the tonic, through a 'development section' (which might actually develop the material of the exposition, or might introduce new material) to a recapitulation of the material of the first section (still part of the second section), except that, rather than modulating, it stayed in and ended in the tonic. Both sections (the first being the exposition, and the second comprised of the development and recapitulation) were repeated, with the convention of repetition becoming less utilized over time. For these composers the melodic materials, being merely markers for the progress of keys in the movement, were of less importance than the tonal scheme. Since the themes were markers, the same theme (or more or less the same theme) could serve as the marker for the second key as well as for the tonic, as happens in certain movements of Haydn's that are said to be 'monothematic'. One might assume that for

[3] Davies, liner notes to Naxos String Quartet No. 3 (CD, Naxos, 8. 557397, 2005).

[4] For a comprehensive survey of sonata form, see James Hepokoski and Warren Darcy, *Elements of Sonata Theory: Norms, Types, and Deformations in the Late-Eighteenth-Century Sonata* (Oxford and New York: Oxford University Press, 2006); Charles Rosen, *Sonata Forms* (New York: Norton, 1988); and James Webster, 'Sonata Form', *The New Grove Dictionary of Music and Musicians*, 2nd edn, ed. Stanley Sadie and John Tyrrell (London: Macmillan, 2001), 23, 687–701.

Classical composers the coincidence of form and general musical process and progress was just about complete, so that they may not have thought of it as a form so much as a procedure.

With Beethoven, the development section tended to become more extended, dramatic, and harmonically intense and directed (and more completely organic to the material of the exposition). The shifted proportions of the sections as well as the greatly increased drama of the return of the tonic at the recapitulation, which gave much more emphasis to that point in the form, served to make a repeat of the development and recapitulation superfluous. As a result of these changes the form morphed from a two-part form to a three-part form, and the expressive nature of the themes, and the contrast afforded by their greater differentiation, tended to make the character of the themes more important than previously had been the case – without, as in Beethoven, lessening the importance of the tonal drama.[5] In the second third of the nineteenth century the form became more standardized – more like a mould into which a composer would pour his material – and less dynamic. There was a much greater emphasis on sonata form as a patterned sequence of themes, whose differentiation of character was of paramount importance; the tonal workings, although not unimportant, nonetheless could be considered more as constituents of another means of articulating the different characteristics of the contrasting melodic materials than as a driving organizational factor of a work on their own accord.

By the end of the nineteenth century, sonata form had become a highly standardized textbook form, and in the last third of the century a generation of composers, including Mahler, Elgar, Strauss, and Sibelius, further adapted sonata form in consideration of changing musical and dramatic attitudes and languages by means of what James Hepokoski calls 'sonata-deformational procedures', including 'breakthrough deformation, introduction-coda framing, various sonata-strophic hybrids, and multi-movement forms in a single movement'.[6] Although not sonata form in any strict sense, Hepokoski writes, these adapted forms are 'in dialogue' with the expectation of the textbook form, and depend to some extent on the listeners' knowledge of its conventions.

Sonata form, then, has been different things at different times, but its constant feature over time is the contrast, conflict, and resolution (and recapitulation) of differing elements, either thematic or tonal, and the difference between statement (stability) and development or movement.

---

[5] At times Beethoven added a coda at the end of the recapitulation; this coda could be as long as the development section, and possibly made the proportions resemble the earlier binary layout. The first movement of the Eighth Symphony, for instance, has the following proportions: exposition, 103 bars (28% of overall structure); development, 85 bars (23%); recapitulation, 110 bars (29%); coda, 72 bars (20%).

[6] James Hepokoski, *Sibelius: Symphony No. 5* (Cambridge University Press, 1993), 4–5.

## The 'ghost' of sonata form

The aspects of sonata form that seem to have been most problematic for Davies in his earlier music were those of development and recapitulation. Classical development is a process that involves fragmenting the melodic materials and expanding, contracting or reassembling the fragments in some new way, leading to them being somehow reshaped. In contrast to these procedures, Davies developed a method of transformation of material whereby a sequence of notes, treated more or less as a cantus firmus, is subjected to an isorhythmic process in which it is repeated a number of times and altered very slightly with each repetition, so that in the end it becomes effectively a new element of the material. This process, as outlined by Gerald Abraham in relation to Sibelius's technique of continuous thematic transformation, 'reminds one of the child's game of altering a word letter by letter, so that "cat" becomes "dog" through the intermediate stages of "cot" and "cog"'.[7]

This method evolved over Davies's career in two stages: early on he began to use quasi-serial isorhythmic procedures derived from his study of medieval and Renaissance formal procedures using isorhythmic tenors; while he was a student at Princeton University, under the influence of Sibelius, particularly the Fourth Symphony, he began, with *Seven In Nomine* (1963–5), to combine isorhythmic repetition with transformational techniques. Davies speaks of that process as being a 'line of connection' rather than development;[8] he apparently finds these two methods irreconcilable and sees the latter as being required by the tenets of sonata form. In his transformation processes the material is in a continual state of flux from beginning to end, and lacks the definite statement of material with clearly different character and the examination and manipulation of the contrast of those characteristics which might be seen as a prerequisite for sonata form. Hans Keller pinpointed the absence of clear contrast of statement–stability and development–lability and the large-scale integration of them to be what was for him a fault in the first movement of Davies's First Symphony.[9] In addition, like many composers since Mahler, Davies also has an abhorrence of repetition, so the idea of anything like literal recapitulation is, to say the least, problematic.

The *Second Taverner Fantasia*, written in 1964, is a complex orchestral work, intimately connected to the prolonged gestation of Davies's opera *Taverner*, which was finally finished in 1968 (but partly reconstructed in

---

[7] Gerald Abraham, quoted in Nicholas Jones, 'Playing the "Great Game"?', 72.
[8] Peter Maxwell Davies, programme note for the *Second Taverner Fantasia*, in Griffiths, *Peter Maxwell Davies*, 141.

[9] Hans Keller, 'The State of the Symphony: Not Only Maxwell Davies's', *Tempo*, 125 (1978), 6–11.

1970), and performed in 1972. Much of the music is very close, if not identical, to music that appears in the opera. Nevertheless the *Second Taverner Fantasia* itself was a major milestone in Davies's development of his personal musical language and in his career, and it remains one of his most important works; it is not in any way some kind of 'suite' of selections from the opera. The *Second Taverner Fantasia* is concerned with the continual transformation over the work's entire span of three melodic figures that are presented in its very beginning,[10] but this progress is deployed in a way that suggests a continuous large-scale work in three movements, the first of which, as mentioned above, is 'roughly a sonata-form movement', with an introduction and a coda. The introduction to the movement leads to fanfare music derived from the third figure.[11] Material derived from the second figure is presented as the first subject at the beginning of the 'exposition' (bar 128), and from the first as the 'second theme' (bar 163), with the first subject returning as a 'closing theme'. The 'development' begins with music referring (mainly through its texture) to the introduction of the work, starting with a version of the 'first subject' in augmentation (bar 219), and gradually bringing in material related to the other fragments, leading to a return of the fanfare music (bar 259) before the 'development proper' (bar 267) begins with the introduction of a four-note whole-tone chord (D-F♯-E-G♯) which, as Davies writes, 'comes to dominate and unify the whole melodic and harmonic structure of the work'.[12] The development section 'explores particularly techniques of isorhythm and mensural canon',[13] with its peroration being an appearance of John Taverner's In Nomine melody, derived from his *Gloria Tibi Trinitas* Mass, which is the source of all three of the figures on which the *Fantasia* is based. In the recapitulation (which begins with a restatement of the whole-tone chord) (bar 447), the subjects come back, clearly recognizable, but in inversion. The movement concludes with a climactic coda based on the fanfare music (which is identical to the music for a scene in the opera in which the Jester, as Death, is seen as the centre of a Wheel of Fortune with which he controls the destinies of all people) (bar 505), and, after the crystallizing out

---

[10] The first figure is heard in the cello in bars 1–5, the second in the viola, bars 5–14, and the third in the second violin in bars 15–20. 'Development' of these figures constitutes the rest of the introduction, up to bar 116.

[11] This music appears in Act I, Scene 3 of *Taverner*, where it is, in fact, a fanfare introducing the King.

[12] Davies, programme note for the *Second Taverner Fantasia*, in Griffiths, *Peter Maxwell Davies*, 142. This chord, in exactly those

pitches, is an important element in a whole constellation of pieces which are related in various ways to *Taverner*, including *Worldes Blis* (1966–9), *Revelation and Fall* (1965–6), *Vesalii Icones* (1969), *Eight Songs for a Mad King* (1969), and *St Thomas Wake* (1966–9). In the opera the chord is associated with the Jester, who is, in turn, the personification of Death, hence its description as the 'Death chord'.

[13] Ibid.

into the aforementioned whole-tone chord (bar 546), moves on to the second movement, a scherzo, and the concluding slow movement.

The 'first movement' of the *Second Taverner Fantasia* conforms to the template of the post-Beethovenian sonata form, with some important differences. One might point to the fact that the harmonic strategy of the work relies on the gradual emergence and repetition of the so-called 'Death Chord', which becomes a fixed reference point at important structural moments. The harmonic movement of the work is away from and back to those fixed points, rather than those points being markers of a large movement away from one clearly defined tonal area to another clearly opposing one and then back to the original. Embedded in the layout of the movement is the strand of fanfare music, which reappears at important points in the unfolding of the form: at the end of the introduction before the entrance of the first subject, which is the beginning of the sonata-form argument of the movement; at the end of the 'introduction' of the development section, before the beginning of the 'development proper'; and at the end of the 'recapitulation', as the coda, which is, in fact, the climax of the movement (rather than the recapitulation). In a sense this strand could be seen as progressing on its own ever increasingly intense course outside of the argument of the movement and serving as another fixed reference point. In this instance, Davies's strategy for dealing with the problem of recapitulation is to present all the original material in inversion, so that even if it is a recapitulation, it is not a literal repetition.

The central dramatic trope of Davies's opera *Taverner* is the uncertainty of apparently clear and undeniable truth: nothing is as it seems and everything is undermined. Aside from this being the central problem for the protagonist, caught in the religious, philosophical, and political turmoil of the English Reformation, which is a political and economic power struggle disguised and presented as an issue of religion, it is manifested in many details of the libretto: the actions that justify condemning a person to death for treason in Act I are exactly the opposite of those that justify the same penalty in Act II; the Cardinal and the Archbishop are in fact the same character, motivated by the same political concerns; the apparently buffoonish and powerless Jester is revealed to be first the Joking Jesus, then Death, and finally the Antichrist who in fact controls the lives of all persons. These ideas are also played out by analogous musical means, where certain musical entities are parodied in other music, and period forms are found to be only surface details of different, more far-ranging musical processes. In the *Second Taverner Fantasia*, an instrumental work so intimately connected with the opera, it is dramatically logical that a section that appears to be a 'sonata movement' would turn out, over the course of the whole work, to be subsumed into a larger design operating on different musical principles with different processes, a sort of (deadly serious) joke on the listener.

Davies has been preoccupied with the music of Beethoven since his student days, and his study and contemplation of this music has been an important factor in his thinking about, among other things, structure. One work he has often referred to in his teaching has been the Piano Sonata in A♭, Op. 110, a work whose 'form' extends over the whole span of the piece and subsumes the individual movements which ostensibly are self-contained forms such as sonata, fugue, scherzo, or recitative and aria. The *Second Taverner Fantasia* applies this principle in a parodistic, ironic manner, but Davies has also used it without irony as a means of structuring larger works.

The first movement of the First Symphony, as already mentioned, has been described by its composer as having 'a ghost of a sonata form somewhere behind it'.[14] The movement can be read, like the first movement of the *Second Taverner Fantasia*, as a sonata movement of the post-Beethovenian type with an introduction and a coda. The introduction features brass chords and *pizzicato* strings playing in octaves; it also presents the basic harmonic and melodic material of the movement, most prominently a minor third (E♭–G♭) which is associated with notes a seventh away from one or both of the notes (Ex. 5.1)

When the main part of the movement begins, at Fig. 1:10,[15] a sonority of this type (F–A♭–G♭) is present both harmonically in the crotales and melodically (and somewhat extended) in hammer strokes of the timpani (F–A♭–G–B–G♭), which are anchored by the note that Davies identifies as the tonic, F (Ex. 5.2 (a)). The note sequence played by the timpani is what one might consider to be the 'first theme'. A quieter section that begins at Fig. 8, after an explosively emphatic cadence, would seem to be the 'second theme' (Ex. 5.2 (b)). It is a note sequence, played by the cellos, which is very similar to the timpani sequence (D♭–F–C–E–A) starting on what Davies considers to be the 'dominant' of the movement, D♭, incorporating a rhythmic feature, a long note followed by two short notes, which becomes more and more prominent over the course of the first section.

The 'development section', described by Davies as forming 'large-scale interlocking isorhythmic cycles',[16] begins at Fig. 21 with an inverted version of the sonority of the first subject: B♯-C♯-E♯ (Ex. 5.3; one will notice that this third chord (C) contains – enharmonically – the tonic and dominant notes of the movement).

The isorhythmic cycles are articulated by timpani strokes and crotales evoking the manner of the first subject, juxtaposed with longer lines, increasingly penetrated by string *pizzicato* figures in various registers which are reminiscent of the *pizzicato* lines from the very beginning of the movement.

---

[14] Peter Maxwell Davies, programme for the First Symphony, in Griffiths, *Peter Maxwell Davies*, 159.

[15] References to specific bars in the First Symphony are based on the composer's rehearsal figures in the score,

with for example, Fig. 1:10 indicating a reference to 10 bars after rehearsal figure 1.

[16] Davies, programme note for the First Symphony, in Griffiths, *Peter Maxwell Davies*, 160.

**Ex. 5.1**  First Symphony, first movement, opening

**Ex. 5.2 (a)** First Symphony, first movement, Fig. 1:10–15, crotales and timpani only: 'first theme'

**Ex. 5.2 (b)** First Symphony, first movement, Fig. 8–8:10, crotales and cellos only: 'second theme'

**Ex. 5.3** First Symphony, first movement, main structural chords

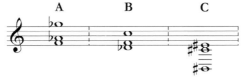

This leads to what seems to be the recapitulation, which is not so much of the first subject as it is of the brass chords of the introduction. This is followed not by the first subject material, but rather by a sort of continuation of the long lines of the 'development section' which become increasingly more active and lead – at Fig. 40 – to the beginning of the coda, in which the exact *pizzicato* string lines from the introduction return in augmentation (Ex. 5.4), the whole texture being broad and expansive leading to an intense climax, somewhat like

**Ex. 5.4** First Symphony, first movement, Fig. 40–40:6

the climax of the 'first movement' of the *Second Taverner Fantasia*, with which the movement ends. As in the first section of the *Fantasia*, the most intense climactic moment of the first movement of the First Symphony is not, as in the Beethoven model, at the beginning of the recapitulation, but rather at the very end of the movement. In both cases, where the argument of the piece extends over the span of the whole work, beyond that movement, this would be a logical means of continuing, rather than closing off, the continuity of overarching form.

It is the general outline of the sectioning of this movement that seems to evoke sonata form. As Davies's programme note points out, 'there is no first or second subject material as such'.[17] He does, however, use similar note sequences, each beginning with an outline of the featured harmonic sonority, somewhat in the manner of Haydnesque 'monothematic' themes, as markers of the places that correspond to the sections of the form. (It is perhaps noteworthy that the interval of a third in the 'first theme' sequence is a minor third, as opposed to the third in the 'second theme', which is major.) The introductory brass and string music is used in a way very similar to the way the fanfare music operates in the *Second Taverner Fantasia*, an independent argument 'developing' across the movement. It enables Davies to mimic the outline of sonata form, while at the same time maintaining a progress that, while it involves an isorhythmic and transformational argument of the material that initially appeared to be the first and second themes, in fact flows not only through the movement, but over the course of the whole work; a process that is independent of that suggested by the movement's outline. It is also another, different, strategy for dealing with the problem of recapitulation.

Both of these movements display certain of the deformational qualities of late nineteenth-century procedures, perhaps most noticeably the breakthrough deformation characterized by fanfare music in the *Second Taverner Fantasia* and the introductory brass and string music that provides the element of recapitulation in the first movement of the First Symphony. In both cases one senses that it is somehow this element, cutting across the outline of the standard sonata form, that is driving the tension and continuity of the movement. Even though both of the movements discussed here have prominent introductions and codas, in neither do those outer sections frame an otherwise separate continuity.

## Sonata form in a multi-movement work

In a reversal of the idea above (where something that on first impression appears to be a sonata-form movement turns out in actual fact to be subsumed into a larger overarching form over a longer span), there have also

---

[17] Ibid., 159.

been times in Davies's works where principles of sonata form have informed his strategies for organizing a sequence of apparently independent movements that comprise the span of a whole work. *Image, Reflection, Shadow* (1982), one example of this manifestation, makes use of material generated from two cells, both of which are derived from the plainchant melody *Lux Aeterna*.[18] Each of the two cells (A and B) is put through a magic square and a transposition matrix, central components of Davies's compositional strategies, the significance of which will be returned to throughout this discussion. Further matrices are used for charting and rhythmizing a gradual process by which a series of notes consisting of the first row of the A matrix, the sixth row of the B matrix, the retrograde of the sixth row of the A matrix, and the retrograde of the first row of the B matrix is transformed into another series of notes consisting of the first row of the B matrix, the sixth row of the A matrix, the retrograde of the sixth row of the B matrix, and the retrograde of the first row of the A matrix – the result of which more or less turns the beginning note sequence inside out. Since each of the two magic squares (and their related transposition matrices) generates collections of notes that are different and distinct, as well as different configurations of intervals, they are treated somewhat as though they signify two different thematic complexes, each associated with its own distinct tonal area. The whole of *Image, Reflection, Shadow* is laid out somewhat in the manner of a sonata movement, with the first movement unfolding square A and then square B, as though they were the two themes in an exposition. The second movement deals primarily with the complex matrix which turns its material inside out so that the squares are reversed, and combines that material with yet other notes, freely derived from the original plainchant source; it thus acts as a sort of development section. The third movement, which begins with a slow section based on square A combined with material drawn from the plainchant source before moving into music that involves another elaborate transformation sequence (transforming notes related to square B into those of square A, not only in a thematic sense, but in a way that mimics tonal operations), is a form of recapitulation.[19]

## Sonata form in a later work

The central works of the most recent, late phase of Davies's career are the ten string quartets that comprise the cycle commissioned by Naxos Records.

---

[18] *Liber Usualis* (Tournai, Belgium: Desclée & Co., 1953), 1815.

[19] For a more detailed examination of the form of *Image, Reflection, Shadow*, including discussion of the work's manuscripts and pre-compositional sketches, see Rodney Lister, 'Steps Through the Maze: *Image, Reflection, Shadow* and Aspects of Magic Squares in the Works of Sir Peter Maxwell Davies' (PhD thesis, Brandeis University, 2001).

These quartets stand as a chamber music equivalent to the ten Strathclyde Concertos and the eight symphonies whose composition occupied the bulk of his attention between 1973 and 2000. Neither the concerto nor the symphony series were initially conceived of as a unified cycle, although each developed cross-referenced relationships over the course of the composition of the set. The string quartets, however, enabled Davies to think from the outset of an architecture spanning the whole cycle: 'I felt like a novelist who issues a book chapter by chapter at regular intervals in the pages of a periodical.'[20]

Most of the stylistic shifts in Davies's career mirror changes in his life as a practising musician: for instance, the theatre works coincide with the beginnings of The Fires of London, while the symphonies and concertos emerge from his post-Fires career as a conductor of orchestras, particularly the Scottish Chamber Orchestra and the BBC Philharmonic. His latest music is the result of the evolution of his musical life brought on by the winding down of his orchestral conducting, and is associated with a greater, indeed practically exclusive, concentration on music for traditional chamber music ensembles. Davies's orchestra conducting of the 1980s and 1990s brought him into direct, hands-on contact with orchestral repertory, particularly from the Classical period and most especially the symphonies of Haydn. It is clear that this work as a performer caused him to think in a deep way about the music of the Classical period, and during that time the music he was writing also reflected a concern and engagement with traditional forms and materials and how they could be adapted to his particular compositional outlook. This exploration of the means and methods of older music seemed to be much more apparent in the concertos and symphonies than the highly evocative, landscape-inspired character which is such a striking aspect of the preceding works, even though that evocative quality has never been completely absent from any of his music. When he turned to the project of writing a string quartet cycle, the quartets of Haydn in particular, as well as those by Mozart and Beethoven, were the source of yet further engagement with older tonal forms. This engagement resulted in works that Davies began to consider as being actually in sonata form, not merely mimicking it.[21]

One of the constants in Davies's music from *Ave Maris Stella* in 1975 is his use of magic squares, as already highlighted in the discussion above of *Image, Reflection, Shadow*. When he began to use them, they were the logical next development of the isorhythmic and transformation procedures he had developed up to that point, providing similar but more complex methods of organization of rhythms and pitches than those which he was using (which

[20] Peter Maxwell Davies, liner notes to Naxos String Quartet No. 1 (CD, Naxos: 8. 557396, 2004).

[21] Nicholas Jones discusses the influence of Haydn in the First Naxos String Quartet in 'Playing the "Great Game"?', 73–7.

were already quite complex) and also allowing him to make even more far-reaching connections and transformations of material in a very systematic way. Initially Davies used the squares given in John Michell's *The View Over Atlantis*,[22] which were the 'classic' magic squares having European occult associations with the Ptolemaic planets. The square he would choose for a work would have a more or less obvious iconographic association with that particular piece – for instance the 9×9 square, the square of the Moon, for *Ave Maris Stella* (referencing a connection between the Moon and the Virgin); the 6×6 square, the square of the Sun, for *Image, Reflection, Shadow* (whose material is based on the plainchant *Lux Aeterna*); or the 8×8 square, the square of Mercury, for *A Mirror of Whitening Light* (whose title is the alchemical name for the element mercury). With time, however, he has come to use more and different kinds of matrices, including magic squares of larger orders (Michell gives no squares of an order greater than nine), and squares organized in different ways, which, therefore, cannot strictly be described as 'magic'.[23] Although he may still consider the iconographic element in his choice of a square, Davies is now sometimes interested 'merely' in their abstract patterns and the compositional possibilities they may provide.

Davies's use of magic squares followed from his interest in medieval music, but as he has come to be more directly involved with the consideration of classical tonal forms he has continued to use them. The intertwining of the two concerns and their associated techniques and procedures has made possible the development of a language and a method of shaping pieces that are both remarkably powerful and flexible. In an earlier article on the Naxos String Quartets, I outlined Davies's recurring engagement with magic squares and presented an analysis of the Third String Quartet.[24] The following discussion, which repeats that analysis, focuses on the first movement of the quartet, as this movement offers one of the best examples of the current state of Davies's compositional concerns and practices, including his most recent engagement with sonata form.

Davies first planned the quartet to be 'a concentrated attempt at virtuoso composition', prompted by a restudy of the two- and three-part inventions of Bach, which would be 'an honest contribution to musical literature' honouring St Cecilia, the patron saint of music.[25] As he was beginning the quartet in 2003, however, the impending war in Iraq and the global debate preceding it claimed greater and greater hold on his attention and left their mark on the

---

[22] London: Garnstone Press, 1969.
[23] For a number square to be called 'magic', the sum of each row, column or diagonal must always be the same number. For instance, the 'magic number' for Saturn (3×3) is 15; for Jupiter (4×4), 34.

[24] Rodney Lister, 'Peter Maxwell Davies's "Naxos" Quartets', *Tempo*, 232 (2005), 2–12.
[25] Peter Maxwell Davies, liner notes to Naxos String Quartet No. 3.

**Ex. 5.5**  Sketch transcription, Naxos String Quartet No. 3: derivation of source cells A and B from the plainchant

composition of the quartet, which in certain ways documents his thoughts on the situation.

The source notes of the quartet are drawn from *Audi Filia et Vide*, a plainchant gradual hymn for St Cecilia's Day.[26] Ex. 5.5 transcribes a sketch

[26] *Liber Usualis*, 1755.

of Davies's demonstrating the derivation from the plainchant of the two cells A and B whose notes are the source for the squares.[27]

Each of the two source cells for the work is put through a magic square, whose structure is unusually intricate. (The complexity of the squares and the resulting compositional challenges were part and parcel of the conception of the tribute to the saint.) The first, Square A, is a 7×7 square in which is nested a 5×5 square, which in turn has a 3×3 square nested in it (Ex. 5.6). The second, Square B, is a 9×9 square – but not strictly speaking a magic square. In this square the content of each row is maintained and the order within the row is shuffled. So, the sum of each column and of each of the longest diagonals is the same, but the sum of each row down is 81 more than that of the row above it (Ex. 5.7).[28]

The beginning of the first movement (Ex. 5.8), titled 'March', unfolds the nested elements of Square A: at the beginning the 3×3 square (starting row 3, column 3) in the second violin part; this is followed by the 5×5 square, starting in bar 8, in the viola, moving in bar 10 into the cello part, and then in bar 12 back to the second violin part (for the notes the two squares have in common), then back, in bar 16, to the viola part. From bar 18 the connection to the notes of the square becomes a little less clear. In small deviations from the order of the notes (as in bar 14), and in his willingness occasionally to alter them chromatically (as in bar 12), Davies is exercising the prerogative of any composer to adjust notes as his ear tells him to do; there are few enough of these differences, however, that the reference is still clear.

Although the notes of the square are used as a cantus firmus around which counterpoint is written, in more or less the same way that a medieval or Renaissance composer would, the music is also concerned with tonal issues. The work begins with an F major/minor harmony. Although the texture is strewn with contradictory notes, the end of the first phrase (bars 5–7) has a sort of $G^7$ harmony superimposed over a C harmony in the bass. The second phrase also ends (bars 13–14) with a G (minor) harmony which moves to an A♭ harmony with a low C in the cello. The third phrase (bars 15–20) ends on a high C, supported by an E, over a D harmony. Meanwhile the bass, picking up from the low C in bar 14, moves by step up to G and then down the notes of a C minor triad (bar 22). In bars 23 and 24 there are octaves, echoing the brief bass notes at the beginning of bar 22, outlining a

[27] I am indebted to Peter Maxwell Davies for lending me the sketch material for the Third Naxos String Quartet. This material has now been deposited at the British Library (MS Mus. 1464–8).

[28] There is insufficient space here to demonstrate the method by which one arrives at the squares from the cells, but this has been written about with some frequency. See, for example, David Roberts, 'Techniques of Composition in the Music of Peter Maxwell Davies' (PhD thesis, Birmingham University, 1985); Nicholas Jones: '"Preliminary Workings": the Precompositional Process in Maxwell Davies's Third Symphony', *Tempo*, 204 (1998), 14–22; and Lister, 'Steps Through the Maze'.

Ex. 5.6  Matrix and Square A

*Matrix A*

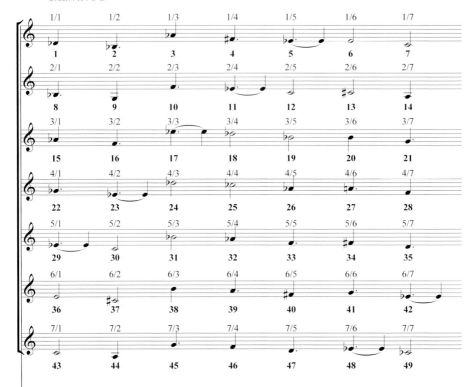

*Square A*

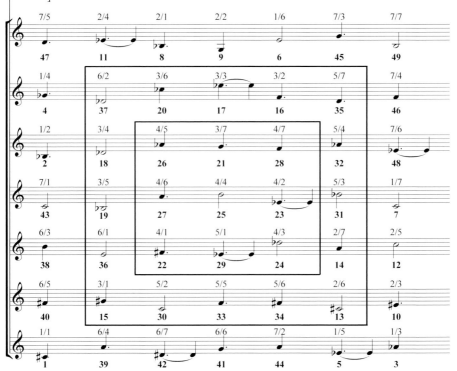

**Ex. 5.7**  Matrix and Square B

**Ex. 5.8**  Naxos String Quartet No. 3, first movement, bars 1–24

4–♭5–1 melodic cadence on C, supported by an E♭. Although not at all straightforward, the section can be heard as being in C. This interpretation is suggested by the movement of each of the very prominent phrases of the first violin to notes of the C harmony, by the fact that the preponderant number of the notes in that line are diatonic in C minor, by the repeated low Cs in the cello part, and by the stepwise motion in the bass leading to the arpeggiated C minor triad; it is reinforced by the C and E♭ in bar 24.

This section corresponds to the first-theme group of a sonata movement. The following section (bars 25–41), which is equivalent to the second-theme group, is based on the notes of the 3×3 matrix of Matrix A[29] which, in the cello part, are the main melodic material of the section, and tonally emphasizes G. These two sections are followed by what could be considered to be a written-out, although varied, repeat. The part that corresponds to the first theme (bars 42–56) is different melodic material: it uses notes of the 5×5 square of Square A, representing a further expansion out from the 3×3 square which is the centre of this whole square complex, and emphasizes A as a tonal centre, rather than C. The repeated second section (bars 57–66), which is clearly recognizable as the same music (the *Hauptstimme* uses the same notes, also in the cello), still emphasizes G. While these four sections together represent a repeated exposition of a classical sonata movement (or a double exposition), at the same time they are not static but present the continual unfolding of the melodic possibilities and tonal implications of the square's materials.

The development section (Ex. 5.9) is developmental on two levels. The cantus firmus which anchors most of it is a further development of the square in that it is goes through the diagonals of Matrix A (in the cello), starting from the northeast corner (Ex. 5.10), first using those notes exactly, implying A minor, and later (in the first violin) a transposition of those notes up a minor third, in C minor.

At the same time, though, reference is made to the viola part at the beginning (referring freely to the 3×3 square of Square A), and to the music that was in the first violin. The three-note, minor-third scalic figure that begins both the viola and first violin parts – at the beginning of the exposition and development sections – also becomes an element of increasing importance. The development section builds to a violently explosive and grotesque march, which is the music that gives the movement its title. The aftermath of the march music is a recapitulation of the generating material, but not the

[29] Like the 3×3 square, the notes of the 3×3 matrix are embedded in the 7×7 matrix, but can be seen less clearly. Of the 49 notes of Matrix A, numbers 21–9 are the 3×3 matrix; those nine notes, along with the eight preceding and following notes, numbers 13–37, are the notes of the 5×5 matrix. In his sketches for the squares, Davies isolates the nine notes of the 3×3 matrix and the first eight notes of the 5×5 matrix. Both are used extensively throughout the quartet as melodic material.

**Ex. 5.9** Naxos String Quartet No. 3, first movement, bars 67–70

**Ex. 5.10** Matrix A: northeast diagonals

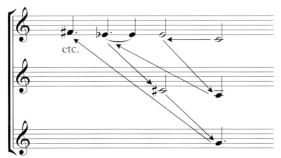

melodic shapes or manner, of the exposition. As Ex. 5.11 shows, there is none of the activity of the beginning, and none of the neat expository divisions and references to sonata form. Into a sort of void is placed, in the first violin, the first line of Square A (bars 141–4) and the notes of the 3×3 (bars 145–9) and 5×5 (bars 150–3) matrices of Matrix A (i.e. notes 21–9 and 13–20 respectively: see Ex. 5.6). This is followed (bars 154–65) by a slow mensuration canon based on two diagonal systems of Matrix A, which were the basis of the development section and the march. After a loud harmonized presentation of the notes of the 3×3 square of Square A (bars 166–70), which were the first notes of the movement, and a crunching glimpse of C major (bars 175–6), the proper resolution of the movement, there is a final ambiguous F major chord, soured by an F♯.

The model for this particular movement, if not other sonata movements in later works,[30] is, rather than the post-Beethovenian three-part version, the

[30] The first movement of the First Naxos String Quartet (2002), which begins with an evocation of the first movement of the Beethoven Piano Sonata in F♯ major, Op. 78, also has a double exposition and development section (see Jones, 'Playing the "Great Game"?', 73–80).

**Ex. 5.11**  Naxos String Quartet No. 3, first movement, bars 141–53

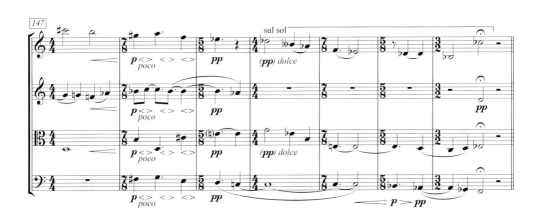

extended rounded binary form used by Haydn, whose music has become increasingly a major focus of Davies's thinking. This focus results in the tracing of the outline of sonata form and a genuine use of its tonal precepts with an intricate manipulation of material through the workings of the magic squares used in its composition. All these elements are balanced in a way that is reflective of Davies's personal compositional methods and is also congruent with the tenets of sonata form. In fact it is his use of magic squares that allows him to be reconciled with aspects of the form that were previously problematic for him. The squares are used to process thematic cells in a way that produces note sequences that are varied and that reveal the basic cells with greater or lesser degrees of clarity. Certain of the resulting note sequences are used here as 'themes' in this movement, and the different paths along which the notes of the squares are unfolded, along with the use of small fragments of material freely derived from the cells that the squares process, can be managed in a way that could accurately be described as developmental. In the recapitulation, the basic cells that are the source of the 'themes' can be stated, giving the most concentrated essence of them without actually presenting their repetition: a method that is both striking and unique.

Just as sonata form evolved over time, from before it had a name, Davies's use of the form, or at least its outward appearance, has changed over the course of his career. Davies's development of the form goes in rather the opposite direction, though, beginning with forms that do not exactly follow the outlines of the form, manifesting certain deformational procedures in dialogue with the textbook version of the form and therefore dependent on the listener's prior knowledge of its conventions. He progressed over time to a highly personal version of an extended binary form dependent on the integrated contrast of thematic and tonal identities. How this progression was coordinated with the development of his use of magic squares is a matter of speculation, but it is clear that through them he was able to arrive at personal methods for the development of material and for the recapitulation of the essence of thematic identities without their literal repetition. This progress is one aspect of Davies's continued dialogue with and synthesis of music and musical procedures of the past – what he calls a 'great game'[31] – and is an important characteristic of his distinctive compositional voice.

[31] Davies, in conversation with Paul Griffiths,
*Peter Maxwell Davies*, 123.

# 6    Questions of form and genre in Peter Maxwell Davies's First Symphony

*Kenneth Gloag*

## Genre – symphony

Peter Maxwell Davies's turn to symphonic composition with the First Symphony (1973–6) now seems to have followed logically from a sequence of extended orchestral works, including *Worldes Blis* (1966–9). However, the generic identity of the First Symphony still stands as a seminal moment in Davies's career, one that initiates an ongoing commitment to recognizable generic frameworks – symphony, concerto, string quartet.

If this move towards the symphonic genre appeared both somewhat isolated and surprising at the time, Davies had followed a careful path through several large orchestral works to the point at which the composition of a symphony might now, in retrospect, seem almost inevitable.[1] Paul Griffiths, from the closer perspective of the early 1980s, states:

> The announcement of this work caused some surprise, even though the symphonic qualities of the Second Taverner Fantasia [1964] and *Worldes Blis* had long been recognized, for in the mid-Seventies it still seemed very odd that an 'advanced' composer should take up the most orthodox of musical forms.[2]

Clearly an image had been formed of Davies as a composer and that image was of a radical, avant-garde composer of challenging modernist music, which included the development of music theatre as a genre throughout the 1960s, and projected an aesthetic position that seemed hostile towards the

---

[1] In his programme note to the First Symphony, the composer draws attention to the work's tentative origins:

> When I started my Symphony in 1973, I had no idea that that was what it would grow into. The Philharmonia Orchestra had commissioned an orchestral work for 1974, and I wrote a moderately long single movement, provisionally called *Black Pentecost* … However, I felt very keenly that this single movement was incomplete, and withdrew it before performance. It was, as it were,

budding and putting out shoots, and although I had firmly drawn a final double barline, the music was reaching out across it, suggesting transformations beyond the confines of a single movement.

Peter Maxwell Davies, 'Symphony', *Tempo*, 124 (1978), 2, reprinted in Paul Griffiths, *Peter Maxwell Davies* (London: Robson Books, 1982), 157–62. In this chapter, all references to this programme note will be based on the *Tempo* source.

[2] Griffiths, *Peter Maxwell Davies*, 89.

existing, traditional genres of music.[3] However, within the prevailing new orthodoxies of the period the symphony was no longer 'the most orthodox of musical forms' and the turn towards this genre was in itself a challenging and radical move.

Griffiths is accurate in his description of previous orchestral works such as the *Second Taverner Fantasia* and *Worldes Blis* as having a symphonic dimension and able to be seen in retrospect as preparatory for, or anticipations of, a first symphony. This line of thought had also been pursued by Stephen Pruslin, who suggests that several orchestral works can be grouped together into what he terms

> a kind of 'hyper-Symphony': *Worldes Blis* is a huge first-movement structure that spawns the suggestions of a scherzo and slow movement … *St Thomas Wake* [1969] is the scherzo, as much related in its grim humour to the scherzi of Chopin as to any orchestral models. Then comes *Stone Litany* [1973], the slow movement. With its mezzo-soprano solo, it has a similar place in Davies's hyper-Symphony to that of 'Urlicht' in Mahler 2 or the midnight song in Mahler 3.[4]

While the pursuit of anticipations of the First Symphony and, more specifically, suggestion of a 'hyper-Symphony' may seem somewhat excessive and difficult to substantiate, obscuring the identity of works that are important in their own right, such an approach does, effectively, highlight their symphonic aspects, even though they do not actually form or shape an identity that could be defined as symphonic. However, what these works do have in common is the fact that they establish the primacy of an orchestral soundscape in Davies's thinking and, particularly in the case of *Worldes Blis*, outline the powerful attraction of expanded forms, gestures and textures.

Before this turn to the symphonic genre Davies's relationship to historical, generic models was rather concealed and perhaps at times marginal. However, the projection of generic identities and affiliations had been evident in a number of earlier works, from the early Trumpet Sonata (1955) through the *Leopardi Fragments* (1961), with its definition of cantata, to the opera *Taverner* (1962–8; partly reconstructed 1970). Although somewhat

---

[3] Music theatre works such as *Notre Dame des Fleurs* (1966), *Missa Super l'Homme Armé* (1968) and *Miss Donnithorne's Maggot* (1974) helped define music theatre as a distinct genre. However, the image of Davies and his music was largely shaped by *Eight Songs for a Mad King* (1969), a work that situated music theatre within the context of the avant-garde aspirations of the period. However, Robert Adlington, in a useful summary of music theatre and the problems involved in defining it as a genre, makes the good point that the development of music theatre in the 1960s could be seen as a move away from some of the prevailing ideologies of the avant-garde: 'music theatre is in many ways intrinsically at odds with the aesthetics of the avant-garde. The referentiality of staged enactions compromises the autonomy that avant-garde composers like to claim for their music' (Adlington, 'Music-Theatre since the 1960s', in *Cambridge Companion to Twentieth Century Opera*, ed. Mervyn Cooke (Cambridge University Press, 2005), 233).

[4] Stephen Pruslin, 'Maxwell Davies's Symphony – an Introduction', *Tempo*, 124 (1978), 6–7.

concealed, the emerging nature of a generic affiliation can be illustrated through reference to *From Stone to Thorn* (1971), a work that is effectively a cantata for soprano and ensemble and is in close chronological proximity to the First Symphony.[5] *From Stone to Thorn*, with its continuation of cantata from the *Leopardi Fragments*, represents a certain departure from Davies's voice-text-based works of the past in that it is primarily song, cantata rather than drama, and it may be seen to begin to signify a changing perspective towards genre.

If *From Stone to Thorn* involves a subtle acknowledgement of the presence of genre, then the First Symphony projects that presence in the most explicit and emphatic manner possible. By naming the work 'Symphony' the composer generates a network of expectations and assumptions about the music around the question of what constitutes a symphony and what the relationship might be between a symphony composed in the later twentieth century and both the historical model and the legacy of this most canonical of genres.

Within the contexts of music, we might think of genre as essentially taxonomic, a way of sifting works into broad categories and classifications, such as 'symphony'. However, more specifically, John Frow, writing from a literary-theoretic perspective, states:

> Genre, we might say, is a set of conventional and highly organized constraints on the production and interpretation of meaning.[6]

On this account, a text, which, from the perspective of this discussion, can be transferred into the context of music, not only enters into its generic category but also, in some way, forms a relationship to a set of conventions that have to be met, or at least reflected, for the presence of a genre to become recognizable. Central to this description of genre is the suggestion of constraint, which seems to imply that the work is somehow bound or restricted by the genre. However, this is qualified by Frow:

> In using the word 'constraint' I don't mean to say that genre is simply a restriction. Rather, its structuring effects are productive of meaning; they shape and guide, in the way that a builder's form gives shape to a pour of concrete, or a sculptor's mould shapes and gives structure to its materials.[7]

---

[5] The *Leopardi Fragments* is interesting because this work is defined by Davies as cantata as part of the subtitle ('cantata' for soprano, contralto and instrumental ensemble) in the score. *From Stone to Thorn* does not have this designation but its song-based vocal part in conjunction with the instrumental ensemble makes the relationship to cantata clear enough. For discussion of this work from this perspective, see Griffiths, *Peter Maxwell Davies*, 81–2.

[6] John Frow, *Genre* (London: Routledge, 2005), 10. Frow's text is a good introduction to the operations of genre within primarily literary contexts. The key texts and key thinkers on genre – Propp, Bakhtin, Jauss, Jameson, Derrida, among others – are conveniently anthologized in *Modern Genre Theory*, ed. David Duff (Harlow: Longman, 2000).

[7] Frow, *Genre*, 10.

In theory and practice, the 'constraint' of genre is a frame that gives shape to a material, with Frow's building metaphor suggesting a certain physical presence. In purely musical terms, such a generic constraint may overlap or intersect with the formal dimension to construct what might be perceived as the frame that both surrounds and contains the musical details. But constraint can also be understood as the boundary beyond which the genre may begin to disappear.

It is, according to Frow, such a construction of genre that shapes the production and interpretation of meaning. It is not the objective of this discussion to determine what Davies's First Symphony might 'mean', but how this work is interpreted may be intertwined with the composer's decision to name the work 'Symphony' and the related questions of form and genre that flow from that decision. Any meaningful response to this work may be contingent on how the constraints that could be used to determine what constitutes a symphony are constructed and interpreted.

One such interpretative response is that of Hans Keller. For Keller, writing in relation to the first performance in 1978, this work represented an opportunity to reflect on the 'State of the Symphony', a process that involved questions of what constitutes a symphony and whether Davies's work met those conditions. There are several ingrained expectations of what a symphony is – number and contrast of movements, specific forms, orchestral – but, moving beyond the obvious, Keller claims that one 'essential characteristic of symphonic thought' is 'large-scale integration of contrasts'.[8]

For Keller, then, 'large-scale integration of contrasts' is effectively a generic condition that has to be met for any work to truly become a symphony and forms a constraint upon the interpretation of a work. Following the elevation of this condition it is implied that Davies's First Symphony fails to meet it, a point to which I will return.

In order to bring these issues into a clearer focus what follows is an analytical account of the first movement of the First Symphony that is formed around the role that contrast – harmonic, textural, dynamic – plays in this large-scale movement. This analysis will return to Frow's definition of genre in dialogue with Keller's critical commentary on the work, and will continue

[8] Hans Keller, 'The State of the Symphony: Not Only Maxwell Davies's', *Tempo*, 125 (1978), 8. Of course, there are many symphonies that do not meet some, or all, of the most basic expectations of what constitutes a symphony through, for example, the number of movements. One powerful reference here is the three movements of the Fifth Symphony of Sibelius, an important precursor for Davies, and, more notably, Sibelius's Seventh Symphony, which consists of a single-movement form that achieves a remarkably intense integration of form, tonality and thematic material, and would be an interesting work to project against Keller's 'essential characteristic of symphonic thought'. For a good discussion of these issues within the context of Sibelius see Tim Howell, *Jean Sibelius: Progressive Techniques in the Symphonies and Tone Poems* (New York and London: Garland, 1989).

to make reference to Davies's own programme note, a secondary but important text that Keller also utilizes. This analysis will be followed by some more general reflections on the relationships between this first movement and the three movements that follow.

## Exposition – climax – contrast

Davies describes the first movement of the First Symphony as having the 'ghost of a sonata form somewhere behind it, there is no first or second subject material as such, and any "development" consists of transformation processes'.[9] For Keller, Davies 'pays more than lip service to the sonata concept'; Keller comments that the fact that 'there is no first or second subject material as such' need not reduce sonata form to a 'ghost' as there are numerous historical precedents for the absence of such thematic contrast.[10] However, it is surely of some significance that Davies draws attention to the possibility of sonata form, and its implied sense of contrast and resolution, and it will be useful to speculate on the extent to which this sense of form may be an active force in shaping and directing this movement.[11]

Throughout the first movement there is a real feeling of return and recurrence. Ideas seem to emerge and reappear through a clearly audible process of development and expansion, with the ongoing nature of this process effectively determining the shape and identity of the movement. The most notable point of recurrence is the short melodic figure X (B♭–F–G) first introduced at Fig. 2 (Ex. 6.1), which Davies describes as 'very evident' and suggests 'forms a main feature of the movement's arguments'.[12] This figure appears in many contexts and assumes a number of different images as the music unfolds, with the dynamic *crescendo* through the sustained note as much as any specific detail of pitch providing its defining character, a gesture that had become recursive and had its origins in Davies's first orchestral work, *Prolation* (1957–8).[13]

[9] Davies, 'Symphony', 3.
[10] Keller goes on to mention the *Magic Flute* overture, among other works by Mozart, and the monothematicism of Haydn as precedents for this absence of thematic contrast (see Keller, 'State of the Symphony', 8).
[11] Just as there was a development towards the realization of the symphonic genre in the First Symphony, so is the reference to sonata form framed within a wider context: Rodney Lister, in Chapter 5 of this book, outlines one path through a selection of works that are in some way defined through Davies's own understanding of sonata form. See also Nicholas Jones, 'Playing the "Great Game"?: Maxwell Davies, Sonata Form and the *Naxos String Quartet* No. 1', *Musical Times*, 146 (Autumn 2005), 71–81.
[12] Davies, 'Symphony', 3.
[13] According to Paul Griffiths, *Prolation* demonstrates 'the use of particular gestures (most obviously the pressing single-note crescendos of the opening vivace, looking forward as far as the first movement of the First Symphony)' (Griffiths, *Peter Maxwell Davies*, 30).

**Ex. 6.1**  First Symphony, first movement, melodic figure X

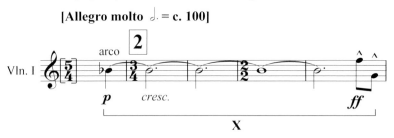

The reappearances of this figure cut across any notional sectionalization of the movement. In other words, although its first appearance comes at a moment that could be defined as the 'first subject' of a sonata form, its repetitions and transformations would seem to negate such a definition, thus illustrating Davies's claim that there is 'no first or second subject material as such',[14] and apparently justifying Keller's questioning of the large-scale integration of contrast in that repetition indicates the absence of contrast. Of course, Keller's recognition of the monothematic nature of some symphonic works might be relevant in this instance, but this figure is not a theme and its repetitions are often literal and without clearly defined contrast. When the figure is developed it is as part of a process of transformation so pervasive that it would seem to resist the possibility of contrast.

If the first appearance of this figure X indicates at least the possibility of a sonata form 'first subject', I want to complicate this formal resemblance further and propose that what actually constitutes the main defining quality of this movement is actually a very simple but effective archetype which consists of climax followed by contrast, what I will refer to as the climax/ contrast moment. Such moments had already appeared in Davies's music, with *Stone Litany*, the 'slow movement' of Pruslin's proposed 'hyper-Symphony', providing a reference point that forms part of the pathway towards the realization of the First Symphony.[15]

In the first movement of the First Symphony such moments expand upon the importance of the dynamic contour (*crescendo*) of the melodic figure I have defined as X (Ex. 6.1), effectively exploding the microscopic detail of the *crescendo* pressing through the sustained note onto a much wider scale. They

[14] Davies, 'Symphony', 3.
[15] *Stone Litany* forms one of the most meaningful representations of Davies's engagement with the landscape and culture of Orkney. It is the setting of the text, ancient runes, that generates the form of the work through the alternating of instrumental sections and sections that include voice. However, of greater significance in this context is the often sharply contrasted nature of the musical surface. For example, the shift into the first vocal section, at rehearsal letter I, involves a short but dramatic *crescendo* into the change of texture. Similar such moments occur elsewhere: see, for example, letter P, which is a much more expansive use of this dramatic/structural effect than at letter I.

provide points of focus within the parameters of texture, dynamic and form and therefore create a certain skeletal sectionalization of the movement through the construction of a series of moments that disrupt, interrupt or punctuate the musical surface. These moments, of varying degrees of intensity, are formed through the accumulation of texture and dramatic dynamic *crescendo* followed by a sudden change of texture and shift from loud to quiet. They are the primary mechanism through which contrast is generated in this movement. They also, through their basic and direct nature, highlight the gestural qualities of this music, again reflecting continuity from *Stone Litany*.

The first climax/contrast moment occurs at Fig. 1:10 (Ex. 6.2).[16] The rising motion articulated by the strings is effectively defined by the *crescendo* that dramatically intensifies this material. Following the *crescendo* there is a sudden change of texture and dynamic, with the moment of contrast identified by the *pizzicato* texture of the lower strings. This moment of contrast could be seen as the point at which the music moves from 'introduction' to 'first subject' within a sonata form design. The analogy with sonata form at this point is reinforced through the arrival on F, the pitch that Davies describes as 'the pivotal tonal centre' and which will clearly become a recurrent reference point throughout the movement.[17] Following the *crescendo* on G in the timpani part, the change of texture and tempo coincides with this move from G to F. The next bar features a descending minor third

[16] In this chapter references to specific bars are based on the composer's rehearsal figure in the score, with for example, Fig. 1:10 indicating a reference to 10 bars after rehearsal figure 1.

[17] Davies, 'Symphony', 3. Davies's use of the conventional tonal terminology of 'tonic' and 'dominant' is clearly highly individual but reflects only his own understanding of the contextually defined nature of such pitches. For discussion of Davies's use of such terminology see Nicholas Jones, 'Dominant Logic: Peter Maxwell Davies's Basic Unifying Hypothesis', *Musical Times*, 143 (Spring 2002), 37–45. Charles Wilson, in an article on Ligeti's self-representation, suggests that 'private lexicons associated with the work of so many composers – terms such as the "Kernformeln and Superformeln" of Karlheinz Stockhausen, the "tintinnabuli" of Arvo Pärt, and even the idiosyncratically defamiliarized "tonics", "dominants", and other tonal "functions" in the symphonic works of Peter Maxwell Davies – can be read almost as coded warnings to the scholar that comparison of their aesthetic or procedures with those of others is at best misguided, at worst simply futile' (Wilson, 'Gyorgy Ligeti and the Rhetoric of Autonomy', *twentieth-century music*, 1/1 (2004), 17). While I generally agree with Wilson that a composer's own terminology forms part of a construction of individuality that looks towards a 'rhetoric of autonomy', Davies's comments concerning 'tonic' and 'dominant' do provide insights into specific, contextually defined pitch relationships in the music and do therefore provide a useful reference point. Arguably too, a text such as the composer's own programme note forms part of the work's discourse and as such deserves consideration. This is certainly the case with the specific context of Davies's First Symphony. The programme note, although problematic, provides a certain entry point into the work and, from a pragmatic point of view, gives some useful signposts. However, reference to this source, and the ideas and terminology contained within it, need not imply that the resulting analysis is necessarily bound by the composer's intentions and motivations or that his own terminology can be appropriated without qualification or awareness of the wider implications in terms of the composer's self-representation.

**Ex. 6.2**  First movement, Fig. 1:5–14

**Ex. 6.3** First movement, opening, strings only

from A♭ to F (timpani and lower strings), followed a few bars later (1:14) by D♮ (Davies's nominated 'dominant').[18] However, this F–D♭, 'tonic'–'dominant' polarity has already been outlined in the opening material, with the initial A♭ moving through D♭ as the high point of the phrase to F as its conclusion (Ex. 6.3). This very brief linear material could be conceived as an unfolding of a D♭ triad, with the other pitches involved, E♭ and G♭, as neighbour notes to the F, a suggestion that leads to a retrospective hearing of this introduction as a 'dominant' upbeat to the realization of the 'tonic' and 'first subject' at Fig. 1:10 and the first climax/contrast moment.

This analytical interpretation of the opening moments of the movement raises further issues of interpretation when Keller's comments are brought back into focus alongside Frow's definition of genre. If Keller's interpretation of the full-scale integration of contrasts as a condition of, and constraint upon, the symphonic genre is correct, then this analysis would seem to go some way towards suggesting that the opening of this movement begins to both affirm and negate these requirements. On the one hand, the first climax/contrast moment at Fig.1:10 would seem to run against the possibility of integration in that the moment of contrast seems discontinuous and disruptive. On the other hand there is the suggestion that this moment actually presents a potential parallel to the shift from introduction to first subject within a more historically determined understanding of sonata form in conjunction with the appearance of Davies's nominated 'tonic' and 'dominant', with the expectations of that form looking towards ultimate return from difference to familiarity, a move that would seem to underpin Keller's ideas about integration and contrast. However, any possible contrast between 'tonic' and 'dominant' is negated by the fact they are, in this instance, already so well integrated that they do not actually sustain individual identities and functions that could generate contrast *before* a point of integration. The coexistence of these factors projects both a proximity and distance to the conventions and constraints of the genre as defined through Keller's own conditions of interpretation.

[18] Davies, 'Symphony', 3.

The next moment of climax/contrast comes at Fig. 4 (Ex. 6.4). From Fig. 2 the thematic idea defined as X is transformed in a way that provides a microcosm of how it will be treated throughout the movement. The transformations of X at this point generate a sense of momentum, with the dynamic gradations from *pp* to *ff* intensifying this process. The 'basic shape' of X is maintained at this point through its rhythmic identity of sustained note followed by two short notes.[19] However, at the bar before Fig. 4 the dynamic contour actually subsides back to *pp*. Nevertheless, there has been a sense of momentum towards this point and there is an immediate feeling of contrast provided by the change of orchestral texture after Fig. 4.

From this point a sequence of climax/contrast moments occurs at Figs. 8, 10 and 12. The moment at Fig. 8 comes after the most intense accumulation of material up to this point. From Fig. 6 vertical harmonies based on F in the strings, characterized by a *crescendo*, lead to an extended realization of X at Fig. 6:5, with the sustained B leading to the two very short loud notes (Fig. 6:10) that is a defining characteristic of X (Ex. 6.5). An extended *crescendo* again conditions, in fact shapes, this gesture. This articulation of X is continued and accumulates towards the moment of climax/contrast at Fig. 10.

Contrast is again generated by the sudden appearance of the new texture at Fig. 10, with the contrast now seeming greater than previous moments of climax/contrast. While the dynamic contrast, in itself, is not that great – a shift from *ff* to *f* – it is still notable. But more significantly there has been a gradual, accumulative texture towards this point and the emphatic realizations of X in the cello part, a process that begins after Fig. 6 and moves towards the moments of climax/contrast at Figs. 8 and 10, extends X into a quite literal thematic foreground. Contrast is further heightened by the fact that there is also a marked absence of X after Fig. 10. The music has now therefore moved into a condition of greater or higher contrast and now provides a shadow of a 'second subject', which Davies seems to deny the possibility of ('there is no first or second subject material as such').[20] However, it is significant that this condition has been projected primarily through the parameters of thematic material, dynamics and texture, rather than 'tonics' and 'dominants'. If there is a trace of sonata form at this point then this is the

---

[19] The term 'basic shape' (*Grundgestalt*) is borrowed from the theoretical vocabulary of Schoenberg, within which it implies a basic source from which all subsequent events can be seen to be derived, or at least undergo influence. While this is not the context within which to pursue this potential correlation, it would seem to suggest points of connection from the monothematicism of Haydn and the thematic integration of Beethoven and to present a certain parallel to the tightly organized music of later composers such as Davies. However, beyond the suggested parallel it is difficult to see how this theoretical context can actually provide a model of analytical interpretation for such music. For a useful summary and application of Schoenbergian theory from this perspective, see Walter Frisch, *Brahms and the Principle of Developing Variation* (Berkeley and London: University of California Press, 1984).

[20] Davies, 'Symphony', 3.

**Ex. 6.4** First movement, Figs. 3:8–4:3

**Ex. 6.5** First movement, Fig. 6:8–12

moment where one might expect the production of harmonic contrast through a large-scale shift from F to D♭ (Davies's nominated 'tonic' and 'dominant') to occur. The fact that no such explicit shift takes place should come as no surprise: sonata form is a shadow, not a model.

The absence of such contrast is now seemingly consistent with Keller's interpretation in that there is no harmonic contrast that can become integrated. But there is a 'large-scale contrast' – that formed through the dimensions of texture and dynamic – and for it to form a meaningful point of contact with the constraints Keller places around this work it must become integrated. But how can we hear such moments of contrast as integrated? We might hear points of harmonic contrast reaching towards synthesis and/or resolution and therefore resulting in integration, but how can it be possible to both construct and interpret a contrast formed through the parameters of texture and dynamic that can be heard as merging into a moment that can be defined as a point of integration?

## Development – transformation – contrast

The next most notable and direct climax/contrast moment occurs at Fig. 16 (Ex. 6.6). The three bars leading up to this point feature the now expected sense of climax through a short *crescendo* from *f* to *ff*, with a simultaneous focus on F and D♭ in the timpani part. The articulation of these two pitches adds significance to this specific moment through the coming together, perhaps integration, of Davies's 'tonic' and 'dominant'. It is also notable that the timpani articulate them, a sonority that has already been used at significant points in the work.[21]

This moment of climax, in conjunction with the simultaneous focus on F and D♭, is followed by a change of texture at Fig. 16. Change through contrast is now more clearly defined than at earlier moments. It is also significant that this is the point at which statements of X, which are now developed but still literally identifiable, again become apparent, with, for example, the piccolo part at Fig. 16:1, featuring a condensed but immediately identifiable version of X as defined by the sustained note followed by two short notes and underpinned by a rapid *crescendo*. Further appearances of X occur, with, for example, the cello again acting as an articulative force. The glockenspiel line also provides an expanded articulation of X in

---

[21] Such points include the initial gesture of the roll on G leading towards the articulation of F–A♭–G–B–G♭, at Fig. 1:10, the gesture with which Davies claims 'the argument proper starts' (Davies, 'Symphony', 3).

**Ex. 6.6**  First movement, Fig. 16–16:6

contrast to some of the more condensed, fragmentary statements that surround it.

The process of recollection through transformation of X at the outset of the new moment of contrast now allows for the projection of a 'development' section, but one that remains in the shadow and is still open for interpretation. This suggestion of development now raises questions concerning Davies's approach towards the generation of materials. It also brings Keller's critical response to this work back into focus. For Davies, 'any "development" consists of transformation processes'.[22] Transformation of pitch material through a highly complex pre-compositional process was already central to Davies's musical language and is definitive of this work, with even the conspicuous detail that is X being part, but not the starting point, of a process of transformation of the *Ave Maris Stella* plainchant with which the second movement of the First Symphony begins.[23] However, it can be argued that the methodological consistency of this process leads to an absence of contrast as we hear the ongoing unfolding through transformation of the materials as a process that may result in the familiar becoming unfamiliar but is still essentially singular, a possibility that seems to be central to Keller's questions about contrast and integration.

Following consideration of contrasts such as that between first and second subject in sonata form, thematic contrast and, in tonal music, key contrast, Keller goes on to highlight what he sees as the defining contrast situated at the centre of sonata form and, by extension, the symphony:

> … the elementary and elemental contrast in the sonata's modes of thought is independent of the contrasts between themes and between keys: *it is the contrast between statements* (whether monothematic or polythematic) and *developments* (whether they concern themselves with the statements or not).[24]

Presumably this elemental contrast must be integrated in a large-scale manner, although Keller does not make this clear; nor does he make it clear how this might work in theory or practice. It is clear that we do not hear the first movement of this symphony as a contrast between statement and

---

[22] Ibid.

[23] According to Davies, 'there is no common vocabulary to describe such processes' (ibid.). However, since then a body of literature has emerged which even if it does not constitute a common vocabulary does bring these processes into focus. See Richard McGregor, 'The Maxwell Davies Sketch Material in the British Library', *Tempo*, 196 (1996), 9–19; Peter Owens, 'Revelation and Fallacy: Observations on Compositional Technique in the Music of Peter Maxwell

Davies', *Music Analysis*, 13/2–3 (1994), 161–202; David Roberts, 'Techniques of Composition in the Music of Peter Maxwell Davies' (PhD thesis, University of Birmingham, 1985). In this instance the initial B♭–F–G (X) is a basic transformation through transposition of the initial D–A–B of the chant source. For more detailed discussion of this transformational process see Roberts, 'Techniques of Composition', 342.

[24] Keller, 'State of the Symphony', 9.

development. There is no point of division between the two, no sense of a thematic idea, or subject, stated and then developed, or of a development that stands as a point of contrast in relation to statement. What has emerged up to this point is the absence of such contrast, and where contrast does occur, often of a fundamental nature, it is generated through the musical dimensions of texture, dynamic and orchestration.

Keller, following comments on Davies's understanding of orchestration, goes on to state:

> there are countless spots in the work which evince maximal musical intensity – of an order, however, which precludes their symphonic integration, not because there is disintegration, but, on the contrary, because there isn't enough to integrate from the symphonic point of view, because characterization, definition, and articulation don't heed the demands for incisive contrast. Above all, the contrast between statement and development is neglected, if not indeed largely ignored.[25]

In Davies's First Symphony the initial material as defined in this analysis (X) is not a theme as such, and it is part of an ongoing process of transformation, which, according to Keller, is not necessarily development: 'transformation processes are not, in their turn, a distinguishing mark of development'.[26] However, if there is a lack of integration in this movement then it is a meaningful one, with the point of non-integration formed not between statement and development as Keller suggests but between the ongoing momentum and continuity of thematic transformation ('monothematicism'?) and the textural disruptions, presumably some of the 'countless spots' that 'evince maximal musical intensity', defined by the climax/contrast moments that, at specific points, provide a parallel with sonata form, Davies's formal 'ghost'.

## Recapitulations – conclusions

As repetitions and recurrences have been active throughout the movement the search for a moment of recapitulation is a seemingly impossible one. However, the moment of climax/contrast at Fig. 40 presents, like that at Fig. 16, a heightened sense of contrast (Ex. 6.7). This moment is dramatized through the ascending motions and their dynamic imperative which is followed by the now expected change of texture and dynamic. The resulting contrast also involves the evocation of the initial material of the movement through the *pizzicato* texture in the strings. But this sense of return also coexists with a point of transformation. The linear texture articulates E♭, F and A♭ in an abbreviated form, leading to the sustained F in the cello part.

---

[25] Ibid., 10.                    [26] Ibid., 9.

**Ex. 6.7**  First movement, Fig. 40–40:6

It is this focus on F, the 'tonic', that signifies a structural move, one that in conjunction with the restatement of X gives a tentative yet meaningful indication of 'recapitulation'. It also again encapsulates the suggestion of the sonata form as functioning as a shadow to the movement in that we can see the trace of such a return but it is not as powerfully affirmative as its historical, formal and generic precursors.

In itself the conclusion of the first movement continues to pose questions of form and genre in that the audible impression it leaves is not necessarily that of resolution or, by extension, integration. The focus of the final chord is D♭, not Davies's self-defined 'tonic' of F (Ex. 6.8). This suggests that, within the context of the movement as a whole, there is no return to this particular source; rather there has been a shift between two poles, with a potential polarity between F and D♭ now effectively framing the movement. This interpretation would seem to connect with the discussion of Keller's response in that it projects contrast through juxtaposition on a large-scale formal and harmonic basis and therefore continues to generate a distance between what we hear in this movement and Keller's understanding of what constitutes a symphony.

Although this discussion has been focused exclusively on the first movement, it is worth remembering that within the context of the four-movement model of the Classical symphony the contrast between movements was one of the main factors in defining contrast within the work as a whole. However, either in terms of an outline of a genre in general or in relation to the specifics of Davies's First Symphony, Keller's generic constraint of 'large-scale integration of contrasts' is not directed towards this the largest of scales: the symphonic work as a 'whole'. The three movements that follow the first all in their own way present a meaningful relationship to the expectations and constraints of the genre. The second movement moves from its initial Lento into Scherzo in a way that is modelled on the first movement of Sibelius's Fifth Symphony, the third movement is described by Davies as 'the slow movement proper',[27] and the fourth is the fast finale that is now expected. While each movement then provides contrast to what comes before or after through different tempi, it is notable that the *Ave Maris Stella* chant, from which X of the first movement is derived, is sounded as the beginning of the second movement, a move that displaces the thematic origin of the work from what might be its expected place at the beginning of the first movement. The transformation of this material is an ongoing process through the work and therefore provides an underlying consistency and continuity that resists expectations of contrast and integration.

---

[27] Davies, 'Symphony', 4.

**Ex. 6.8**  First movement, concluding bars

If the ending of the first movement continued to pose questions about contrast and integration, the conclusion to the fourth movement (and to the work as a whole) intensifies these questions. The concluding gesture, described by Davies as 'the stabbing chords', is 'an adaptation of Sibelius's solution'[28] to the end of his Fifth Symphony. It is also notable that Davies himself saw this ending as effectively inconclusive, claiming that he could not 'write a (falsely) "affirmative" conclusion'.[29]

Regardless of compositional intent or process, the effect is not that of an 'ending', there being no sense of a moment of resolution that brings closure. As with the end of the first movement, this moment again points towards a resistance to Keller's generic constraints and, if his understanding of both the symphony in general and Davies's First Symphony in particular are accepted, questions the relevance of the generic title for this work.

However, the purpose of this chapter has been neither to defend the symphonic status of Davies's First Symphony nor to dismiss Keller's critical response, which was immediate and stimulating. Rather, the process of revisiting the form of the first movement through consideration of one attempt to place a generic constraint around it has brought several issues and questions into a clearer focus. The analysis of this movement can now be summarized as a tripartite sequence of interrelated issues – the climax/contrast moments, their parallel with sonata form, the repetition and transformation of the thematic idea defined as X. The intersection of these issues suggests that this is a highly complex movement that goes some way to acknowledging the presence of the genre's past but is not necessarily affirmative of it. In other words, it suggests a simultaneous sense of proximity and distance. Keller claims that large-scale integration of contrast and the elemental contrast of statement and development are effectively the generic conventions and conditions that form a constraint around a symphony. On the basis of the analysis presented above, this work would seem to fail to meet these conditions. There is a powerful sense of contrast throughout the first movement but it is neither harmonic nor thematic and therefore does not result in a resolution or synthesis that could be interpreted as a 'large-scale integration of contrasts'. Where contrast does exist, through texture and dynamic, it cannot by its very nature become integrated. On this basis, Keller's questioning of the symphonic status and identity of this work would seem to be justified. However, any such conclusion only poses further questions in relation to the accuracy and authority of Keller's own construction of what is implicitly a generic constraint.

[28] Ibid., 3.

[29] 'I did not want the last gesture to sound "final" in a rhetorical way, giving the impression that I thought I had completely worked through and solved the problems posed by the Symphony and could therefore afford to write a (falsely) "affirmative" conclusion' (ibid., 4).

Keller's modelling of what constitutes a symphony would seem to be both historically and stylistically contingent. The evolution of compositional practice in relation to a shifting sense of context throughout the twentieth century was such that the generic reference can only be allusive, not affirmative, suggesting that the constraints that help shape the genre are not so securely fixed as to allow any one set of conditions to be definitive. The basic fact is that Davies's First Symphony actually makes a powerful allusion to the historical legacy of the symphonic genre through such obviously basic features as the number of movements (four) and the orchestral scale (large). That it does not meet Keller's constraint of large-scale integration of contrast may only suggest that this constraint did not have the determining level of relevance Keller attaches to it and further suggests that issues of contrast and integration of contrast no longer hold the same theoretical and practical relevance as they might have done from within the common vocabulary of tonality. Ultimately, it may be the case that in the later twentieth century and beyond it is enough to say that a work is a symphony because the composer has named it as such and while this naming can never fully in itself define the work or the interpretative response, it can begin to shape the questions we ask of it.

## 7 Peter Maxwell Davies's sources: reflections on origins, meanings and significance

*Richard McGregor*

In his examination of Paul Griffiths's *Peter Maxwell Davies*, David Roberts warns against reading too much into the levels of meaning suggested by Davies's statements regarding any particular work, or engaging in too much speculation about the 'meaning' or 'reasoning' that lies behind the choice of a particular source or technique:

> we begin to get into the kind of deep water where Davies's work so often lures us, for such chains of association, connotation, and resemblance, once begun, have no logical conclusion, and the point at which we cross the boundary from what is directly signified by a work to what is nothing more than free association quite independent of it is difficult to judge.[1]

This interpretation suggests that the composer's understanding and expression of his purposes is the metanarrative that gets in the way of a critically detached understanding of the work in question.

Roberts's injunction is also cited by Raymond Monelle in his discussion of Davies's *Antechrist* (1967).[2] As a musical semiologist, Monelle remarks that the commentator, when seeking '"what is directly signified by a work" … can only reach trivial conclusions'.[3] Nevertheless Monelle is content to speculate on some of the possible, or perhaps potential, cross-references that Davies might be making in *Antechrist* in relating one plainchant to another in order to 'turn the meaning [of the work at a given point] inside out'.[4] Having spent much of his book review correcting factual inaccuracies in Paul Griffiths's analysis of *Antechrist*,[5] Roberts would no doubt be less than content with such speculation.

[1] David Roberts, review of Paul Griffiths, *Peter Maxwell Davies* (London: Robson Books, 1982), in *Contact*, 24 (1982), 24–6.
[2] Raymond Monelle, 'An Allegory of *Ars Antiqua*: Peter Maxwell Davies's *Antechrist*', in *Interdisciplinary Studies in Musicology*, ed. Maciej Jablonski and Jan Steszewski (Poznan: Publishing House of the Poznan Society for the Advancement of the Arts and Sciences, 1995), 209–26.
[3] Ibid., 221.
[4] Ibid. Monelle is making reference to Davies's own programme note for *Antechrist*, in Griffiths, *Peter Maxwell Davies*, 144–5.
[5] Roberts, review of Griffiths, *Peter Maxwell Davies*. For Griffiths's analysis of *Antechrist*, see *Peter Maxwell Davies*, 55–61.

# The problem of 'meaning' in the music of Peter Maxwell Davies

In his seminal article which creates a vocabulary for discussing Davies's musical language, Peter Owens refers to 'a body of "received wisdom"' existing regarding Davies's compositional technique, one which is concerned with the metaphorical allusions that can be drawn from the composer's own writings and pronouncements.[6] As an alternative, Owens seeks a path that goes beyond such mythology surrounding the composer's compositional processes in order to illuminate the background material that underpins these processes. He does this, in part, by showing how the set-based components relate to the plainchants that generate them, and thus constructs a vocabulary for analysing, classifying and articulating some of the relationships that exist within the musical material.

The essential problem of Owens's methodology is that it is different from the way in which Davies himself chooses to label and classify his material as revealed by study of his score annotations when translated from the personal script in which they are written.[7] It is not the intention of this chapter either to rake over old ground, or to try to reconcile Owens's system with the composer's. However, risking the approbation of David Roberts, I want to examine Davies's 'starting points' across his output to engage in some, I hope, informed speculation as to the reasons behind his choice of initial generating idea(s). After the mid-1970s these 'starting points' are often, but not exclusively, plainchant, while in the earlier works there is a rather diverse collection of source ideas, which, as we shall see in due course, appear to have at least one thing in common.[8] After discussion of the sources, detailed consideration is given to a pair of works under the title *Ecce Manus Tradentis* (1969): *Eram Quasi Agnus*, the instrumental introduction, added in 1969, and the earlier choral work *In Illo Tempore* (1964–5). The latter has received very little scholarly attention and yet contains a significant number of key compositional ideas related to the set transformation processes contained in works written at and after this time, as well as being one of the first works to deal explicitly with the idea of betrayal. By way of a comparison of sorts, this consideration is followed by a brief discussion of some aspects of *Veni Creator Spiritus*, the 2002 duo for flute and bass clarinet, which, equally, lies at an important 'turning point' in the composer's output.

[6] Peter Owens, 'Revelation and Fallacy: Observations on Compositional Techniques in the Music of Peter Maxwell Davies', *Music Analysis*, 13/2–3 (1994), 161–202. In this article Owens builds upon the initial ideas for an analytical model contained in David Roberts's pioneering study 'Techniques of Composition in the Music of Peter Maxwell Davies' (PhD thesis, Birmingham University, 1985).

[7] See Richard McGregor, 'Reading the Runes', *Perspectives of New Music*, 38/2 (2000), 5–29.

[8] For a comprehensive listing of the source material used by Davies in his works, see Appendix II.

## The importance of plainchant

I take as my cue for this chapter Davies's own words from a programme note to the 2002 Mass (a work related to *Veni Creator Spiritus*):

> Several times a week [while in Rome as a student of Petrassi, 1957–8], I ascended the Aventine Hill to the Benedictine Monastery [S. Anselmo], armed with the 'Liber Usualis' … and came to know plainsong in normal everyday use.[9]

This comment feeds the presumption that Davies has regularly had recourse to the *Liber Usualis* as a repository of ideas,[10] a notion given even more force by statements such as the following, made in relation to *A Mirror of Whitening Light* (1976–7):

> The number eight governs the whole structure, and the sharp listener who knows his *Liber Usualis* will recognise emerging from the constant transformation processes at key points eight-note summaries of the plainchants *Veni Sancte Spiritus* and *Sederunt Principes*, whose implied texts (if you are prepared to play my game!) have some bearing on the implied alchemy involved.[11]

This statement is significant because it seems to imply a number of things. Firstly, that the composer knows the *Liber Usualis* back to front. Secondly, if 'the message' of the work and all the cross-references contained therein are to be understood and appreciated completely, then he expects his listeners also to know the *Liber Usualis* thoroughly. Thirdly, that Davies is prepared to concede that he *is* building a personal mythology round the processes of extraction – that there may be some significance to the choice of plainchant on the basis of the texts to which they are connected. The Christian underpinning of such texts is not an issue for Davies, whereas institutionalized religion has both attracted and repelled him, and he has contrasted the transcendental nature of some religious ideas with the hypocrisy of human interpretation and religious practice. Nevertheless he is not above recourse to superstition, such as when he remarks:

> There are also purely superstitious deviations – something done first in *Prolation* (1958), where I broke absolutely perfect arithmetic symmetry, out of a conviction that it was presumptuous – possibly even dangerous! – to attempt any exact imitation of higher natural perfection … the forces generated during the composition of *The Lighthouse* [1979] and *Resurrection* [1986–7], on the other hand, were such that I felt they had to be 'spiked' – I therefore introduced specific 'wrong' notes into various sequences including magic squares, to neutralize any 'Nekuomanteia' (evocation of shades).[12]

[9] Davies, programme note for the Mass, *MaxOpus*, www.maxopus.com/works/mass.htm.
[10] *Liber Usualis* (Tournai, Belgium: Desclée & Co., 1953).

[11] Davies, programme note for *A Mirror of Whitening Light*, reproduced in Griffiths, *Peter Maxwell Davies*, 164.
[12] Davies, 'Four Composition Questions Answered', *MaxOpus*, www.maxopus.com/

Such statements are certainly fuel for the Davies mythology but I would suggest they indicate that the choice of pre-compositional material is hardly likely to be arbitrary and it *is* possible to speculate on the meaning for the composer of certain choices.

The earliest published works do not use plainchant and the first clear example occurs in *St Michael*, composed in 1957, of which Davies says:

> A basic shape (hardly a series) consciously underlies the design in large forms and in the detail of the whole work, containing features common to and determined by the various plainchant fragments.[13]

Chief among these fragments, as the programme note goes on to highlight, is the *Dies Irae* (used in the second movement) and the *Sanctus* (in the third), but the work probably also contains references to the chant *Requiem Aeternam*, the *Kyrie Eleison, Dona Eis Pacem* and possibly the *Agnus Dei* of the Requiem Mass.[14]

It is, however, the other work of 1957 that has generated a certain amount of heated debate. In brief, *Alma Redemptoris Mater* has always been assumed to have been based on a work by John Dunstable, or at least the plainchant, which David Roberts identifies as *Liber Usualis* (henceforth *LU*), 273.[15] Various attempts to ascertain exactly *which* Dunstable work have met with varying degrees of failure. However, I suggest that the composer to whom the Davies work should be related is Dufay, and specifically his *Alma Redemptoris Mater* found in the *Historical Anthology of Music*, Vol. 1, No. 65 (Exx. 7.1 (a) and 7.1 (b)).[16]

---

essays/question.htm. This seems to be a 'superstitious' answer or explanation for a 'problem' that emerges from analysis of earlier works, such as *Sinfonia* (1962), where it is found that a change in one area of the melodic sequence as it is expanded and contracted by, usually small, intervals (and later likewise in the working out of transformation sets) has to be counterbalanced by its opposite somewhere else in the sequence.
[13] Quoted in Peter Owens, 'Revelation and Fallacy', 162 (the programme note is reproduced in full in Roberts, 'Techniques of Composition', 235–6). Owens observes that Davies later reduced 'technical' detail in his programme notes, and this note for *St Michael* was replaced with a spoken introduction on the *MaxOpus* website. Either he now feels that such programme notes get in the way of audience perception, or, that being rather more vague contributes to the mystique of the compositional process.

[14] See British Library Add. Ms. 71444, fols. 1–6 (or 7), which almost certainly relate to this work. Many of Davies's manuscripts were sold in the early 1990s to the British Library where they are to be found under the catalogue numbers Add. Ms. 71252–71445. For further discussion, see Richard McGregor, 'The Maxwell Davies Sketch Material in the British Library', *Tempo*, 196 (1996), 9–19, and 197 (1996), 20–22. At the time of writing, the British Library has acquired a second batch of manuscripts, MS Mus. 1400–98.
[15] David Roberts, '*Alma Redemptoris Mater*', in *Perspectives on Peter Maxwell Davies*, ed. Richard McGregor (Aldershot: Ashgate, 2000), 15. However, Roberts does not attempt to make any such connection.
[16] Willi Apel and Archibald T. Davidson, *Historical Anthology of Music*, Vol. 1: *Oriental, Medieval and Renaissance Music*, 2nd rev. edn (Cambridge, Mass.: Harvard University Press, 1949).

**Ex. 7.1 (a)**  Dufay, *Alma Redemptoris Mater*, opening (*HAM1*, 65)

**Ex. 7.1 (b)**  Davies, *Alma Redemptoris Mater*, third movement, oboe line

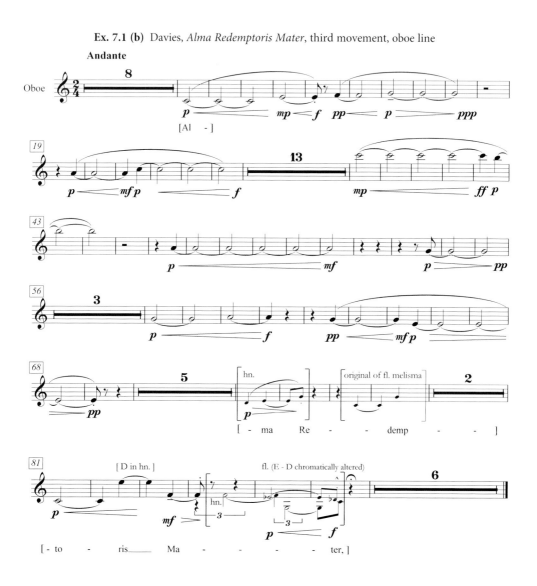

## The *Historical Anthology of Music* as source

This proposed relationship to Dufay is by no means the only reference to material contained in the *Historical Anthology of Music* (hereafter *HAM1*) that relates directly to the source material for a work by Davies in the period up to the early 1970s. The *Dies Irae* just mentioned is found at *HAM1*, 14; *Veni Sancte Spiritus* and *Veni Creator Spiritus* are found together in a *Quodlibet* by Heinrich Finck at *HAM1*, 80 (I will return to this pair in due course); *Haec Dies* (the plainchant itself), which is used in *Antechrist*, is at *HAM1*, 12 and contains the words 'Confitemini Deo', which, as Monelle suggests,[17] may be linked with *Deo Confitemini Domino* (*HAM1*, 32a) and *Benedicamus Domino* (*HAM1*, 28a). *Haec Dies* resurfaces again in *Chat Moss* (1993) and Symphony No. 5 (1994) where, given Davies's fondness for cross-referencing, it almost certainly refers back to *Antechrist*,[18] with all its attendant allusions. The plainchant *Victimae Paschali Laudes* is to be found at *HAM1*, 16b and is often present in Davies's works that touch on betrayal (such as *Vesalii Icones* (1969),[19] *Missa Super L'Homme Armé* (1968), *Ecce Manus Tradentis* and *Resurrection* (1986–7; conceived 1963)), but it became one of his favoured sources and therefore reappeared in, for example, *From Stone to Thorn* (1971), *Into the Labyrinth* (1983) and *Sinfonietta Accademica* (1983).

In other words, many of Davies's early sources were not for the most part from the *Liber Usualis* but from the *Historical Anthology of Music*, and this, when taken with *Musica Britannica* and the Monteverdi Vespers, provided by far the majority of the early sources used by Davies. There are very few examples of plainchant written out in the early sketches (1955–65), and most are contained in the unlisted volumes at the end of the first collection of Davies's manuscripts at the British Library.[20] It was probably the case that Davies introduced his pupils to some during his time at Cirencester but only four are to be found in the sketches, simply in written-out form and not otherwise developed compositionally by him.[21] Three of the four have a connection with the Virgin Mary: they include *Ave Maris Stella* (*LU*, 1259),

---

[17] Monelle, 'Allegory', 219–21.
[18] Ibid., 220.
[19] See Peter Owens, '*Worldes Blis* and Its Satellites', in *Perspectives*, ed. McGregor, 48–50. For Davies's programme note for *Vesalii Icones*, which makes reference to the use of *Eram Quasi Agnus* in that work, see Griffiths, *Peter Maxwell Davies*, 154.
[20] Add. Ms. 71442–5.
[21] Stewart Craggs suggests that they were arranged for soprano and alto and performed between 1959 and 1961 at Cirencester (see Craggs, *Peter Maxwell Davies: A Source Book* (Aldershot: Ashgate, 2002), 74–81). One grouping of these in the sketches (in Add. Ms. 71444) includes the *Ave Verum Corpus*, whereas another (Add. Ms. 71437) instead has *Plangiamo Qual Crudel Basciare*, which is a plainchant not actually from the *Liber Usualis* but from the *Laudario di Cortona* (Biblioteca Comunale di Cortona, Ms. 91), a collection of 46 *laude* (Italian vernacular sacred songs) from the thirteenth century.

as later used in the work of that name written in 1975, and *Ave Maria Gratia Plena* (*LU*, 1861). 'Ave Maris Stella on a plainsong – Dunstable +1453' in three parts, written in ink, is found in Add. Ms. 71444, but the hand is not Davies's. The third of these plainchants is *Ave Verum Corpus* (*LU*, 1856); the fourth, *Tantum Ergo* (*LU*, 1852), the chant of Spanish origin that he subsequently used in *In Illo Tempore*, will be discussed in due course.

Aside from the Requiem references in *St Michael*, plainchant made slow progress into becoming the mainstay of Davies's pre-compositional resource. Even when it became common for a work's starting point to be a plainchant, many works and their satellites utilized the same chant, and some chants reappeared time and again over the years.[22] Thus *O Magnum Mysterium* (1960) utilized two plainchants of the nativity: *Puer Natus* (*LU*, 408), and *Lux Fulgebit* (*LU*, 403 or 382), the former reappearing (no doubt 'resurrected') in *Resurrection*. Perhaps the most striking of these chant groupings is *Veni Creator Spiritus*, *Veni Sancte Spiritus*, and *Dum Compleréntur*. The latter pair are first apparent in Davies's own *Veni Sancte Spiritus* written in 1963, and one or more of them reappear in a surprising number of works.[23] Although not professing a Christian faith Davies has always had some kind of fascination with the mysteries of religious faith, and the idea of a creative spirit 'invoked' by the chants suggests that he sometimes uses these chants in an almost superstitious way, to 'assist', as it were, in the creation of new music.

It is remarkable how many of the source plainchants fall into one of three broad categories: concerning either Death and/or Betrayal (of Christ); invoking the Creator Spirit; or associated with the Virgin Mary. The use of Marian plainchants in some key works suggests that it was not just at the time of the composition of the Symphony No. 2 (1980) where he used the plainchant *Nativitas Tuas* (the plainchant for the nativity of the Virgin celebrated on 8 September, which happens also to be Davies's birthday) that Davies considered there to be some 'connection' between himself and the Virgin Mary.

## Touching the methodology of the magic square

Equally, once Davies began regularly using magic squares, the choice of which square to use was hardly random. The connection between *Ave Maris Stella* (1975) and the Moon square used in the work is probably well known, and

---

[22] For a discussion of the significance of 'satellite' works, see Owens, '*Worldes Blis* and Its Satellites', 27.

[23] *Veni Sancte – Veni Creator Spiritus (Dunstable)* (1972), *A Mirror of Whitening Light* (1976–7), *Westerlings* (1977), Strathclyde Concertos Nos. 1 (1987), 2 (1987–8) and (probably) 3 (1989), Symphony No. 4 (1988–9), Strathclyde Concerto No. 9 (1994), Symphony No. 8 (2000), and, it seems, almost every work from 2000 to 2003.

obvious, and yet there could be other allusions such as the equating of Diana, Goddess of the Moon, with the Virgin Mary as an archetypal feminine figure.[24]

Davies himself has written in his programme note for *A Mirror of Whitening Light* of the use of a Mercury square to invoke the alchemical properties of the element mercury as actually suggested by the title of the work.[25] Elsewhere, Davies has stated that the work reflects

> [t]hat very special quality of light which is due, I think, to the fact that the sun strikes not only from above, but is reflected into that window [of his then house, Bunertoon in Rackwick, Hoy] from the crucible, from the bay, from below – so that one has a two-fold light, which puts an extraordinary shimmering edge … on everything you see.[26]

This statement gives a clear indication that the square of the Sun is involved in the work. Having stated that the plainchant *Veni Sancte Spiritus* (the creative light again) is used as the starting point,[27] Davies then suggests that he 'took as a principle of design the magic square of the sun', which is a 6×6 square.[28] However, immediately he begins to describe the magic square creation process for the Mercury square, which does not quite make sense. Davies makes an alternative statement in his programme note for *A Mirror of Whitening Light* with regard to the plainchants *Veni Sancte Spiritus* and *Sederunt Principes*: he asserts that their 'implied texts … have some bearing on the implied alchemy involved', but does not, rather frustratingly, elaborate on what he means.[29]

*Sederunt Principes* is a reused plainchant, first found in Davies's First Symphony (1973–6). One of the multiple meanings therefore being suggested here is that of the transformation of the material of the symphony into something new, and hence the generally used term of 'satellite' connoting a smaller work 'orbiting' a larger is not really so helpful in this case when trying to work out the relationship between *A Mirror of Whitening Light* and the

---

[24] There are a variety of magic square species. Davies uses numerical squares, often (but not always) ranging from 3×3 to 9×9, where the sum of each row, column or diagonal is always the same number. These seven magic squares have been associated with the seven Ptolemaic planets: Saturn (3×3), Jupiter (4×4), Mars (5×5), the Sun (6×6), Venus (7×7), Mercury (8×8) and the Moon (9×9). For a good introduction to this subject, see David Roberts, review of Davies's scores, in *Contact*, 19 (1978), 26–9, and 23 (1981), 26–9; see also Roberts's 'Techniques of Composition', 336–69.

[25] Davies, programme note for *A Mirror of Whitening Light*, in Griffiths, *Peter Maxwell Davies*, 163–5.

[26] Davies, introductory talk for the first broadcast performance of *A Mirror of Whitening Light*, transcript available on *MaxOpus*, www.maxopus.com/works/mirror.htm.

[27] David Roberts identifies this as the antiphon *Ad Invocantem Spiritum Sanctum* (*LU*, 1837), but the allusion remains valid.

[28] Davies, introductory talk for the first broadcast performance of *A Mirror of Whitening Light*.

[29] Davies, in Griffiths, *Peter Maxwell Davies*, 164.

First Symphony.[30] Moreover, since the text translates as 'Princes sat, and spoke against me; and the wicked persecuted me; help me, O Lord my God, for Thy servant was employed in Thy justifications', it is hard to imagine what possible connection this has with the 'alchemy' of the Mercury square.[31]

Some other connections between the magic squares and individual works would include the use of the Venus square as a representative of the potential seductress Salome in the ballet of that name (1978); the Sun and Moon squares associated with the choice of *Lux Aeterna* ('Eternal light'; *LU*, 1815) in *Image, Reflection, Shadow* (1982); and the use of the Sun square, figuring a source of light, to represent Metin, Davies's partner at the time of the composition of the Third Symphony (1984). It also seems likely that the reducing magic square sequence (Venus (7×7) to Mars (5×5) to Jupiter (3×3)), with the plainchants *Domini Audivi* (Habbakuk's prayer; *LU*, 695), and *Haec Dies* (*LU*, 783 – the Easter plainchant used previously in *Antechrist*) are recalled later in the 'nested' square charts of the Third Naxos String Quartet and its plainchant, *Audi Filia et Vide* ('Listen daughter and see'; *LU*, 1755).[32]

In the discussion above I have suggested some reasons for Davies's choice of source material. Given his large output there is clearly a good deal more that could be said about any particular work. With the limitation of space I confine the discussion to just two works: *Ecce Manus Tradentis* and the instrumental duo *Veni Creator Spiritus*.

## *In Illo Tempore*

The motet *In Illo Tempore* was first performed in 1965 at the Wardour Castle Summer School as *Ecce Manus Tradentis*, and although the score published in 1982 includes a brief introduction by Davies in which he states that it was written in 1965, the work itself is dated 'Tollard Royal 1964' which makes it more or less contemporary with most of the *Seven In Nomine* (1963–5) which are similarly dated. *In Illo Tempore* contains, apparently, a number of 'firsts'. The third of Davies's *Seven In Nomine*, dated 'Princeton Nov. 1963', was, Davies suggests, 'one of the first works where … the creative evolution of

[30] I mean here not helpful if one thinks of a satellite as being in orbit round a planet. However, the idea of a satellite slung out into space in a trajectory away from the orbit of the planet is actually a useful metaphor for what happens in this work (and indeed in other works where a similar process occurs).
[31] Mike Seabrook's biography of Davies hints at various troubles at this time, with The Fires of London, and, slightly later, with Murray Melvin over the staging of *The Martyrdom of*

*St Magnus*, which might have occasioned a metaphorical reference to 'princes' (see Mike Seabrook, *Max: The Life and Music of Peter Maxwell Davies* (London: Gollancz, 1994), 158–67).
[32] See Rodney Lister, 'Peter Maxwell Davies's "Naxos" Quartets', *Tempo*, 232 (2005), 2–12. In the context of this article Lister makes reference to Davies's reuse of the Taverner In Nomine in the Third Naxos String Quartet to make a protest about the Iraq War: 'a not-*In Nomine*': 'Not In My Name'.

material was more "real" for me … [and] involved a transformation process … a line of melodic material … here derived from John Taverner's old
*In Nomine* tune – in turn related to the plainsong Gloria Tibi Trinitas'.[33]
However, *In Illo Tempore* is the first work to clearly use actual plainchants
as the starting point for the transformation process,[34] and it is also the first
work performed in which the plainchant might be said to underline the
meaning of the text. Finally, and in a related way, it was the first work in
which the so-called 'Death Chord' makes its appearance allied to a text that
gives it meaning.[35] These are the aspects that will now be explored in more
detail.

The extant sketches suggest that Davies was already familiar with the
*Tantum Ergo* (*LU*, 1852) Spanish chant at the time he was teaching in
Cirencester; it shares certain important characteristics with *Eram Quasi
Agnus* (*LU*, 649), the plainchant that is its 'partner' in this work and is used
as the basis of the instrumental first movement, *Eram Quasi Agnus*.
Davies's decision to set a religious text about betrayal may simply reflect
his thinking concerning the opera *Taverner* at the time. Both *Tantum Ergo*
('Let us therefore, bending low, venerate so great a Sacrament') and *Eram
Quasi Agnus Innocens* ('I was like an innocent lamb') are chants associated
with Maundy Thursday which is no doubt why Davies says on the score
'I should like the work to be performed in a liturgical setting on Maundy
Thursday or Good Friday'.[36] When the work was eventually published in
1982 having acquired the opening instrumental movement, the pairing
was given the title *Ecce Manus Tradentis* ('Behold the hand of the one
that betrays'), a quotation from the Vulgate that Davies had set, or rather
sent up, in his caricature of communion/the Last Supper in *Missa super
L'Homme Armé*.

This earlier vocal setting has none of the later histrionics of Davies's
'expressionistic' period and, as already suggested, the choice of these particular chants reflects musical relationships only. The broad similarities between

[33] Davies, 'Four Composition Questions Answered', *MaxOpus*, www.maxopus.com/essays/question.htm.
[34] I am not discounting the earlier use of *Gloria Tibi Trinitas* in other works but there is a difference between on the one hand using the Taverner In Nomine and then drawing on the plainchant that lies behind it for transformation processes, and on the other using the plainchant itself as the actual generator of transformation processes.
[35] The identification of this chord with death stems from the use made by other commentators of an association noted by Stephen Arnold in 1972 writing about Act I, Scene 4 of Davies's opera *Taverner*: 'The scene introduces the one *Leitmotiv*-like idea in the opera. When Taverner realizes that he is in the presence of Death, the low brass sound the chord of superimposed major thirds based on the whole tone tetrachord [D-F♯-E-G♯] … which is henceforth associated with the idea of death, real or symbolic' (Arnold, 'The Music of *Taverner*', *Tempo*, 101 (1972), 26). Clearly this chord was heard in works related to *Taverner* long before the opera made it to the stage.
[36] Davies, *Ecce Manus Tradentis*, full score (London: Boosey & Hawkes, 1978/1982).

**Ex. 7.2**  *Tantum Ergo* plainchant (*LU*, 1852)

[added sixth profile]

[square brackets indicate pitches Davies has not repeated]

**Ex. 7.3**  *Eram Quasi Agnus* plainchant (*LU*, 644)

[F    B ] in *Tantum Ergo*

[added sixth profile]

the two plainchants are obvious: *Tantum Ergo* contains a strong what we would now term tonic and dominant polarity and the same can be seen in *Eram Quasi Agnus* – including, in both, a strong outline of 'tonic' triad which Davies does not obscure (Exx. 7.2 and 7.3).

In subsequent works the texts of the chants might have a bearing on the choice of partner chants, as is the case, for example, with *Dum Compleréntur* and *Veni Sancte Spiritus*. Here what determined the choice is almost certainly the coincidence of intervallic shape. Davies at this point in his career was still more concerned with gestures that might be relevant to the compositional process for himself as the composer, rather than directly or necessarily perceivable by the audience.

Thus, for example, the opening pitch sequence, with four-part homophonic voices and trombones with handbell, becomes, in the next phrase, voices with bassoons and oboes. The handbell, not uncommon in later works by Davies, is probably here symbolic of the Sanctus bell, and the trombones, though perhaps carrying echoes of *St Michael*, are more likely chosen for their traditionally 'supernatural' connotations (for example as in the 'Tuba Mirum' in Mozart's Requiem or as the presagers of hell where Don Giovanni is bound), but these are 'betrayed' immediately at the second phrase through the use of bassoons (with oboes), traditionally the comedians of the orchestra. And in the pitch sequences 'betrayal' is also taking place. From Davies's sketches (Add. Ms. 71423, fol. 8), the pitch sequence of the opening of the chant *Tantum Ergo* with its exact pitch inversion is to be found (Ex. 7.2 transposed onto D), followed by the first bars of *In Illo Tempore* – in which the pitch sequence starts as expected but is quickly 'betrayed' – pulled away to pitches not in the 'true' sequence: and the chorus begins with a vertical articulation of the 'Death Chord':

**Ex. 7.4** Davies, *In Illo Tempore*, opening section, trombone and bassoon parts (intruded pitches shown as diamond noteheads)

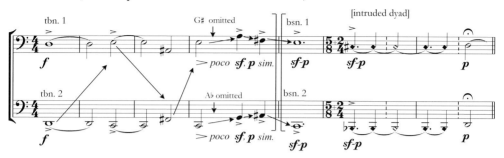

**Ex. 7.5** 21-note set derived from *Tantum Ergo* plainchant

D-F♯-E-G♯.[37] These are the first four distinct pitches of the transposed *Tantum Ergo* chant, another reason for its choice (Ex. 7.4).[38]

The initial compositional workings that exist show what would become normal procedures for Davies, but because they were largely new at the time of the composition of *In Illo Tempore*, some comment on their nature and function is appropriate. Firstly, Davies has taken the *Tantum Ergo* chant and used each of its first four phrases (the fifth and sixth just repeat the first and second). Although most of the repeated pitches are removed from within each phrase, Davies retains four, one each in phrases one and three, and two pitches in the fourth phrase. None of the pitches are chromatically altered at this stage in the sketches (Ex. 7.5). Those familiar with Davies's music will see that this preference for longer lines is an essential feature of his style, and that the means of generating long lines was eventually solved for the composer in a more elegant and thoroughgoing way in the tracing of lines and patterns through the magic squares.

This 21-note set is then subjected to a 13-stage transformation process (from F to F) changing the prime form to the inversion by way of the tritone pivot B on the seventh line – or rather, all 20 pitches, except one, are B: the fourth pitch of the seventh line is B♭. Since this pitch could easily have been

[37] Thus Davies may have originally thought of this chord as a harbinger of imminent betrayal, rather than, necessarily, death. This would better explain the chord's usage in *Eight Songs for a Mad King*, as for example in the middle of the first song where there is a sudden switch from 'you are a pretty fellow: next month I shall give you a cabbage' (occurrence of 'Death Chord' on violin and cello) to 'Undo the door' – a change from madness to sanity and panic as the King realizes that by being locked in he has been betrayed by 'his people'.

[38] The *Tantum Ergo* chant, transposed by Davies onto D here, has echoes of the *Gloria Tibi Trinitas* chant used in the Taverner works which likewise began on D, a point that is discussed later in this chapter.

**Ex. 7.6** *Eram Quasi Agnus* set: Davies's chromatic alterations

manipulated to become B♮, it may be possible that this is an example of Davies's 'superstition' that such manipulations should not be 'perfect'. In this vein, the number of lines required to go chromatically from F to F is 13, and this would be a rather convenient number in the context of the work itself.

The set from *Eram Quasi Agnus* is treated is a similar way. The first phrase is given as a separate entity as a transposition set but the derived transformation set is based on 10 steps, using five phrases and 33 notes in length. Whether these are intended to have any symbolic significance is not clear although 33 is traditionally, if not actually, Jesus's age when he was crucified. Ex. 7.6 shows the whole prime form of this set and it typically demonstrates Davies's penchant for symmetry in that the chromatic alterations balance each other – four up and four down. Given the four years that separate these works the use of the latter chant shows some evidence of a development in compositional thinking. However it should be said that in analytical terms the exposition of the transformation set in the instrumental *Eram Quasi Agnus* is much less complicated and possibly more assured in its relative simplicity than the pitch manipulations in the earlier vocal work.

As David Roberts has noted,[39] Davies used the *Gloria Tibi Trinitas* plainchant fragment in many works of the period, and *In Illo Tempore* is no exception. The fragment's appearance in *In Illo Tempore* is clearly symbolic. It 'floats' over the section of the text that includes the words of Jesus in the Last Supper in a version obviously related to the second of the *Seven In Nomine* – only the final pitch is altered (D–F–E–D–C–B♭–A♭→A), and with textural similarities to the floating cantus in bar 633 or 677 of the *Second Fantasia on John Taverner's 'In Nomine'*, completed also in 1964. The *Gloria Tibi Trinitas* fragment is not altered by transformation at any of its three early appearances and therefore must represent a sort of 'holy purity' – even Jesus himself. However, in contrast to this, a final 'bastardized' version of the chant which appears at very end of the work at the words 'Et osculatus est eum' ('And he kissed him') – C♯–G–E–D–F–E♭–B–A♯ – surely represents Judas with the Devil's mark upon him (C♯–G).

[39] Roberts, 'Techniques of Composition', 282.

## Structural significance in *In Illo Tempore*

The derivation of the pitch material actually used in *In Illo Tempore* is not as obvious as the surviving sketches suggest. Davies constructs textures in which the instruments and voices create elaborate canonic devices (for example, canons by diminution, crab canons, and so on). The exact pitch-generating processes applied to the *Tantum Ergo* chant are unclear. However the deployment of pitch-set-derived thematic ideas is relatively uncomplicated for most of the work's duration, and therefore in order to interrogate any possible 'meanings' contained in Davies's setting some discussion of the structure and articulation of thematic material is necessary.

The opening section is essentially a setting of the Biblical text of the Last Supper. The thematic material has its origins in the *Tantum Ergo* plainchant, with virtually every statement beginning or ending with the pitch sequence as set out in Ex. 7.7 (a) or an obvious derivation of it, including inversion. A typical example of this, on trombone 1, is given in Ex. 7.7 (b). At the key point of the raising of the chalice Davies inserts an extended instrumental passage for flute, bassoons 1 and 2, horn, trombone 1 and oboe. Though there are echoes of the procedure he employed in *O Magnum Mysterium*, this instrumental passage functions as a commentary on the 'significance' of the Last Supper, expressed through, by implication, the text of the *Tantum Ergo* plainchant 'Let us venerate … so great a Sacrament'. The instrumental lines are enclosed within a tritone and utilize the four forms of set statement, most obviously in the flute part, which begins on F♯ with the inverted form, pivots round the tritone C and returns to F♯ by way of a retrograde statement (Ex. 7.8).

**Ex. 7.7 (a)** *Tantum Ergo pitch sequence in* In Illo Tempore

**Ex. 7.7 (b)** *In Illo Tempore, 4 bars after Letter J, trombone 1 part*

Tbn. 1

***p*** *(always slightly detached)*

**Ex. 7.8** *In Illo Tempore, Letter F, flute part*

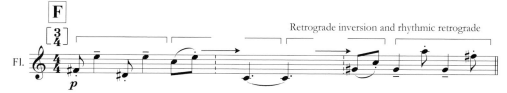

Retrograde inversion and rhythmic retrograde

Fl.

*p*

**Ex. 7.9** *In Illo Tempore*, Letter L, flute part

The breaking of the bread and sharing of the wine are symbolized by the juxtaposition of the unaltered *Gloria Tibi Trinitas* plainchant fragment on flute referred to earlier with the *Tantum Ergo* plainchant derivations in trombone 1 and bassoon 1, which leads to the climactic, though very quiet 'Verumtamen ecce manus tradentis me, mecum est in mensa' ('In very truth I tell you, behold the hand of him that betrays me is with me at the table'). Davies would later set this text in a much more expressionist and irreverent fashion in *Missa Super L'Homme Armé*. Betrayal here is quiet and insidious and inevitable.

Thus far in *In Illo Tempore* the text and musical setting have followed the event sequence of the Last Supper; at this point, however, Davies interjects an 'out of time' sequence relating to Jesus's prediction and the actual occurrence of Peter's denial of him. To suggest the change of emphasis and to underline Peter's denial as a form of betrayal, Davies introduces a 'new' thematic element in the form of two statements of an extended pitch series on flute and harp. The actual original of the material is obscure despite there being some prefiguring of it in the extant sketches.[40] One might draw an inference from the linear version of the 'Death Chord', which opens the third phrase, that death and betrayal are closely linked (Ex. 7.9). A solo tenor invokes Peter's declaration that he is 'ready to go to prison and to die', through a newly derived inverted version of the *Tantum Ergo* pitch set, accompanied by prime and retrograde inverted forms in the instrumental parts. Peter's declaration is not 'true' and Davies's use of the inverted pitch set may be intended to point up this 'falseness'. Peter's tearful exit is followed by a harp solo based on elements of the *Tantum Ergo* plainchant, although as it proceeds the actual detail of this becomes more obscure.

A second time-shift occurs and the text returns to Judas's bargain with the authorities. This is prefigured by the chorus chanting 'secundum Marcum' ('according to Mark') on the 'Death Chord'. The pitch set used from this point on is the new one which came before Peter's denial. This is the 'true' betrayal and the pitch sets operate in the same way as at letter F (see Ex. 7.8), but this time the central pivot does *not* lead to a retrograde, and thus back ultimately to the starting pitch, and so the very pitch sequence 'embodies' the betrayal: we have been led away to something 'new', not encountered before. Judas's

[40] Add. Ms. 71423, fol. 11.

betrayal is symbolized through the musical substance that expresses it. The complete absence of any obvious references to *Tantum Ergo* might represent the cutting-off of Judas from the Great Sacrament.

Whether or not the 'new' material is in fact derived from *Tantum Ergo*, for which there is no evidence one way or another, is largely irrelevant: if completely new (though no doubt based on something which if it could be identified would undoubtedly change the 'meaning'), the fact that it is not recognizably *Tantum Ergo* suggests dissociation. Judas is here one of the first of Davies's Antichrist figures.

Davies's use of *Tantum Ergo* in this work is significant in that it lays the groundwork for later works in which some kind of symbolism or meaning is embedded in the choice of source material, and particularly where the choice of source and the processes applied to it are pertinent to an interpretation of the compositional idea expressed in the work.

## *Veni Creator Spiritus* – nearly thirty years on

To illustrate this point in relation to later work we can examine the flute and bass clarinet duo *Veni Creator Spiritus*. A relatively short work, it is termed an 'instrumental motet', as indeed *In Illo Tempore* was a motet. It is one of the series of shorter works – satellites – written in tandem with the Mass composed for Westminster Cathedral for use at Pentecost. Although the Mass and related works were written to commission it is interesting to note the liturgical connections between these works and the earlier *Ecce Manus Tradentis*, which Davies suggests should be used on Maundy Thursday. In a sense the works related to the Mass are commentaries on the Mass in the same way that the instrumental interludes of *In Illo Tempore* are commentaries on the choral and solo parts of that work.

In terms of the liturgical season to which the Mass belongs it would have been surprising if Davies had not chosen to work with the plainchants *Dum Compleréntur* and *Veni Creator Spiritus*. However given the number of other occasions, liturgical and non-liturgical, in which Davies has used these same chants and the likelihood that the notion of some kind of 'creator spirit' in relation to his own creativity is implied in their use, there are likely to be levels of meaning to be discovered within these works.[41]

In his programme note for the work Davies makes explicit some of the symbolism. So the *Veni Creator Spiritus* chant is presented within a magic square framework as a 'folded-in-upon-itself' version 'building up a magic

---

[41] It could be argued of course that Davies's use of plainchant means that many of his works would have at least an implied liturgical context even if it is not explicit.

square of the Moon'.[42] Although the Moon square is one of Davies's favoured versions, it is not unlikely that he makes this explicit because we are intended to draw some significance from it; I will return to this later. The pitch series is taken up 'isometrically' by the bass clarinet (hence the designation 'instrumental motet', no doubt), and later is subjected to a rhythmic process which Davies describes as creating 'corrugated time' (adding or subtracting a semi-quaver duration on each successive hearing to an initially 'straight' crotchet statement).

David Fallows has suggested that Davies's interest in 9-pitch series was in fact generated by his discovery (in 1957) of the fifteenth-century *L'homme armé* mass where the 'tenor [was] built of a nine-note fragment, followed by its precise retrograde inversion, then its inversion, and then a retrograde, before a return to the original series [of notes]'.[43] Fallows's statement hints at a continuity here linking the prime to retrograde inversion manipulation referred to earlier in the discussion of *In Illo Tempore*, to Davies's own *Missa Super L'Homme Armé*, and from there to the astrological/metaphysical associations of the magic squares. In *Veni Creator Spiritus* at least one of these associations is applied to the pitch values in the 'corrugated time' section where the use of the Moon square clearly leads to the idea of the temporal modifications through rhythmic 'waxing and waning'.

The initial bass clarinet lines of the work play out the magic square backwards, that is, from row 9, with one slight deviation (following, no doubt, Davies's insistence that such things should not be perfect lest one 'invoke the shades'), in that pitch durations are extended not just by repetition but by the insertion of tritone-related pitches (as for example at bar 24: A–E♭).

The source transposition set for the work does not at first glance give up its connection to the *Veni Creator Spiritus* chant with its pitch sequence: E♭–F–D♭–A♭–B♭–A–E–F♯–B. However, remembering that this is a well-used chant in the composer's output leads to the conclusion that a relatively uncomplicated sieving process is in operation, with transposition – a process that allows for the repetition of chant pitches (Ex. 7.10).

The final flute version (Ex. 7.11) restores the original pitch level of the chant, while simultaneously making a link, through the chromatic alteration of pitches, to both the First Symphony – whose third movement uses the *Veni Creator Spiritus* chant and, like Davies's own *Ave Maris Stella* before it, the magic square of the Moon – and Strathclyde Concertos Nos. 1 and 3, whose

[42] Davies, programme note, *Veni Creator Spiritus* (London: Chester Music, 2003).
[43] David Fallows, 'Peter Maxwell Davies, Laurence Feininger and the *L'homme armé* Tradition', in *Contemporary Classical Music: Collected Papers from the 2006 Intercongressional Symposium in Göteborg of the International Musicological Society*, ed. Chris Walton and Stephanus Muller (Pretoria: University of South Africa Press, 2008).

**Ex. 7.10** Sieved, transposed set derived from *Veni Creator Spiritus* plainchant

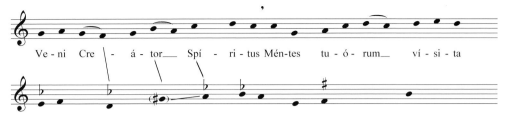

**Ex. 7.11** Davies, *Veni Creator Spiritus*, bars 180–5, flute part, and 9-note set derived from *Veni Creator Spiritus* plainchant

various sets have a strong connection in pitch terms with the set/square of the present work.[44]

The magic square for the work is set out in Table 7.1 (see Ex. 7.10 for the first line of the transposition square: E♭ = pitch number 1, F = 2, D♭ = 3, A♭ = 4, etc.). The symbolism of the 'folded-in' square, which Davies refers to in relation to the opening pitch sequences on flute, is simply the composer's conceit to express the fact that the magic square, as is not uncommon in his works, limits the choice of pitches by containing internal repetition. In this case, the pitch sequence pivots round the middle line when read in the inversion or inversion retrograde forms: reading from top left (37/D) straight down to bottom left (77/D) yields the pitch sequence D–A–D–B–E♭–B–D–A–D (note the pivotal role of the E♭).[45]

The significance for Davies of the square of the Moon probably lies in the fact that it was the first magic square that he worked with, in both *Ave Maris Stella* and the First Symphony, works that established his reputation once and for all in the mid-1970s. The square may represent something of a talisman for him, in much the same way that I have suggested the Pentecost

[44] I discuss the connections between the two plainchants *Veni Creator Spiritus* and *Dum Compleréntur* and similar pitch sequences at some length in 'Compositional Processes in Some Works of the 1980s' and 'Max the Symphonist', in *Perspectives*, ed. McGregor, 93–137 (see especially 109–14).

[45] As will be noted, the magic square here has 37 at top left, 77 bottom left, 5 top right, and 45 bottom right – its most common orientation in Davies's usage. It follows that the diagonals emanating out from these corners converge towards the middle – left top and left bottom being the same, and likewise right top and right bottom. The implied analogy of folding paper in on itself is as apt as any.

**Table 7.1** Davies, *Veni Creator Spiritus*, magic square of the Moon

| | | | | | | | | |
|---|---|---|---|---|---|---|---|---|
| 37 | 78 | 29 | 70 | 21 | 62 | 13 | 54 | 5 |
| D | D♭ | E♭ | B♭ | G♭ | A♭ | E♭ | A♭ | B♭ |
| 6 | 38 | 79 | 30 | 71 | 22 | 63 | 14 | 46 |
| A | E | A♭ | C♭ | C | D♭ | D♭ | F | C |
| 47 | 7 | 39 | 80 | 31 | 72 | 23 | 55 | 15 |
| D | E | C | B♭ | G♭ | F | E♭ | F | E |
| 16 | 48 | 8 | 40 | 81 | 32 | 64 | 24 | 56 |
| B | B♭ | G♭ | G | E♭ | A♭ | A | D | G |
| 57 | 17 | 49 | 9 | 41 | 73 | 33 | 65 | 25 |
| E♭ | D♭ | F | B | A | G | G | B | A |
| 26 | 58 | 18 | 50 | 1 | 42 | 74 | 34 | 66 |
| B | B♭ | G♭ | G | E♭ | A♭ | A | D | G |
| 67 | 27 | 59 | 10 | 51 | 2 | 43 | 75 | 35 |
| D | E | C | B♭ | G♭ | F | E♭ | F | E |
| 36 | 68 | 19 | 60 | 11 | 52 | 3 | 44 | 76 |
| A | E | A♭ | C♭ | C | D♭ | D♭ | F | C |
| 77 | 28 | 69 | 20 | 61 | 12 | 53 | 4 | 45 |
| D | D♭ | E♭ | B♭ | G♭ | A♭ | E♭ | A♭ | B♭ |

plainchants do. Moreover, the wish to explore fully the different possibilities of the same material is now a defining characteristic of Davies's compositional method.

## Conclusion

There is, unquestionably, a 'mythology' surrounding the 'meanings' that one might draw out of Davies's work, and the compositional choices he makes. In this chapter I have demonstrated that much is to be learned from a close study of the origins of the source material and other background details underpinning Davies's compositional decisions. There is a sense also in which the written or spoken text a composer like Davies chooses to make public about a work becomes part of the fabric of that work, whether or not it represents a metanarrative, albeit an informed one, derived from the composer's perception.

In the works I have chosen for discussion it is clear that there is much more to be learned by taking a critical stance which allows for the interpretation of allied linguistic statements and the symbolic musical gestures that go with them, rather than dismissing them as part of the 'mythology'.

*In Illo Tempore* and *Veni Creator Spiritus* are both works that group with other related scores and, taken together, stand at the crossroads of changes in Davies's compositional direction. While this fact might give them extra significance in his output as a whole, it is not unreasonable to assume that their influence on the shape, form, and direction of succeeding works is not to be underestimated. Despite the body of scholarship that has been generated round works of the 1970s and 1980s, much still needs to be done to truly understand the 'meaning' of many of the key works in Davies's output.

# 8    Setting it in stone: the problems of an *Urtext* in the music of Peter Maxwell Davies

*Peter Owens*

Since April 1994, the availability of sketch materials relating to a large number of Peter Maxwell Davies's compositions for consultation at the British Library has led to several important commentaries that benefit from direct study of primary manuscript sources. The writings of Nicholas Jones, Rodney Lister and Richard McGregor are notable among them.[1] It is nevertheless a truism that the format in which the works are most readily and widely accessible for perusal remains the printed study-score, and that listeners' experience of the music in performance will likewise stem from materials supplied for sale or hire by the publishers. Although it may verge, therefore, on the prosaic to register a concern that these should embody the composer's intentions as faithfully as possible, an illustration from music of the past might usefully heighten awareness of the potential significance in any apparently simple discrepancy.

## Historical precedent

In order to help create a sense of context and provide a point of departure, reference to a specific historical precedent – Monteverdi's Vespers, an influential work for the young Davies – is appropriate. This work is preserved for us from 1610 in eight separate printed partbooks, from Cantus to Bassus Generalis, of which copies are to be found in Bologna, Brescia, Lucca and Warsaw; only the Warsaw copy contains handwritten annotations, though of a later date. This published source presents singers with an unlikely sonority on which to chant the words 'Dominus a dextris' in the psalm 'Dixit Dominus' (Table 8.1).[2] Familiarity with the harmonic style suggests that

---

[1] See, for instance, Nicholas Jones, '"Preliminary Workings": The Precompositional Process in Maxwell Davies's Third Symphony', *Tempo*, 204 (1998), 14–22; Richard McGregor, 'Composition Processes in Some Works of the 1980s' and 'Max the Symphonist' in *Perspectives on Peter Maxwell Davies*, ed. McGregor (Aldershot: Ashgate,

2000), 93–137; and Rodney Lister, 'Steps Through the Maze: *Image, Reflection, Shadow* and Aspects of Magic Squares in the Works of Sir Peter Maxwell Davies' (PhD thesis, Brandeis University, 2001).

[2] The registral designations in Table 8.1 and elsewhere in this chapter adopt the Helmholtz notation (see Llewelyn S. Lloyd and Richard

**Table 8.1** Monteverdi, *Vespers*, 'Dixit Dominus':
fifth *falsobordone* sonority (Warsaw partbook)

| | |
|---|---|
| Cantus: | c♯″ |
| Sextus: | a′ |
| Altus: | e′ |
| Tenor: | a |
| Quintus: | c[♮]′ |
| Bassus: | a |
| Bassus generalis: | a |

**Table 8.2** Monteverdi, *Vespers*, 'Dixit Dominus': Cantus
and Quintus solutions from four modern editions

| | Wolters (1966) | Stevens (1961/94) | Bartlett (1990/91) | Roche (1994) |
|---|---|---|---|---|
| Cantus: | c♯″ | c[♮]″ | c♯″ | c[♮]″ |
| Quintus: | a | a | e′ | c[♮]′ |

this is almost certainly not the sound that Monteverdi intended here, and
modern editors have proposed a variety of solutions (Table 8.2).[3]

These solutions are differently justified in accompanying editorial notes.
For instance, Roche notes that 'C[antus], sharp; cannot be right because of c′
natural in Quint[us]',[4] whilst Bartlett states that:

> Quintus C with no sharp in 1610, [clashes] with Cantus C sharp. Some editors have
> emended the Cantus to C natural, justifying it by noting that it completes the
> alternating pattern of recitation chords between A minor and G [major]. [This is the
> basis of Stevens's argument.] 1615[5] leaves the Cantus as C sharp and prints E for
> Quintus, which we have followed. This completes another pattern: the Quintus
> reciting notes become ABCD<u>E</u>DCB (completed by A as the final chord).[6]

Wolters, on the other hand, apparently considers no explanation necessary,
although a g♯ in the Tenor against g♮ in the Bassus and Bassus Generalis two

Rastall, 'Pitch Nomenclature', *The New Grove Dictionary of Music and Musicians*, 2nd edn, ed. Stanley Sadie and John Tyrrell (London: Macmillan, 2001), 19, 806).
[3] *Claudio Monteverdi: Vesperae Beatae Mariae Virginis 1610 – Vespro della beata vergine da concerto composto sopra canti fermi*, ed. Gottfried Wolters (Wolfenbüttel: Möseler-Verlag, 1966); *Claudio Monteverdi: Vespers 1610*, ed. Denis Stevens (London: Novello, 1961, rev. 1994); *Claudio Monteverdi: Vespers 1610*, ed. Clifford Bartlett (Wyton: Kings Music, revised 1990/91); *Claudio Monteverdi: Vespro della Beata Vergine*, ed. Jerome Roche (London: Eulenburg, 1994).
[4] Roche, ibid., xxii.
[5] 'The first two movements were reprinted five years after the original edition in *Reliquiae sacrorum concentuum Giovan Gabrielis, Iohan-Leonis Hasleri, utriusque praestantissimi musici*, Nuremberg, 1615; there are no contemporary manuscripts' (Bartlett, *Claudio Monteverdi*, 5).
[6] Ibid., 23.

bars earlier (a false relation about which there is no dissent among these editions) merits a footnote: '*Original!*'[7]

It is not uncharacteristic of such comments that they address the matter essentially from a musical perspective, although, as Jeffrey Kurtzman has noted,[8] it may further be illuminated by an appreciation of how technical slips are likely to have arisen in the typesetting. The method used – that of laying down single blocks cut with the five staff lines and the required note (together with its accidental, if appropriate) – might arguably imply greater clarity of intent in the selection of c♯″ for the Cantus; whereas the placing of the Quintus pitch – a 'long', and thus without benefit of a stem – as the first note on a new system in the partbook, offers a highly probable context for simple error.

Discussion of similarly intriguing details (by their nature, forever moot) fills the critical commentaries in *Urtext* editions of a growing number of composers' works, now including those of the earlier twentieth century. Their relevance potentially extends indefinitely, however, to the work of living artists, since the transmission of musical thought in notated form will always remain susceptible to mistakes. It is entirely to be expected, therefore, that instances are to be found among the published output of Peter Maxwell Davies. Before reviewing a number that touch on the music's compositional substance, it will be helpful to consider the process through which his works might typically progress from genesis to public dissemination.

## From concept to score and parts

Fig. 8.1 offers an archetypal stemmatic diagram for the stages in this sequence, not all of which will be in evidence for each individual work. It draws on terminology applied in Arthur Searle's catalogue of Davies's manuscripts and further elucidated in McGregor's overview of Davies's sketch material in the British Library,[9] implicitly also accepting David Roberts's metaphor of 'the compositional workshop' for the initial autograph phases.[10]

Fig. 8.1's nomenclature and filiation can be more fully understood from the following outline definitions:

(A)  Pre-compositional charts: pitch sets, together with prototypical sets of transpositions, transformations, permutations, durational proportions, etc.

[7] Wolters, *Claudio Monteverdi*, 28.
[8] Jeffrey Kurtzman, *Essays on the Monteverdi Mass and Vespers of 1610* (Houston: Rice University Press, 1978).
[9] Richard McGregor, 'The Maxwell Davies Sketch Material in the British Library', *Tempo*, 196 (1996), 9–19. The British Library has recently acquired a second set of sketch materials: MS Mus. 1400–98.
[10] David Roberts, 'Techniques of Composition in the Music of Peter Maxwell Davies' (PhD thesis, University of Birmingham, 1985), 260.

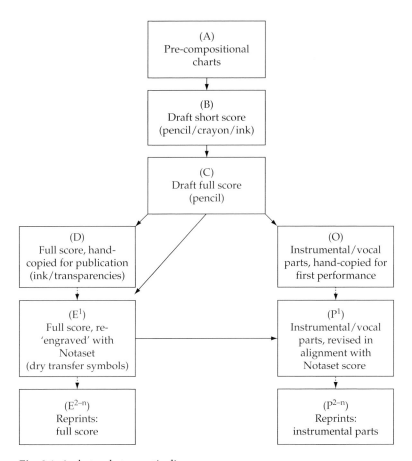

**Fig. 8.1** Archetypal stemmatic diagram

(B) Draft short score: an initial 'composing out' of the material, generally on no more than four staves, with indications of underlying set-forms, structural procedures and selective instrumentation.

(C) Draft full score: the summation of the creative process, in which all details of the completed work are thoroughly specified.

(D) Full score: a fair copy of (C), focused on improved legibility, and not necessarily in the composer's hand. For works of the late 1970s onwards, this stage is frequently bypassed.

(E) Engraved full score: professionally typeset under the supervision of the publisher's editorial staff. Minor errors are corrected on reprint.

(O) Instrumental parts: hand-copied from (C). As with (D), this separate phase is passed over for later works directly to its successor, (P).

(P) Instrumental parts: professionally revised and/or recopied in conformity with the editorial procedures of (E). Photocopied sets are supplied from masters in the publisher's hire library, incorporating minor corrections when implemented.

Discrepancies may arise between each successive stage in this sequence, and determining their significance in respect of the composer's intentions will depend on an interpretation of them as (i) oversights or (ii) considered interventions. Instances of the latter category may be further classified as (a) intended equivalence (for example, enharmonic respelling) or (b) calculated alteration.

Specific examples, chosen to highlight a range of issues, now focus on four works from early in the composer's mature oeuvre – *Revelation and Fall* (1965–6), *Worldes Blis* (1966–9), *Hymn to St Magnus* (1972) and *Stone Litany* (1973). The available materials for these works, relative to Fig. 8.1's proposed stemma, are identified in Table 8.3 by the following means: shelf marks of manuscripts in the British Library; copyright dates, catalogue and plate numbers of publications; master sets of current Boosey & Hawkes hire materials.[11]

## Copying errors, supported by pre-compositional paradigms

The most trivial of anomalies between published scores concern instances where entirely empty bars stand in place of previously composed material: simple errors of transcription, for which graphic clues are readily to hand. A number are listed in Table 8.4, and the appropriateness of the correction can easily be verified with respect to sources (B) and (C) for each. As with the illustration of Monteverdi's Quintus part noted above, these typically arise at the start of a new system and/or page.

Likewise, telling idiosyncrasies in the enharmonic notation of pitches and the melodic octave leaps (a taboo of classical serial composition that Davies has long since relaxed), highlighted in Table 8.5, would quickly raise suspicions, whose correction is easy to check by consulting antecedent sources.

Since the orchestral parts (O) relating to Tables 8.4 and 8.5 will have been copied directly from the unpublished pencil manuscripts (C), these remain untainted by the errors in the first-printed scores. A more complex situation is illustrated in Fig. 8.2, however, showing how recopying of both the score and parts has the potential to correct the former while corrupting the latter. It relates to a deceptively simple figure for glockenspiel (four dotted crotchets)

---

[11] I would like to thank Boosey & Hawkes for kindly allowing me access to the master sets of their current hire materials for comparison; these were consulted on 29 August 2007. The notion of a work being a 'satellite' of another larger work – as suggested in Table 8.3 between *Revelation and Fall* and the *Second Taverner Fantasia* – is one that is discussed more fully in Peter Owens, 'Worldes Blis and Its Satellites', in *Perspectives on Peter Maxwell Davies*, ed. Richard McGregor (Aldershot: Ashgate, 2000), 27.

**Table 8.3** Available materials for *Revelation and Fall*, *Worldes Blis*, *Hymn to St Magnus* and *Stone Litany*

| | *Revelation and Fall* (1965–6; rev. 1980) | *Worldes Blis* (1966–9) | *Hymn to St Magnus* (1972) | *Stone Litany* (1973) |
|---|---|---|---|---|
| (A) Pre-compositional charts | Add. Ms. 71252; Add. Ms. 71253: fols. 1v–2; essentially a 'satellite' of the *Second Taverner Fantasia*, bb. 1–548 | Add. Ms. 71320: fols. 1–7 | Location unknown | Add. Ms. 71324: fols. 8–14 |
| (B) Draft short score | Add. Ms. 71253: fols. 3v–102 (1965–6); facsimiles of fols. 7v–9, 56v–59 and 90v–91 are reproduced as an appendix to (D) | Add. Ms. 71320: photocopy of material held by Karl Renner; fol. 10 (bars 212–240) with Stephen Pruslin | Location unknown | Add. Ms. 71324: fols. 15–40 (n.d.); see also Add. Ms. 71408 |
| (C) Draft full score (pencil) | Washington, Library of Congress | Add. Ms. 71320: fols. 8ff. (Adelaide 1966, Barters Town Feb. 1967); with conductor's markings | Add. Ms. 71407 (Sept. 1972) | Add. Ms. 71325 (1973) |
| (D) Published MS full score | = Facsimile of (C); published Boosey & Hawkes, © 1971, The Markham Press of Kingston Ltd: M.P. 6.71 | Add. Ms. 71321 (ink, 1973; lacking bars 197–211); in the hand of Jonathan Lloyd from bar 382 (bars 482ff. and 585ff. are renumbered from 1); published Boosey & Hawkes, © 1975: B. & H. 20299 | N/A | Add. Ms. 71326 (transparencies, 1973, 1975); published Boosey & Hawkes, © 1975: B. & H. 20304 |
| (E) Engraved full score | Revised 1980: B. & H. 20648 | HPS 1198 (1993): Halstan & Co. Ltd. | © 1978 by Boosey & Hawkes; first publication for sale 1980; B. & H. 20457 | HPS 1110 (1983): B. & H. 20670 |

**Table 8.4** Copying errors and corrections in *Worldes Blis* and *Stone Litany*

|  | **Error** Published MS full score (D) | **Correction** Engraved full score (E) |
|---|---|---|
| *Worldes Blis* Viola | p. 3, b. 30: the last note at the end of this upper system carries a tie to an empty bar at the start of the next; the whole of this lower system is left blank | pp. 3–4, bb. 30–2: the phrase is completed |
| *Worldes Blis* Horns 1–4 | pp. 132–3, bb. 83–7: full bars' rests throughout, although clef changes are marked (bass to treble) for horns 1–3 at the end of p. 132 (for horn 2, this change proves entirely redundant) | pp. 126–7, bb. 667–71: material is restored for all four instruments (now without clef changes) |
| *Stone Litany* Clarinet, Bass Clarinet | p. 2, Letters A–B: neither instrument is named on the two staves between flute and bassoon in the accolade; the staff for bass clarinet is entirely blank (lacking even a clef) | pp. 2–3, Letters A–B: the accolade specifies both instruments; material for bass clarinet is restored |

**Table 8.5** Notation errors and corrections in *Stone Litany*

|  | **Error** Published MS full score (D) | **Correction** Engraved full score (E) |
|---|---|---|
| Violin II | p. 38, 3 bars before Letter CC, note 4 onwards: e♯″– g♯″– f♮″– 𝄽 – f‴– etc. | p. 45, 3 bars before Letter C1, note 4 onwards: e♯″– g♯″– f♮″– 𝄽 – f♮‴– etc. |
| Violin I | p. 38, 2 bars before Letter CC: e[♮]′– e♮″– g♭″– e♭″– etc. | p. 45, 2 bars before Letter C1: e♮′– e♭″– g♭″– e[♭]″– etc. |

in *Stone Litany*, based on a transformation process I have fully transcribed elsewhere.[12] Davies's choice of double flats for notation of the draft short score (B) has led to confusion in the published transparency, although the pitches can be heard correctly in his recording of the work.[13] Subsequent editorial attention, while faithfully restoring the transformation process in a new enharmonically equivalent solution, has failed to ensure concordance with this in freshly made hire materials (lacking a full dotted-crotchet beat in the part).

It seems important to stress that nothing noted here should be taken to reflect at all negatively on the level of attention from Davies's publishers, who are clearly concerned to prepare his works to the highest of professional standards. Proofreading and copy-editing in line with the needs of performances

[12] Peter Owens, 'Revelation and Fallacy: Observations on Compositional Technique in the Music of Peter Maxwell Davies', *Music Analysis*, 13/2–3 (1994), 161–202, Ex. 24.

[13] *Stone Litany*, Collins Classics (CD, 13662, 1993): Della Jones (mezzo-soprano), BBC Philharmonic, conducted by Davies.

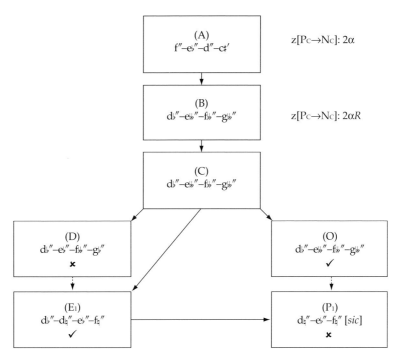

**Fig. 8.2** *Stone Litany*, Letter J, glockenspiel part

(especially premieres) and readily available study scores, however, are necessarily deprived of the luxurious time-scale associated with work on scholarly critical editions:[14] it is only over a comparably extended period that the present observations have been made.

## Adjustments to pre-compositional paradigms and second thoughts

Ex. 8.1 shows two decorative figures for celesta, deriving from a left-hand melodic sequence with superimposed chords in the first published score (D) of *Stone Litany*. The instrument plays ten figures of this kind in the orchestral interlude between songs 1 and 2, from which it is apparent that the vocabulary of chords for deployment above each melody note is pre-compositionally determined. This is made explicit in a sketch (A), summarizing twelve chords above successive notes of the chromatic scale, c to b (Ex. 8.2).

Only by prefixing the final figure with a treble clef for the left hand – absent also in the score as later engraved (E), but correctly copied into the part from

[14] See Helen Wallace, *Boosey & Hawkes: The Publishing Story* (London, Boosey & Hawkes, 2007), 158–9.

Ex. 8.1 *Stone Litany* (1975 edn), 4 bars before Letter P to Letter P, celesta part

Ex. 8.2 *Stone Litany*: transcription of a pre-compositional sketch (A)

Ex. 8.3 *Stone Litany*: transcription of an extract from the draft short score (B)

the pencil draft full score (C) – do the harmonies emerge as consistent with this principle. The correctness of this adjustment is additionally supported by a melodic sketch for the melisma as unstemmed notes in the short score (B) (Ex. 8.3).

The ante-penultimate sonority is of more particular interest, however, since the a′ in the melody of the sketch is realized as c♭″ in the draft full score (C); and we may infer that this is a genuinely structural change, as the superimposed harmonies are those 'appropriate' for C♭, not A. Cases like the celesta figure in *Stone Litany* support an important qualification to our understanding of Davies's serial-based technique: although the organization of pitch and rhythm derives fundamentally from pre-compositionally defined paradigms, in his 'composing out' from these paradigms Davies exercises creative choice – strictly to conform, or otherwise – on various levels.

For instance, the pre-compositional chart (A) for the main transformation process underlying *Stone Litany*[15] shows the second pitch of the central subunit ($z[P_C \rightarrow N_C]$: 5: 2) to be e♭″, and it is realized as such – though notated as d♯′ – in the melodic unfolding with which the work opens, in all sources (B–E) following the draft short score (Table 8.6).[16]

[15] See Owens, 'Revelation and Fallacy', Ex. 24.

[16] The labelling here and elsewhere in the chapter of sets and pre-compositional processes is consistent with my development of David Roberts's terminology as demonstrated in Owens, 'Revelation and Fallacy' and '*Worldes Blis*'.

**Table 8.6** *Stone Litany*, Letter D to Letter E: subunit z[$P_C$→$N_C$]: 5

| Letter: | D | | | E |
|---|---|---|---|---|
| z[$P_C$→$N_C$]: 5 | α | β | γ | |
| Cl. B. Cl. Tpt. 1 | e  **d♯'**  f'  A | g♯  f'  e''  d'  b♭ | d♭  e♭'  c | |

**Table 8.7** *Stone Litany*, Letter Y to Letter Z: subunit z[$P_C$→$N_C$]: 5

| Letter: | Y | | | Z |
|---|---|---|---|---|
| z[$P_C$→$N_C$]: 5 | γR | βR | αR | |
| Tbn. 1, 2 | C  e♭  B♭'  d♭ | d  e  f  g♯  A | **d♭**  f  e | |

**Table 8.8** Pitch durations and interval-dependent ratios in *Stone Litany*

| | |
|---|---|
| **m**[inor[ **2**[nd] | 1 : 1 |
| **M**[ajor] **2**[nd] | 2 : 1 |
| **m**[inor] **3**[rd] | 3 : 1 |
| **M**[ajor] **3**[rd] | 3 : 2 |
| **p**[erfect] **4**[th] | 4 : 1 |
| **A**[ugmented] **4**[th] | 4 : 3 |
| **P**[erfect] **5**[th] | 1 : 1 |

Yet when later this transformation process is used in a retrograde realization to generate a dyadic sequence on trombones, underlying the orchestral interlude that separates songs 2 and 3, the expected pitch class E♭/D♯ is replaced by the pitch class D♭ (Table 8.7).

The structural status of this modification, however, is supported by other variants of the transformation encountered elsewhere in the work, most obviously in the melody of song 3, which immediately follows. Here, an annotation in the pre-compositional charts (A) summarizes how durations for successive pitches are calculated according to interval-dependent ratios in the melodic sequence (Table 8.8).

The resulting rhythm – treating the melody note as pitch class D♭, not E♭ – is analysed in Table 8.9, lending support to Roberts's view that:

> the editorial problem of establishing a definitive version of a serial score is particularly extreme in Davies's case owing to his propensity for making decisions in later stages of the compositional process on the basis of musical events produced at earlier stages:

**Table 8.9** *Stone Litany*, 2 bars before Letter I1 to 5 bars after
Letter I1: subunit z[$P_C$→$N_C$]: 5 and durational ratios

| Letter: | | | | I1 | | | | | | | |
|---|---|---|---|---|---|---|---|---|---|---|---|
| z[$P_C$→$N_C$]: 5 | α | | | | β minus vector interval 1 | | | γ plus vector interval 1 | | | |
| Cl. in E♭ | e″ | d♭″ | f″ | g♯″ | g‴ | e″ | e♭‴ | d♭″ | b′ | d″ | e″ | c♯″ |

|   | 3 : | 1 |   | 1 : | 3 |   | 3 : | 1 |   | 1 : | 2 | 1 | 3 |   | 3 : | 1 |
|---|---|---|---|---|---|---|---|---|---|---|---|---|---|---|---|---|

:

|   | 2 : | 3 |   | 1 : | 1 |   | 1 : | 1 |   | 2 : | 1 | 1 : | 2 |
|---|---|---|---|---|---|---|---|---|---|---|---|---|---|

**Table 8.10** Pitch durations and interval-dependent ratios for final
5 bars of *Stone Litany*

| z[$P_C$→$N_C$]: | | | | | | |
|---|---|---|---|---|---|---|
| 3γ⁻³: | B♭ | | D♭ | E♭ | | D |
| 7αR: | | A　B♭ | | G♭ | A♭ | (9γ4 = F) |

|   | 1: | 1 | 1 : | 3 | 1 : | 3 | 3 : | 4 |
|---|---|---|---|---|---|---|---|---|

|   | 1 : | 1 | 2 : | 1 | 2 : | 1 | 1 : | 3 |
|---|---|---|---|---|---|---|---|---|

**Ex. 8.4** *Stone Litany*, final 5 bars, voice part

potentially 'correctable' 'wrong' events thus become inextricably enmeshed in the
compositional fabric.[17]

Just as pitches may be subject to departure from an initial model, so too
can *a priori* rhythmic principles adjust to local considerations in different
contexts. The haunting vocal line that closes *Stone Litany* is a 75-note melody
(interlocking retrograde and transposed-prime subsets of z[$P_C$→$N_C$]: 9R/1,
8/2R, 7R/3) whose durations conform to the interval-dependent ratios illustrated above. The final phrase is shown in Ex. 8.4, with the strict realization of
these proportions illustrated in Table 8.10.

---

[17] Roberts, 'Techniques of Composition', 7.

**Ex. 8.5** *Stone Litany*, 4 bars before Letter P to Letter P, trombone and trumpet parts

This same melody features earlier in the work, however, most significantly in the orchestral interlude between songs 1 and 2 (Letters K–P) as the basis for a four-voice canon: the leading voice on brass, followed at the proportion of 5:4 and transposed up a major second on bassoons and clarinets; at the proportion of 3:2 in retrograde on marimba, and finally at the proportion of 2:1 in retrograde and transposed down a major second on cello and first violins. The movement is structured to end with the voices' simultaneous completion of their respective realizations. Durations for each are identical with those of the concluding vocal line though, as Ex. 8.5 shows, the governing principles are relaxed and varied in the final phrase, allowing the larger-scale rhythmic complexities to be accommodated within a whole number of 4/4 bars. Cases of this kind clearly bear out Roberts's observation that noting what is 'wrong from the point of view of the chart is not at all the same as saying that it is wrong from the point of view of the composition'.[18]

## Reconstructing paradigms in the arbitration of discrepancies

The immediately preceding examples have focused on discrepancies in the first two consecutive stages of a work's generation: within the pre-compositional charts (A) or between them and the draft short score (B). As with Exx. 8.1–8.3, McGregor has also illustrated, in the context of Davies's Symphony No. 2, 'the alteration of some detail between sketch and first draft', extending at least to modification of register and of the rhythmic articulation of durations from stages (B) to (C).[19] A further instance is shown in Ex. 8.6 from *Worldes Blis*, where repeated *pianissimo* statements from bar 2 of the bass-drum motif with which the work culminates *ffff* in bars 736–7 are transcribed according to the draft short score (B), although Davies subsequently reduced their number by omitting the bracketed figures in the draft full score (C).

[18] Ibid.

[19] McGregor, 'The Maxwell Davies Sketch Material', 15–16.

**Ex. 8.6**  *Worldes Blis*: draft short score (B); bracketed motifs are omitted in (C)

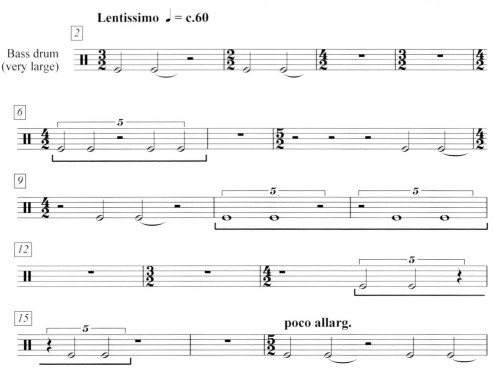

Evidence is also offered in *Hymn to St Magnus* of details revised between the next successive phases, (C) and (E$^1$) – in other words, the full score as drafted in pencil and subsequently engraved. The singer ('mezzo-soprano obbligato'), for example, was originally to have added an extra layer of percussion sounds, striking a 'small suspended cymbal' six times (*p, mp, mf, f, ff, fff*) between letters R2 and S2 ; a 'large bell' (*f*) at letters S2, V2, B3, E3, the start of her last phrase ('Sanc-[te Magne]'), and Letter F3; and both instruments simultaneously in a *crescendo* from *mf* to *fff* to reinforce the supplication 'ora pro nobis' with which the third movement ends.

A clear indication that such contributions were reconsidered in perform-ance – since the pencil score is annotated throughout with cues for members of The Fires of London, with whom Davies first directed it ('Judith [Pearce]', 'Steve [Pruslin]', 'Mary [Thomas]', etc.) – is given by the cancelling in the vocal part of the direction '4 large bells (unusually long tubular bells will suffice) – free "carillon", allegro/*ff* – allegretto/*f* – moderato/*mf* – andante/*mp–p* – ada-gio/*pp* – lento/*ppp*', which extends from the climactic entry of the clarinet in Movement 4 to the *fermata* e♭′ that ends the handbells' recapitulation of fragments from the twelfth-century Hymn ('Nobilis, humilis'). The printed score (E$^1$) is not entirely consistent in its respect for this revision, however, in that 'four large bells (or unusually large [*sic*] tubular bells)' remain listed in the instrumentation: yet the only other appearance of these in the pencil score (C) is between letters Y2 and two bars after Z2 in the percussionist's part, notated unpitched as '1st, 2nd, 3rd and 4th bell' but transcribed as $c\sharp''$, $a\sharp'$, $f\sharp'$ and $d\sharp'$ respectively for 'Handbells (or crotales)' in the printed edition.

While the foregoing discussion of percussion parts certainly indicates Davies's readiness to rethink practical, dramatic and colouristic elements of a work after completion of the draft full score, Tables 8.4–8.5 and Fig. 8.2 suggest that this stage, (C), might otherwise be considered authoritative as regards substantive matters of pitch and rhythmic organization. A surprising advantage with these earlier cases, however, is the *mis*-match between instrumental parts and full score at parallel stages of the materials (see Fig 8.2: (D) ≠ (O), $(E^1)$ ≠ $(P^1)$), which might potentially prompt comparison with (C) to arbitrate between them.

A difficulty illustrated by the current score $(E^1)$ and parts $(P^1)$ of *Hymn to St Magnus* is where editorial attention has made these fully congruent with one another (so that no debate would arise, for example, between conductor and players in rehearsal), yet both materials actually depart from the draft full score (C). Confirmation that mistakes have thus been identified is, however, rendered less secure for this work, since the whereabouts is unknown of any earlier material, (A) or (B), that would make structural paradigms explicit. Similar lacunae apply for a number of works in the British Library collection, of which partial manuscripts are presumed lost or destroyed (for instance, in the fire at Davies's home in 1969),[20] or else are no longer to be traced having been gifted into private ownership by the composer.[21] It can, nevertheless, prove possible to reconstruct the matrices governing the organization of pitch and duration for such works,[22] and I have previously attempted a broad outline of these in respect of *Hymn to St Magnus*.[23] It was, ironically, the otherwise most inconsequential of slips in the engraved published score that provided the key to modelling of the work's genesis from the *Dies Irae* plainchant: the double bar line for flute alone at the end of bar 3 in 'Sonata Seconda' (which, in the pencil full score, extends also to the clarinet). Three examples will serve to demonstrate the capacity of such reconstruction to prompt questions on the basis of the published source.

The harpsichord part, entering after Letter B of 'Sonata Prima', is reproduced in Ex. 8.7. It is based on the squares shown in Ex. 8.8, derived from a first-note-only sieving of the *Dies Irae* incipit in inversion.

[20] See Mike Seabrook, *Max: The Life and Music of Peter Maxwell Davies* (London, Victor Gollancz, 1994), 118.
[21] See McGregor, 'The Maxwell Davies Sketch Material', 9.
[22] See Roberts, 'Techniques of Composition' and Owens, '*Worldes Blis*'.
[23] Owens, 'Revelation and Fallacy', Exx. 12–13; '*Worldes Blis*', Exx. 2.9–2.12.

**Ex. 8.7** *Hymn to St Magnus*, 'Sonata Prima' after Letter B, harpsichord part

**Ex. 8.8** H_F Squares 2: A–E

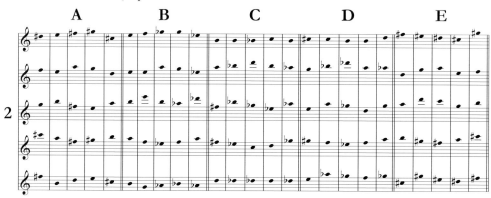

The ten beamed groups of chords present a twofold realization of the squares, initially creating ripple-like verticalizations, radiating from or decaying to the bottom right-hand-corner note and subsequently according to variations of this pattern, as summarized in Fig. 8.3.

The printed chords depart from their putative model, however, in three instances:

Beamed group 3, chord 1:    c♯″, not c♮″
Beamed group 7, chord 2:    d″, not e″
Beamed group 10, chord 4:    f[♮]′, not f♯′

Comparison with the pencil full score (C) confirms that these differences are attributable to simple copying errors. The flute and clarinet parts of the following Moderato section, at Letter C of 'Sonata Prima', derive from a similar matrix, analogously generated from the five-note sieved-incipit set

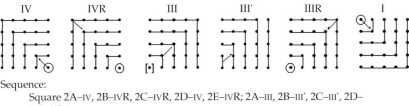

Sequence:
    Square 2A–IV, 2B–IVR, 2C–IVR, 2D–IV, 2E–IVR; 2A–III, 2B–III', 2C–III', 2D–
    IIIR, 2E–I

**Fig. 8.3** Patterns of chordal realizations

**Ex. 8.9** H$_F$ Squares 3: A–E

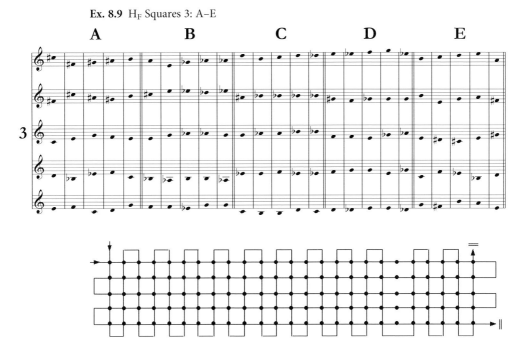

**Fig. 8.4** Paths traced by flute and clarinet

in retrograde, as shown in Ex. 8.9. The counterpoint results from weaving horizontally traced paths for flute with vertical strands for clarinet, in the manner of Fig. 8.4.

Pitches in these realizations are aligned rhythmically one-to-one, and a principle is established from the outset that where this would result in coincidence (or immediate proximity) on a unison, one instrument remains silent (as indicated by bracketed note-names in Ex. 8.10). Most frequently, this is the clarinet, whose omission of the entire last column of Square 3D is marked by a quaver rest at the end of bar 12, and whose last five pitches, like those of the flute, are more freely spaced in the last two bars.

Again, detailed comparison of this reconstructed model with the published source highlights an anomaly – a misplaced quaver rest which, when verified against the pencil full score (C), proves to be a copying error:

**Table 8.11** Copying errors in *Hymn to St Magnus*

|  | W$_G$ | W$_A$R |
|---|---|---|
| Pencil full score (C): | g″– a′ – c″– d♭‴– a♭″ | b♭ – e♭″ – d′ – b″– a″ |
| (E$^1$) and (P$^1$): | b″– a′ – c″– d♭‴– a♭″ | b♭ – e♮″ – d♭′ – b″– a″ |

**Ex. 8.10**  *Hymn to St Magnus*, 'Sonata Prima', Letter C, flute and clarinet parts only

Clarinet, bar 6 (E$^1$):   a♭′ – a♭′ – c♭″ – g″ – g″ – ⅄ – ⅄ – g″
(C):                               a♭′ – ⅄ – a♭′ – c♭″ – g″ – g″ – ⅄ – g″

Two other discrepancies are revealed, however, identical in both sources, for which a rationale is more elusive:

Flute, bar 12, notes 5–6:   b♮′, not a♭′
Flute, bar 16, notes 1–2:   c[♮]″, not c♯″

Although it exceeds the scope of the present discussion to detail all minor departures from the pencil full score in the publisher's current score and parts, revealed by infidelity to a reconstruction of serial workings, a final example is both structurally most significant and readily audible. The clarinet cadenza at the start of Movement 4 is based on a succession of ten transpositions of the five-note set that begins the entire work (on *pizzicato* viola, W$_C$: c″–d′–f′–g♭″–d♭″),[24] alternating prime and retrograde forms (with freer permutations in the *prestissimo* demisemiquaver figures derived from transpositions 4 to 7). The recapitulatory function of this gesture is distorted, however, by the errors in the opening phrase (Table 8.11).

## Revision: practical improvements or distorted paradigms?

In *Revelation and Fall* we have an unequivocal example of specific revisions being undertaken between the publication, in 1971, of the composer's

---

[24] See Owens, '*Worldes Blis*', Ex. 2.9.

manuscript in facsimile (D) and the engraved score of 1980 (E). In a note to the latter, Davies draws attention to his replacement of specially made percussion instruments with more easily found alternatives, and remarks, 'I have also simplified barring and notation in several places'. The nature of these revisions is predominantly of two kinds: (i) where events were originally cued in relation to a guiding *Hauptstimme* – usually the vocal line – complete textures are now fixed metrically under the conductor's control (Exx. 8.11 (a) and (b) illustrate this, and its implications for the listener can be seen as minimal); (ii) where passages originally consisted of superimposed phrases, dependent on one another for their horizontal and vertical cohesion, but without any fixed hierarchy within the texture, these too are brought into a unified metrical frame.

The effects of this latter are of somewhat greater consequence since, as Ex. 8.12 (a) and (b) reveal, the revised score's transcription serves essentially to fix only one possible realization of what was originally composed.

A similar approach is apparent from amendments to the trumpet part of *Stone Litany*, made to the engraved score in the interlude between songs 2 and 3: 'feathered' beaming in Ex. 8.13 (a) gives way to strictly notated rhythms in Ex. 8.13 (b); this is evidence, at least, that preparation of this score was treated as an opportunity for revision.

Recognizing the real possibility of this, however, might conceivably pro-voke uncertainty as to whether apparently minor discrepancies in the later published sources may represent second thoughts – genuine practical adjust-ments in the light of performance experience – or be more simply errors of transcription. In Ex. 8.14(a), for instance, we see a texture created from the technique of what David Roberts has termed 'interfusion', whereby a new melodic line begins imperceptibly from another by overlapping its initial pitch with one in the voice already sounding.

The extract in Ex. 8.14 (a) shows the cello's phrase aligned to begin with the end of the trumpet's. In the revision reproduced in Ex. 8.14 (b), this alignment is disturbed by modification to the rhythm of the trumpet phrase, which now ends a triplet-quaver *before* the cello entry. Although a structural principle of the music thereby seems to have been relaxed at this point, it may be that execution of the passage's metrical subtleties is facilitated as a result.

Davies's use of the harp might also be considered in this light. Throughout the work – as, indeed, elsewhere in Davies's music – the realization of set-forms is regularly accommodated to the practicalities of pedalling (the means by which harpists make notes of the full chromatic scale available from the seven pitch classes of their 'unstopped' strings). The phrases shown in Exx. 8.15(a)–(d) are all to be performed at fast tempi: Exx. 8.15(a), (b) and (d) at ♪ = 184; Ex. 18.15(c) – with its 7:5 relationship to the main tactus – at *circa* ♪ = 246.

**Ex. 8.11 (a)** *Revelation and Fall* (1971 edn), bar 22: accompaniment cued to the vocal line

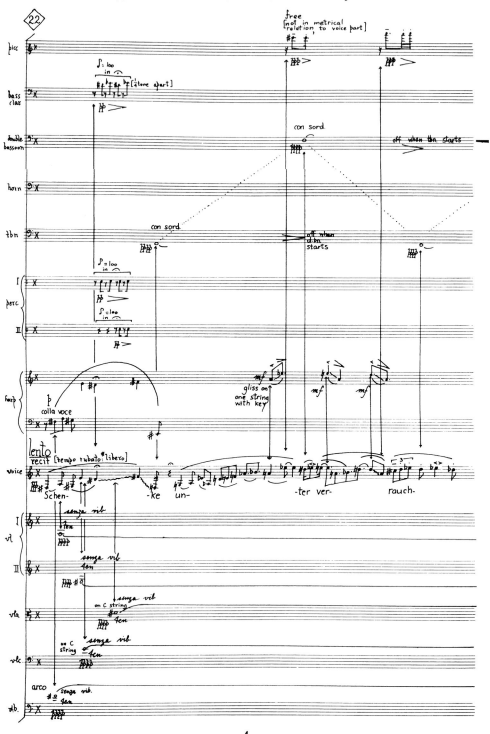

**Ex. 8.11 (b)** *Revelation and Fall* (rev. 1980 edn): measured notation

**Ex. 8.12 (a)** *Revelation and Fall* (1971 edn), bar 181: phrases aligned relative to each other

In the score as first published, the harp's first phrase is an unmodified realization of the seven-note set that it transforms, in subsequent phrases, to its own inversion. In line with the given pedal settings of Ex. 8.15 (a), a change is therefore required to play the final B♮. In the revised score – Ex. 8.15(b) – this B♮ has been substituted by C♯ – a note also present in the set – and the original remark concerning the pedal setting for the glissando immediately following is no longer given, apparently confirming the elimination of a pedal change. In the later, quicker passage of Ex. 8.15 (c), a pedal change in the original and revised scores is avoided by enharmonic respelling, and substitution of the fourth note in the set with its chromatic neighbour (d♭); but one's apprehension of the relevant factors here may not be complete, given that bar 332's recapitulation of bar 178 (at the same tempo) – as shown in Ex. 8.15 (d) – preserves the set with its final B♮ in the revised score, just as it was originally written. And the matter is further complicated on examination of the instrumental part ($P^1$), all of whose pitches remain faithful to those of the pencil full score (C).

**Ex. 8.12 (b)** *Revelation and Fall* (rev. 1980 edn): with fixed metrical realization

**Ex. 8.13 (a)** *Stone Litany* (1975 edn), 3 bars before Letter X to 5 bars after Letter X: written with 'feathered' beaming

**Ex. 8.13 (b)** *Stone Litany* (1983 edn), 3 bars before Letter X to 3 bars after Letter X: fixed metrical notation

**Ex. 8.14 (a)** *Revelation and Fall* (1971 edn), bar 231 onwards: cello entry coincides exactly with the end of the trumpet phrase

At this point, of course, it is perhaps time no longer to ignore the essential difference between the Monteverdi example with which we began and the issues that have since been considered: Davies still is here to be consulted on any matters of doubt that might arise in the publication of his music, and

**Ex. 8.14 (b)** *Revelation and Fall* (1980 edn), bar 291 onwards: cello enters *after* the trumpet phrase

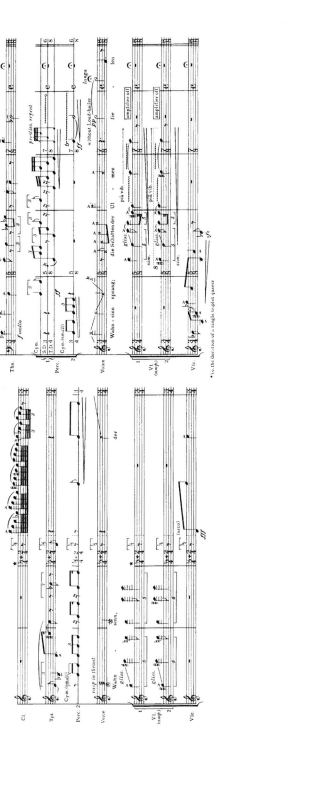

**Ex. 8.15 (a)** *Revelation and Fall* (1971 edn), bar 137: note 7 = B♮

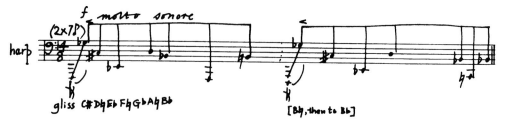

**Ex. 8.15 (b)** *Revelation and Fall* (1980 edn), bar 178 [=137]: note 7 = C♯

**Ex. 8.15 (c)** *Revelation and Fall* (1980 edn), bar 254: note 7 = C♭ (note 4 = D♭)

**Ex. 8.15 (d)** *Revelation and Fall* (1980 edn), bar 332: note 7 = B♮

correction to reprints of the scores from which illustrations have been chosen might proceed – or otherwise – on his ultimate authority. It is merely realistic, however, to note that this will not always be so, and that, in any case, the composer's capacity to respond to such details is necessarily limited. On the one hand, Davies has always been a composer unafraid, in line with the exhortation of other artists, of 'letting go' his works to find their own way in the world; and the concerns of present creativity – there are no signs of any let-up in his prolific writing – are likely always heavily to outweigh those of any retrospection. On the other, it would stretch reason to expect him to recall the minute serial workings of all but the most recent of his pieces, and it is therefore important to recognize the value of any documents in the publisher's archives that might shed light on editorial issues,[25] and invest in the

---

[25] See Kent Underwood *et al.*, 'Archival Guidelines for the Music Publishing Industry', *Notes*, 52/4 (1996), 1112–18.

**Ex. 8.16** *Worldes Blis*, transcription of pre-compositional chart (A): subunit 9,
z[+W$_G$ →( +WI$_A$]

understanding of Davies's compositional processes as recorded for our study
in sketches and drafts such as those at the British Library.

## Generative paradigms retained in recast material

Fortunately, there is much among these materials that can deepen and direct
the nature of this study, illuminating not only the serial paradigms underlying
the music, but also the decisions taken on all levels as these are brought to
fruition in the completed work. Deliberate variance of pitch-class sequences
as generated in pre-compositional charts (A) may be signalled by annotations
in the draft short score (B), such as: 'E statt F', 'G statt A♭' [*statt* being German
for 'instead of'], 'B♭ instead of A', 'omit B♮', and so on. The significance of
these for insights into Davies's melodic and harmonic thinking is considerable
and awaits adequate study.

Even totally unrealized aspects of a pre-compositional model may nevertheless leave traces in the final work. For an example, one might cite the principal
transformation process of *Worldes Blis*,[26] for which durations are calculated on
the basis of interval-dependent ratios similar to those illustrated above in *Stone
Litany*. The seventeen-element +W$_G$ is transformed to its inversion through
sixteen intermediate subunits. In the central subunits (notably 9–11) – whose
aggregate pitch content becomes extremely limited – durations for all seventeen
elements are calculated, before making a representative selection of the notes to
be deployed in subsequent 'composing out'. Ex. 8.16 reproduces the pre-
compositional chart for subunit 9: pitches sieved out, for substitution by rests
in melodic realization, are underlined, and the resulting duration for the subunit
is totalled: '13 (+ 3 𝄽 [an extra rest is inserted to separate subunit 9 from 8] = 16)'.
The missing notes thereby leave their effect on the durational scheme of what
remains, as may be verified in the first trombone part of bars 102–5.

In overtly poetic aspects, also, generative processes are revealed in the study
of drafts and revisions, of which *Stone Litany* provides a particularly clear
illustration. A remark found in both editions, (D) and (E), of the published
score highlights problems that the composer encountered with the third song,

[26] See Owens, '*Worldes Blis*', Ex. 2.6.

**Ex. 8.17**  *Stone Litany*, Song 3: sketch (B) with the text as originally underlaid

based – like the others – on runic inscriptions from the Neolithic cairn of Maeshowe:

> I have selected the text for this song from Stones 19 and 20, having originally set Stone 20, and made little sense of it. Michael Barnes pointed out my error in attempting to read Stones 19 and 20 separately.[27]

An extract from the song as Davies originally sketched it is given in Ex. 8.17 where the vocal line appears on two staves, the upper of them articulating a *Hauptstimme* (here, identical with Table 8.9), and the lower one interpolating melismatic decorations. In this passage it can be seen that the vowels in the melismas essentially repeat and prolong those of the main text. (This is not uniformly the case throughout the song, and other interjections have a paralinguistic quality, e.g.,'HA–A–A', suggestive of laughter, and so on.)

To help clarify the subsequent revision, Fig. 8.5 represents the two stones, which are to be read – in accordance with Michael Barnes's comments – as forming a single page. Having first set only Stone 20, Davies preferred a more aphoristic selection from both stones rather than incorporating their complete text into his music. (It will be remembered, in any case, that this text – in

[27] Davies, 'Composer's Note', *Stone Litany*
(London: Boosey & Hawkes, 1975/1983).

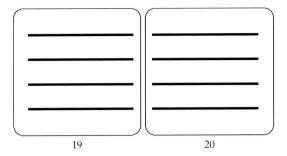

**Fig. 8.5** Layout of Maeshowe Stones 19 and 20, as set in *Stone Litany*, Song 3

**Ex. 8.18** *Stone Litany*, 2 bars before Letter I1 to 5 bars after Letter I1: published version (1975/83) of Ex. 8.17

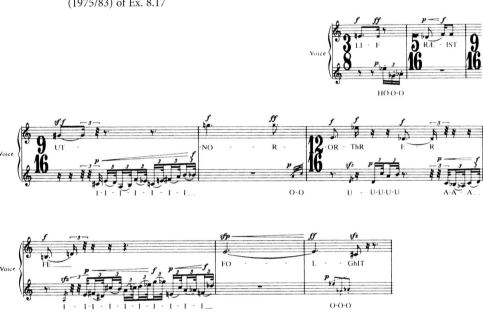

the dead language of Old Norse – is treated as raw phonetic material rather than conventional poetry.) The chosen text is underlined in a transcription of the runes included as a frontispiece to the published scores.

Ex. 8.18 reveals the new textual underlay for the same passage, now referring to one 'Lif the Earl's cook' in whom, Davies records, 'it is tempting to see … Lifolf, Earl Hakon's cook, of the Orkeyinga Saga, who in 1115 was forced by Hakon to behead Earl Magnus'.[28] Although a new melismatic decoration was inserted to the final 'FOLGHIT' at the draft short-score stage – based on the vowel of the word's first syllable – vocalization in the

[28] Davies, programme note for *Stone Litany*, *MaxOpus*, www.maxopus.com/works/ stonelit.htm.

remaining decorations matches that of the original sketch, thus allowing most elegant traces of fortuitous developments in the composition to be preserved in the work as currently published.

Revision of the text in line with Barnes's comments is discussed in a letter to the composer dated 15 November 1974 from Sally Cavender, Davies's editor at Boosey & Hawkes.[29] This document also apparently contains the first mooting of a connection (made by 'John' [Carewe? – Cavender's husband]) with 'Lifolf, Hokon's [*sic*] chef'. Since the work had been premiered more than a year earlier,[30] this calls into question Griffiths's association of the 'knife-like attacks in brass and percussion' with the historical figure and prefiguring of the character in Davies's opera *The Martyrdom of St Magnus*.[31] Of greater relevance to the present discussion, evidence of the conducting score from the publisher's early hire materials confirms that *Stone Litany* was first heard with the original text-setting (i.e., Stone 20 only). As with examples previously cited, then, Davies's conception of the work may be understood to have changed in at least one important aspect between performances.

Should *Stone Litany*, or any of the other three pieces on which the present discussion has focused, ever benefit from publication in a critical edition, the scope for an editorial apparatus to distinguish errors, inconsistencies, minor adjustments or major revisions within and between authoritative sources should now be apparent. This seems likely to be the case for Davies's oeuvre more generally, given the explicitly stratified technique that is innate to his approach to composition and the typical interventions of copyists and publishers, working to the demands of performers and the market, that come between so productive a composer and his audience. As with renowned precedents, optimal resolution of dubious matters in Davies's works can be much enhanced by musicological data:

> In order to reach a decision, [editors] engage in a critical transaction that involves the careful consideration of the evidence bearing on the problem. Understanding of the musical idioms that make up a piece, knowledge of the historical conditions under which it was composed or the social and economic factors that influenced its performance, coupled with an aesthetic sensitivity for the composer's or repertory's style, can all contribute to a heightened critical awareness.[32]

Even so, the quest for an *Urtext* of pieces by Peter Maxwell Davies may ultimately prove to be the chimera for which it is now recognized in so many other historical contexts.

[29] Included in British Library Add. Ms. 71324.
[30] 22 September 1973, City Hall, Glasgow, Jan DeGaetani and the Scottish National Orchestra, conducted by Alexander Gibson.
[31] Paul Griffiths, *Peter Maxwell Davies* (London: Robson Books, 1982), 89.
[32] James Grier, *The Critical Editing of Music: History, Method and Practice* (Cambridge University Press, 1996), 5.

# 9 The composer–performer relationship in the music of Peter Maxwell Davies

*Grenville Hancox*

It is apparent that throughout the long creative output of Peter Maxwell Davies, personal/musical relationships have been fundamental in shaping the outcome of a number of works. This continuity may be considered, in some ways, to be of paramount importance in the creation of a body of work, embroidered as they are with dedications on title pages, regardless of genre. These relationships seem worthy of investigation to discover whether they form the springboard of composition, just as did those between Haydn and Luigi Tommasini, Mozart and Stadler, Brahms and Joachim, Bartók and Szigeti.

The potential for influence from the performer on the composer seems likely in the case of Davies's ten Naxos String Quartets, written over a short period of five years, and following on from the ten Strathclyde Concertos written in similar time-constrained circumstances (a challenge for most composers, but for Davies the long-treasured spur), themselves the result of another significant commission. With regard to the Naxos String Quartets, would the virtuosity of four players act both as a continuing incentive for composition and as a stimulus to the content? Or was the plot so carefully contrived, the compositional drive so intense, the design so complete that the players' ability to realize Davies's ideas was a necessary challenge for them to overcome with little possibility of influencing the compositions themselves? This was the backdrop for one of the most significant commissions of chamber music in contemporary music, bringing together Davies, the Maggini Quartet and Klaus Heymann of Naxos Records.[1]

The desire to write string quartets was long held by Davies, whose initial attempts to write in the genre were returned by the Society for the Promotion of New Music, to his disbelief, in 1952 to be followed in the course of nearly three decades only by the dense and extraordinary twelve-minute quartet of 1961. This work anticipated and exhibited many traits of Davies's later works, with its retrospective view and reworking of plainchant fragments. Two 'Little Quartets' in 1980 and 1987 (revised from 1977) complete the whole output in

[1] Arguably the last composer to have been in a similar position was Beethoven with Prince Lobkowitz, who commissioned the six Op. 18 quartets.

*199*

the genre until the period 2002–7 when the ten Naxos String Quartets were composed.

This fallow period for string quartet writing, however, was itself characterized by an intense period of chamber music composition with The Fires of London (formerly The Pierrot Players) in which many of the traits alluded to above were similarly in evidence. A note by Davies in the final concert given by the group in January 1987 paid tribute to the ensemble and the collective relationship he enjoyed with them:

> The Pierrot Players were founded because the performances Harrison Birtwistle and I were receiving of our music in the sixties were less than satisfactory – underrehearsed and uncommitted. We were both interested in opera and music-theatre, opportunities for which were non-existent for the likes of us in Britain. There emerged a group of friends, willing to spend many hours of unpaid time with two inexperienced conductors, rehearsing difficult new works. Thanks to The Pierrot Players/Fires of London I learned the basics of instrumentation as never before, and the rudiments of theatrical craft – not to mention, out of frightening necessity, how to conduct. The dedication of our musicians, under circumstances of extreme duress, when a new work [for instance *Eight Songs for a Mad King* (1969), *Vesalii Icones* (1969), *Ave Maris Stella* (1975), *Image, Reflection, Shadow* (1982)] in the early stages of rehearsal seemed to be crazy beyond redemption, cannot be over-emphasized. The group has been the most important music experience of my life to date.[2]

What begins to emerge is a sense that everything and anything is possible in musical terms when a composer challenges his performing colleagues. The integrity of the music is everything, and Davies's belief in his colleagues reinforces it. Just as with his belief in children's musical abilities, demonstrated when Davies was at Cirencester Grammar School (1959–62), the compositional process becomes the catalyst for change, thereby strengthening the composer–performer relationship.

## The development of composer–performer relationships

Within this period of composition – 1962–2002 – one is able to draw out examples of works that demonstrate the potential influence of performer on composer as well as composer on performer. In particular, reference can be made to two singers, both of whom had a profound effect on Davies's compositions. The first, mezzo-soprano Mary Thomas, was responsible for the realization of many of the composer's song cycles and vocal chamber works, and perhaps we may judge from the sheer number of works featuring

[2] Peter Maxwell Davies, note in concert programme, Queen Elizabeth Hall, London, 29 January 1987.

her voice that it reflected a personality attractive to him in its unpretentiousness combined with artistic integrity and virtuosity. Thomas's voice was the spur to such luminous instrumental song cycles and vocal chamber music as *From Stone to Thorn* (1971), *Hymn to St Magnus* (1972), *Dark Angels* (1973–4), *The Blind Fiddler* (1975), *Excuse Me* (1986) and *Winterfold* (1986), where she called upon her concentrated intensity of performance and vocal range. The second voice was that of the actor/singer Roy Hart whose vocal techniques allowed the composition of *Eight Songs for a Mad King* to be realized. The extended vocal techniques utilized in the composition were the direct result of Davies hearing Hart's voice.

Here then are not only two examples of the performer influencing the composer but also the confirmation that throughout his composing life Davies has challenged orthodoxy and stretched both performers' expectations and their abilities to the limit, allowing them to go beyond and into regions hitherto unknown to them or indeed the rest of the world. Time and time again we will be reminded of this as Davies composes works for soloists and for performers of the Strathclyde Concertos and the Naxos String Quartets.

Davies's intense concentration on the composition of chamber works with his ensemble The Fires of London in a way anticipated the composition not only of the concertos and quartets but also of the symphonies. Again a pattern begins to emerge of Davies establishing a relationship with an ensemble and a genre through commission. The composition of eight symphonies over a twenty-seven-year period confirms his former manager Judy Arnold's suggestion, made in a 2002 interview, that Davies likes to write in 'lumps':

> Ever since these twenty-seven years I have been with Max he's always had an enormous number of pieces to write – lots and lots of commissions. He tends to do things in what I call 'lumps'. That is to say, in certain times of his life he's doing this and in other times of his life he's doing that, because of circumstances.[3]

The development of relationships and friendships (often intense and sometimes dissipating) extended to ensembles with consequent output:

> So, The Fires' pieces were some theatre pieces and some straight instrumental pieces, some solos and some duos, but on the whole, mostly for the sextet that was The Fires. And then he started with the Scottish Chamber Orchestra, so there were lots and lots of chamber orchestra pieces. Then he went one larger – to the full symphony orchestra working for about ten years with the Royal Philharmonic Orchestra and the BBC Philharmonic Orchestra in Manchester. His title was Conductor and Composer and there were just lots and lots of pieces of all shapes and sizes; big ones, small ones, big symphonies, small, little overtures, light pieces and all kinds of different things.[4]

[3] Grenville Hancox, 'Grenville Hancox Interviews Judy Arnold', 11 October 2002. A full transcription of the interview is available online: www.canterbury.ac.uk/arts-humanities/music/peter-maxwell-davies/pdf/judy_arnold_interview.pdf.
[4] Ibid.

The relationship with the Scottish Chamber Orchestra was particularly fruitful in respect of the writing of ten concertos, again the result of an extraordinary commission: from the Strathclyde Regional Council. The strands of friendship, relationship building, exuberance, the desire to challenge orthodoxy converge in these ten works. Stephen Pruslin sets the scene:

> Several years earlier, Maxwell Davies had composed a triptych of chamber-orchestral sinfonias, which, taken together, form a 'macro-concerto', with the *Sinfonia Concertante* (1982) as its 'classical' first movement, *Into the Labyrinth* (1983) a dark, intense slow movement and *Sinfonietta Accademica* (1983), with its references to folk-fiddling, a 'gypsy rondo' finale.
>
> Through these pieces, Davies forged a relationship with the Scottish Chamber Orchestra, leading to his appointment as Associate Conductor/Composer. This activity entailed not only his own music, but also an exploration of Haydn, Mozart, Beethoven and Schubert. On several occasions, he programmed the Mozart C-major Oboe Concerto, and then decided to write an oboe concerto of his own, which would enable him to further develop aspects of his Violin Concerto.
>
> From this sprouted the idea of a whole concerto-cycle. The Strathclyde Regional Council joined the Scottish Chamber Orchestra in commissioning the ten *Strathclyde Concertos*, with funds provided by the Scottish Arts Council and Strathclyde Regional Council itself.[5]

What attracted Davies to the project was the possibility of creating a whole family of concertos – a series of works for 'first amongst equals' – enabling him to develop the personality of each featured instrument. Orthodoxy was challenged once more by the inclusion of works for bassoon and double bass, instruments not featuring largely in concerto repertoire, whilst the tenth (and last) concerto was written for the whole orchestra – the composer embracing the ensemble in mutually respectful terms.

Virtuosity did attract Davies, however. When the young horn player Richard Watkins joined The Fires of London Davies was immediately taken by the beauty of his sound and the sheer brilliance of his playing, so much so that Davies wrote two works of extraordinary difficulty for Watkins to perform. The first, *Sea Eagle*, was given its first performance at Dartington Summer School in 1982; at a subsequent American premiere it received the following recommendation from the *New York Times*:

> It is difficult to write convincingly for a solo wind instrument, and doubly difficult to write for the cumbersome horn. Peter Maxwell Davies has succeeded spectacularly in his three movement *Sea Eagle* for solo horn which served as the evening's curtain raiser. Mr Davies, an Englishman who established a reputation in this country for a series of riveting and sometimes grotesque theatrical works, has in recent years proven himself to be one of the era's finest composers of concert music; his latest

[5] Stephen Pruslin, 'Background to the Music of the Strathclyde Concertos', *MaxOpus*, www.maxopus.com/essays/strath.htm.

compositions possess a near-Sibelian bleakness. For all that *Sea Eagle* is a largely lyrical utterance, with few gratuitous effects.[6]

On the performance difficulty rating scale, this is a most complex and challenging work. *Sea Eagle* is firmly in the tradition of works that derived from Davies's continual challenging of players for whom he has the utmost respect and affection. What at first appears impossible and unorthodox gradually is realized and sits firmly in the repertoire. *Sea Eagle* was thought at first to have been entirely the preserve of Richard Watkins. Now, it is mainstream repertoire for professional horn players. As Watkins himself states:

> It was rather like when Britten wrote his Serenade for Tenor, Horn and Strings … People said then that only Dennis Brain would have the technique to manage it. Yet only last time round, I noticed *Sea Eagle* was one of the set pieces for the Munich international horn competition.[7]

Watkins, playing as Principal Horn of the Philharmonia Orchestra and as a soloist, continued to impact upon Davies, and in 1999 he wrote a concerto for Watkins. 'When Richard Watkins plays a note it has a lovely authority,' says Davies:

> I can't quite put it into words – it's something to do with the very rounded quality of the sound he makes, which I love. I wanted to create music to exploit Richard's particular lyrical qualities: above all his singing tone and the extraordinary 'presence' of each note – hence, a concerto which 'breathes' in one, long connected argument, from the opening slow introduction through to the final cadenza and coda. The horn writing is extremely virtuoso throughout, not least in exploring the full range of the horn, from the deepest notes in the bass, normally exclusive to an orchestral fourth horn player, to the highest, most exposed sostenuto of a first horn soloist, presenting here challenges of embouchure and sheer stamina I should think fairly unprecedented.[8]

Whatever the challenges, just as so many other players had done in the past, Richard Watkins accepted and met them. But these challenges are very often formidable: looks of amazement, if not horror, on the faces of players when initially presented with one of Davies's scores have been witnessed many times over the years. As Judy Arnold recounts:

> He likes to have an association with a particular ensemble – with a group of people – and write for them and play to their strengths. That's what he did with The Fires over and over again, and he knew what they could all do. He'd give it to them, and they'd be screaming and howling at the difficulties of it. I remember those first rehearsals of

[6] Tim Page, 'Concert: Davies Piece for Solo Horn', *New York Times*, 6 October 1984, 16.
[7] Richard Watkins, in conversation with Nick Kimberley, 'A Lusty Horn and a Roman Carnival', *Independent*, 28 April 2000, 9.
[8] Davies, in conversation with Nick Kimberley (ibid.).

*Image, Reflection, Shadow* – David [Campbell, clarinet player in The Fires of London] will tell you – I thought they would all kill each other. But then they get to it … it just takes an immense amount of excellent time, that devoted people are willing to give.[9]

This challenging approach was to be repeated with the series of Naxos String Quartets. The context for the composition of the string quartets was well defined. It is possible to identify a pattern of mutual admiration and developing trust between composer and performers, as will be discussed in due course. Similarly, Davies's penchant for writing series of works within a relatively short space of time, spurred on by the demanding schedule of premieres (the 'lumps' referred to above), not to mention the enormous gap in his output – including a gestation period of approximately ten years during which time Davies was still engaged with major compositions – led to the decision to engage with the quartet project. With the cycles of ten Strathclyde concertos and eight symphonies completed, major conducting projects terminated and opera writing similarly abandoned, the time was ripe for Davies to seize the opportunity presented to him through Judy Arnold's identification of a potential commission that would enable him to address the notable absence of extensive string quartets in his oeuvre.

I remember having my first meeting with William Lyne [then Director of the Wigmore Hall] at the Wigmore Hall in 1991 to propose doing all these string quartets. He was very interested, but we weren't able to get to it for different reasons. Meanwhile, there were all these huge works that Max had to write. He didn't only get commissions from the orchestras with which he was associated – there were lots of other commissions as well, in between the special associations that he had here and there. Then he said, 'No, I'm not going to do any more orchestral pieces, I'm going to write chamber music.'[10]

Naxos Records was founded in 1987 by Klaus Heymann. Naxos has established a phenomenal reputation for promoting a catalogue of works which not only contributes to the existing canon of recordings but has also added to it through the championing of composers whose works appear neglected. The policy of recording string quartets by British composers in the series 'The Glory of the English String Quartet', featuring the Maggini Quartet, provided an excellent example of this. As Arnold explains:

We got in touch with Naxos, and went to see Klaus Heymann … We met him in London and put the suggestion to him that he might commission these pieces. He said he would like to, and here we are [2002]! That was almost five years ago, to the minute. That's about the time that all of these things take – always five years in advance of when the thing is going to happen, except when Max says 'I'm going to write it tomorrow'. So it's either five years, or it's tomorrow.[11]

[9] 'Grenville Hancox Interviews Judy Arnold'.

[10] Ibid.
[11] Ibid.

Klaus Heymann's commission was the spur for Davies to distil ideas fermenting for so many years and to be prepared musically, in engaging with the genre, to 'dance naked in public'.[12] The opportunity to write a series of string quartets for one group was exactly what he yearned for, rekindling his passion for creating an association of composer with a group of performers, be it chamber ensemble, orchestra or string quartet, always with a desire to find ways to 'play to their strengths'.[13]

## The Naxos String Quartets: a 'novel in ten chapters'

Nineteenth-century authors, notably Charles Dickens, developed a genre of writing based on an episodic model. Weekly or monthly instalments would later be compiled into a complete novel. The general readership, once having tasted the initial parts, hungered for successive episodes. Whilst the comparison with the Naxos String Quartets may seem a little stretched, the parallel has some merit and was confirmed by the composer himself. As late into the series as the Eighth Naxos String Quartet (2005) Davies referred to the series in the following terms:

> The quartets are rather like a novel in ten chapters – the same rhythmic patterns, themes and harmonic designs are developed like characters throughout, also the same magic square matrices, and architectural structures carry over from one quartet to the next.[14]

The set of string quartets was considered to be a series by Davies, like his symphonies, where common elements informed their composition, cast within an overriding architecture which, for Davies, suggested a cyclical form.[15] At the first public exposition of the Naxos String Quartets, Davies referred both to the fact that he had been wishing to write a series of string quartets for 'the last dozen years' and to the developing nature of the series. The countless walks taken as part of his compositional process on the strand of the isle of Sanday had allowed a grand design to emerge and develop, to the extent that even in 2002 with only one quartet completed, the plans for the remaining nine chapters had been clearly laid:

[12] Davies, workshop discussion of Naxos String Quartet No. 1, Canterbury Christ Church University Music Department, 17 October 2002. A recording of this workshop is available online: www.canterbury.ac.uk/arts-humanities/Music/SirPeter/NaxosStringQuartets/StringQuartetNo1/Workshop.aspx. Further interviews, workshop recordings, and premiere recordings of the quartets are also available online: www.canterbury.ac.uk/arts-humanities/Music/SirPeter/Home.aspx.
[13] 'Grenville Hancox Interviews Judy Arnold'.
[14] Davies, liner notes to Naxos String Quartet No. 8 (CD, Naxos, 8.557399, 2007).
[15] See Davies's programme note for Symphony No. 7, *MaxOpus*, www.maxopus.com/works/symph_7.htm.

The chance for me to do ten quartets is very significant as it offers opportunities
for exploration in the architecture of the music which hitherto I have not been able
to indulge in. When I wrote that set [the symphonies], it's really a set of seven
symphonies with Antarctica [Symphony No. 8] sitting outside the set … by the time
that I got to No. 4 I realized this was a cycle of seven symphonies and I could make
symmetries in the architecture of the seven and make link points in the symphonies
and take up points from there. In fact the last one, No. 7, the end bit leads straight
back into the end of No. 1 so that the whole thing forms a loop and in theory could go
on ad infinitum. As an architectural idea I like that, the idea of making a piece that
goes through one piece into the next and into the next. With these string quartets that
is precisely what I am doing.

   The last movement of this quartet [No. 1] is too short for the quartet. It won't really
be a conclusion and it's a scherzo which is very fast and the end just evaporates. It
goes right up to the top of the sound spectrum and disappears. I imagined it going on
being played somewhere up there until it's going to come down again in the Third
Quartet and that's going to continue.[16]

   The first outing of the Naxos series took place at Canterbury Christ Church
University, where the Maggini Quartet (the string quartet in residence since
1994), together with the composer, had agreed to be part of a project to record
and archive the realization of the works during the five-year period 2002–7.
On two occasions each year, prior to the scheduled world premiere of each
quartet, composer and players met in the music department, rehearsing in
camera each new work in turn, every moment recorded and archived.
Further, during each visit a workshop with students took place, the composer
introducing and contextualizing the unfolding novel, with players and composer subjecting each chapter to public scrutiny, as they presented each new
work. Each premiere was also recorded (with the agreement of all parties
including venue management); these recordings, together with the final
Naxos studio recording, have provided a fascinating document tracing the
development in performance terms of each quartet.

   The Maggini Quartet – consisting of Laurence Jackson and David Angel on
violins, Martin Outram on viola and cellist Michal Kaznowski – had only met
Davies once before the first rehearsal (at a photoshoot to publicize the series) –
a fact that added to the inevitable anxiety felt by composer and performers
alike. But the choice of the Maggini Quartet as the conduit group for Davies's
ideas was obvious to all concerned. The quartet's contribution to the growing
realization that the British compositions for string quartet largely written in
the twentieth century were works to celebrate and be proud of had been firmly
established prior to their association with Davies through their 'Glory of the
English String Quartet' series of concerts and recordings released on Naxos.
Over 100,000 discs had been sold worldwide, drawing both public and critical

[16] Davies, workshop discussion of Naxos
String Quartet No. 1.

acclaim for the quartet's performances of neglected, largely twentieth-century repertoire by composers such as Bridge, Elgar, Vaughan Williams and Ireland. Thus their selection as the quartet to be asked to develop further the conception of the English quartet was obvious. However, the fact that their focus had been directed towards the more pastoral repertoire – alongside the mainstream Classical and Romantic repertoire of the canon – did mean that to champion the works of someone who was still considered by many as a radical force in music was for them a radical change in direction.

The agreement between the Maggini Quartet and Judy Arnold, acting as Davies's manager, took place in 2001, the original proposal for five concerts, each premiering two quartets at the Wigmore Hall, having been discounted. This proposal was replaced with ten concerts, six at the Wigmore, with the remaining four to be presented at the Cheltenham Festival, the Purcell Room in London, the Royal Palace in Oslo and St Gregory's Centre for Music, Canterbury.[17] The score and parts of the Naxos String Quartet No. 1 were sent to the Maggini Quartet for reading and rehearsal in August 2002, three months prior to the premiere, while the quartet was leading a string course in Norway. At this point, Davies was nervous about their reaction to the score and to the challenge. He had heard and admired all their recordings but was unsure how they might react to this opening element of a journey that included a continuing scaling of technical mountains. A week before the first Canterbury rehearsal, Judy Arnold reported:

> Max is very nervous because he doesn't really know them. He's heard their recordings and is very keen to go on with them. When he sent the score and the parts off and they were doing their first rehearsal in Norway, he kept saying 'Have you heard back from them?'[18]

Davies was very surprised and delighted not to have received a catalogue of enquiries and complaints from the Maggini players, as often had happened in the past. Indeed there were very few, signalling at the outset of this new

[17] Naxos String Quartet No. 1 (2002), dedicated to Judy Arnold, first performed 23 October 2002, Wigmore Hall, London; No. 2 (2003), dedicated to Ian Kellam, first performed 11 July 2003, Pittville Pump Room, Cheltenham; No. 3 (2003), dedicated to Eric Guest, first performed 15 October 2003, Wigmore Hall; No. 4: *Children's Games* (2004), dedicated to Giuseppe Rebecchini, first performed 20 August 2004, Chapel of the Royal Palace, Oslo; No. 5: *Lighthouses of Orkney and Shetland* (2004), dedicated to Thomas Daniel Schlee, first performed 20 October 2004, Wigmore Hall; No. 6 (2005), dedicated to Alexander Goehr, first performed 26 April 2005, Purcell Room, London; No. 7: *Metafore sul Borromini* (2005), dedicated to Archie Bevan, first performed 19 October 2005, Wigmore Hall; No. 8 (2005), dedicated to her Majesty the Queen Elizabeth on her eightieth birthday, first performed 10 March 2006, St Gregory's Centre for Music, Canterbury Christ Church University, Canterbury; No. 9 (2006), dedicated to Dame Kathleen Ollerenshaw, first performed 18 October 2006, Wigmore Hall; No. 10 (2007), no dedication, first performed 16 October 2007, Wigmore Hall.

[18] 'Grenville Hancox Interviews Judy Arnold'.

relationship a trust that was to be central to its development. The grand plan, the architecture already in Davies's mind, could be preserved if this was the first reaction. Similarly, the players were aware that gesture for Davies was all-important and that access to some of the detail could be modified to enable gestures to happen or to be able to capture the atmosphere of a passage:

> Max was extremely surprised at the lack of queries. I kept saying to Sue [Bailey], 'Can I have the queries? Where are their problems?', and I got a list which was rather small – just half a dozen items, which is not much for a big score. One particular problem was that of the tempo marking. Michal [Kaznowski] said they couldn't do it. I asked Max about it, and he said: 'It's not that I want you to get to that speed. It's just to give an indication of the sort of atmosphere that it ought to be. Do it at the speed you feel you could manage, but that's the atmosphere that I want.'[19]

The first rehearsal and workshop of the project – only the second meeting of performers and composer – took place at Canterbury Christ Church University on 11 October 2002. Motorway traffic delayed Laurence Jackson and Michal Kaznowski, and thus it was left to Martin Outram and David Angel to make the initial introductions and to break the ice. A real sense of nervous energy and anxiety can be detected in the recordings made on that morning. This was perhaps because of the task that lay before the Maggini Quartet, not only in relation to their own realization of this monumental work, but also in the knowledge that this was the first in the series, with a further nine to come at regular intervals. The recordings reveal that Davies too displayed a little anxiety: he was keen to know if the challenge that he had presented to the Maggini Quartet was achievable. All were concerned to discover whether a relationship had started to be forged through the music alone, prior to meeting and working together. This tension, inevitable in any situation similar to this, was exacerbated by the delay of two members of the quartet and only began to be really resolved when the music began to be realized fully.

It is interesting to listen to the conversations about the difficulties encountered, the comparisons between other works hitherto rehearsed, and Davies's gently reassuring comments as the music unfolds. Nervous laughter gives over gradually to shared humour, and very little compromise is necessary to realize Davies's ideas. Thus a relationship begins to be forged between players and composer, setting the scene for the quartets to follow and for the series as a whole.

The challenges presented to each player in the Naxos String Quartet No. 1 were extraordinary, leading to a new (for them) way of learning and playing such music. The first quartet in the series allowed the composer to establish

---

[19] Ibid.

an artistic context, presenting the ensemble with a framework within which they had to be able to work. The composer himself reinforced this:

> If you like it's a 'putting your cards out on the table' sort of quartet rather than one which presents any solutions to problems which may appear in those two big expositions that appear in the first movement.[20]

In many ways the technical demands made in the first three quartets were not exceeded in the remaining seven, though they were constantly redemanded, suggesting again that the architecture was firmly in place prior to the complete set's realization. Yet this technically demanding music required the absolute minimum of rescoring in order to clarify expression – a tribute to Davies's understanding of the instruments and genre, deepening the relationship he began to share and develop with the four Maggini players.

Virtuosic writing in the violin 1 part at the outset of the First Naxos String Quartet was to be the benchmark for all of the players throughout this work and the series of quartets as a whole. After a mysterious and evocative introductory four bars where attention to dynamics is extraordinarily detailed, a Scotch snap rhythm is introduced which permeates this and other quartets. The filigree violin 1 part, from bar 23, underlain with a combination of string writing that includes directions for harmonics, *pizzicato* and *arco* together with *glissando col trillo*, introduces the listener to a soundworld hitherto unknown in string quartet writing (Ex. 9.1).

For the Maggini players the challenges were enormous not least in the area of rhythmic complexity, as they had to learn how to relate to each other's playing. According to Martin Outram, 'We learned to bounce off each other and take cues rather than rely on the metronomic element of our counting':

> The technical demands of the First Quartet, indeed the first three quartets, have not been exceeded in the remaining quartets, whilst the challenges were maintained throughout in many different ways. In rehearsals we would spend many hours cueing parts. The first time we played through the First Quartet with Max in the Stockwell Room we were tense, but he helped us to feel very relaxed. He taught us to feel gestures rather than count them and helped us to feel like jazz players might; never metronomic but listening to and playing off each other.[21]

Davies similarly acknowledged the two-way process of learning when, in his workshop introduction of the First Naxos String Quartet, he recalled that in solving some of the problems faced by a composer when writing string quartets he was indeed fortunate to be working with such an eminent group of players from whom 'I am learning a lot'.[22]

[20] Davies, workshop discussion of Naxos String Quartet No. 1, 17 October 2002.
[21] Martin Outram, interview with the author, October 2007.

[22] Davies, workshop discussion of Naxos String Quartet No. 1.

**Ex. 9.1**  Naxos String Quartet No. 1, first movement, bars 23–5

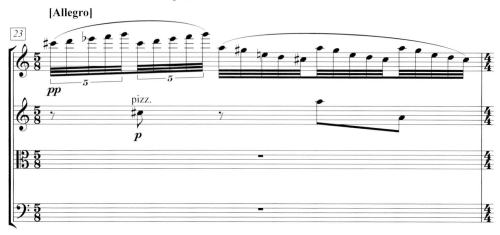

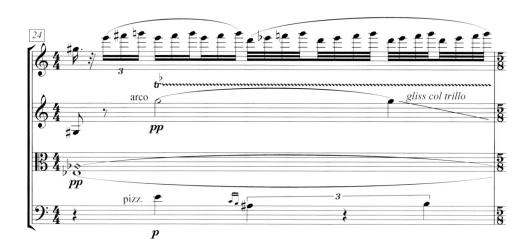

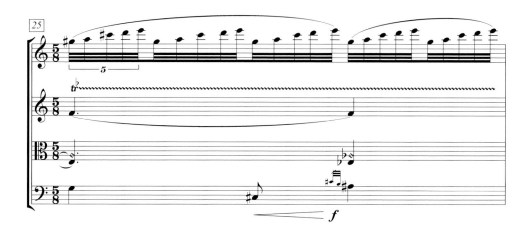

**Ex. 9.2** Naxos String Quartet No. 1, first movement, bar 176, viola part

**[Allegro]**

The major influences of place and people inform each quartet in the series, together with an overriding fascination with architecture (in each quartet and in the whole series), and in one specific instance, No. 7 – which concerns itself with the architecture of Francesco Borromini – with buildings themselves. As Davies himself explains in his programme note for the First Naxos String Quartet:

> Although filtering the extraordinary light, weather and seascape of Orkney through the comparatively restricted medium of the string quartet was of huge interest, it was architectural challenges which preoccupied me in the composition of the first *Naxos String Quartet* … I am very aware that this is the first in a sequence of ten quartets, which enabled me to think from the outset of an architecture spanning the whole cycle.[23]

The architectural plan is itself dependent to some extent on the compositional scaffolding of his magic square technique which Davies refers to often. In his first workshop introduction he suggested that the magic square technique would underpin all that he would write in the series but, following the experience of teaching students this methodology, at the Dartington Summer School of Music, he vowed to himself not to disclose where he uses it until twenty years after the event, and that he would leave it to others to discover! But Davies informs us that the opening material in the first movement of the First Naxos String Quartet was

> subjected to a process of transformation through a twelve-unit 'most perfect pandiagonal magic square'. Perhaps this sounds more daunting than it is – it works as a catalyst to musical invention, engendering enough related but varied basic rhythmic and melodic outline for the whole series, with due harmonic accountability.[24]

Such an approach, demonstrating another aspect of Davies's mastery of compositional technique, inevitably demands much of the players as they seek to expose the framework and all that is laid over it. The virtuosic writing in the first violin referred to above is mirrored by the writing for the other three instrumentalists, producing at times passage work of immense challenge. The viola part, for example, at bar 176 in the first movement (Ex. 9.2) covers nearly three and a half octaves across four beats moving at ♩ = *c.* 132.

[23] Davies, liner notes for Naxos String Quartet    [24] Ibid.
No. 1 (CD, Naxos, 8. 557396, 2004).

Martin Outram points to other examples of almost unprecedented virtuosity in viola writing throughout the works, as in the Naxos String Quartet No. 4:

> In this quartet, *Children's Games*, Max demanded of me writing unprecedented elsewhere in the literature, with left hand *pizzicato* and bow strokes in the same passage. Literally I had a photocopy of this passage (bars 27–38) in my case and would practise it when I could. It is like a Paganini *Caprice*, but not having trained as a virtuoso violinist, the demands were new to me.[25]

The novel in ten chapters was, however, blown off course when world events elicited a response from Davies so characteristic of his life. The invasion of Iraq by American and British forces angered him to such a degree that he changed his long-thought-out plans for the Third Quartet. His demonstration at the front of the anti-war march held in London was the first public manifestation of his total revulsion at the action of the government. His second was to write into the quartet elements that expressed this revulsion:

> The varied ways in which these events impact upon the piece, surfacing almost involuntarily in a deliberately 'nasty' little satirical Mahlerian march, in the intentionally 'cloying, nauseating grotesquerie' at the end of the scherzo and in a consciously malevolent treatment of John Taverner's 'In Nomine' ('Blessed is he that cometh in the name of the Lord') – a bitter, twisted reference to both the 'godlessness' of war and the betrayal at the heart of Davies' first opera [*Taverner*] – confirms that the provocative Davies of the 1960s has certainly not changed his spots.[26]

Thus the quartet medium and the players he trusts implicitly to realize his ideas become the vehicle for the radical artist who shocked the establishment in the 1960s and 1970s and whose later appointment, in 2004, as Master of the Queen's Music was demonstrably not going to affect the central core of his being and his understanding of an artist's role in society. The democracy that he celebrates metaphorically so strongly in his quartet writing had been for him completely abused by the action of the government. Davies and the Maggini Quartet had already developed a mutual trust, understanding and strengthening relationship, and such an overt political statement was received comfortably by the players who endorsed his anger with their passionate interpretation:

> In the final Fugue [of the Third Naxos String Quartet], the Magginis – who played with compelling insight – created a dialogue between ancient and modern, as an archaic-sounding texture was traduced by jagged, dissonant music. In the last moments of the performance, that contrast was amplified, as hollow, stabbing chords exploded over quiet, sinewy lines.

[25] Martin Outram, interview with the author.

[26] Roderic Dunnett, 'Short Note [for Naxos String Quartet No. 3]', *MaxOpus*, www.maxopus.com/works/naxos3.htm#short.

The way Davies transforms his political sentiments into musical structure gives the whole piece a coherent architecture. If anything, his technical manipulations are almost too sophisticated: in the first movement, he composes what he describes as an 'empty, grotesque' march, but in the Maggini's performance, the music was expressively intense, but always refined.[27]

## A two-way process?

The players of the Maggini Quartet have been very generous in their acknowledgement of Davies's influence upon them in the realization of the quartet series. Laurence Jackson (leader until October 2006) suggested that working with Davies was a unique experience, allowing the players to develop the technical side of their playing to a considerable degree. There was, he suggested, opportunity to investigate the workings of an ensemble and to consider – even more so than in other works – the relative positions of the constituent instruments and players. When the Maggini Quartet was presented with Naxos String Quartet No. 2 there was a hiatus in the learning process, as for a little while the challenges proved to be beyond their capabilities. (Even so, they made only one request to Davies to modify any of his writing in this work; as a result, with his approval, two bars – 247–8 inclusive – were re-scored between second violin and cello.)

Jackson suggests that the Maggini Quartet may have influenced Davies from the Third Naxos String Quartet onwards, citing the significant part that the second violin, David Angel, was given in the Fifth:

> I think we may have influenced his writing from the Third Quartet onwards. In Naxos 5 in particular there is an emphasis upon David, where there are incredible outbursts – the writing seems to be more and more on an individual basis.[28]

Similarly, Jackson refers to his own playing perhaps having influenced the composer:

> No. 5 has some incredible serene writing for me – I think he has got my sound in mind; I get the impression of having to be more focused.[29]

The idea of Davies being a part of the quartet in spirit emerges through conversations with the players. Martin Outram suggests that Davies 'imagined himself sitting next to the viola player when writing the quartets',[30] whilst Jackson goes a step further to suggest that the working relationship with the composer was open and frank:

[27] Tom Service, 'Anti-war Protests at the Wigmore Hall', *Guardian*, 17 October 2003, 32.
[28] Laurence Jackson, interview with the author, March 2006.
[29] Ibid.
[30] Martin Outram, interview with the author.

He is a member of the quartet really; we have developed a real understanding and
affection for him, that is why the recordings are so successful. If Max likes something,
the quartet feels very good; he doesn't intervene too much, not wanting to interrupt
the work. He has a quartet voice, writing music with dramatic intensity for us, full of
gesture and experimentation.[31]

Above all Jackson suggests that the quartet has developed a mutual feeling of
trust, with and for Davies:

There is a great element of trust: he is amazingly flexible compared with other
composers. He is not so precious and sometimes physical boundaries are overstepped
and we feel that he trusts us so much that we can say, 'come on Max, you can't be
writing like that at your age'.[32]

David Angel recognizes similar influences on the Maggini Quartet, stating
that they worked with such intensity with Davies that they now view other
works from a composer's perspective. Angel's extensive experience as a player
had never brought him into contact with such challenging writing for the
second violin, but he acknowledges also that Davies is a composer who never
writes anything 'just for effect'; instead he allows imagination free range and
pushes the player to the edge of his ability:

I wonder if we have influenced Max? Texturally No. 3 was far less dense than No. 2,
and No. 4 was even more transparent. He certainly does not approach the second
violin in a traditional manner. No … in the Second Quartet he doesn't use the
instrument in alto register; both violins are used in the same register. It's the highest
quartet writing for second violin that I know. When I asked Max why he had done
this he replied with a twinkle in his eye, 'because I knew you could do it', and we are
both great admirers of Isaac Stern.[33]

Michal Kaznowski has endorsed all the points made by his colleagues,
suggesting further that the quartet of players entered into Davies's soundworld, enticed to do so by the complexity of metric challenge, the sheer beauty
and eloquence of sound, and the multiplicity of textures found throughout
the works. According to Kaznowski, a sense of humour, so essential for
successful relationships when working so intensively, was also a feature of
the learning process:

Max has a wonderful sense of humour and does not mind being teased. It is
sometimes a waggish sense of humour which not only allows the intense learning and
rehearsing to be pleasant and very positive but has also resulted in David having to
play some pretty challenging passages, although the difficulties in the music are not
gratuitous. Undoubtedly, too, Max has spotted more of what Martin can do and
I sense too he has my sound in mind in some of the later writing. When we identify

[31] Laurence Jackson, interview with the author.   [33] David Angel, interview with the author,
[32] Ibid.                                    March 2006.

problems he tries to solve them for us. His love of Haydn provides a very strong common-based grounding, a common language inspiring a trustworthy reference point.[34]

## Conclusion

In his Naxos String Quartets, Peter Maxwell Davies has exhibited characteristics that are the hallmarks of his entire output, with his continued desire to challenge, to stretch and to question. Virtuosity is acknowledged and exploited but always for musical ends and not for its own sake, while the sheer brilliance of understanding, every nuance of the instruments he writes for, is writ large on every page of every score. Similarly, the reflection of a sense of place is paramount in the quartets, as the music powerfully evokes the Orcadian landscape.

Friendship, companionship and relationship similarly inform each quartet, even his friendship with the monarch, for whom the Naxos String Quartet No. 8 was dedicated on the occasion of her eightieth birthday, a dedication that reflects Davies's status as Master of the Queen's Music. The great relationship Davies enjoys is with music itself, informed by relationships with people and place. His understanding of every aspect of composition reflects these relationships, and through the inspired commission of Klaus Heymann the Naxos String Quartets have confirmed that:

> Not least among the ways in which Max's music has always been unmistakably his own is that he has never sought to separate his creation from his own attitudes … Here is the 'intensely moral composer' that [Gerard] McBurney called him, with his horror at cruelty, philistinism, and anti-intellectualism, his detestation of the cheap and nasty, the bogus and the kitsch, his distaste for religion, especially in its authoritarian, thought-policing aspects, his concern for the environment, his hatred of commercialism run amok, all written plainly in his music.[35]

To this list could be added his detestation of the government that invaded another sovereign territory, but definitely not in his name.

The concluding bars of the Tenth (and last) Naxos String Quartet suggest that these are not the last quartets that Davies will write: the final bar is without bar lines. A pause sign (instruction *lunga*) hangs over a semibreve rest, together with the instruction to the players to hold their bows in the air (*archetto in alto*). Ready perhaps for a second novel in the series?

---

[34] Michal Kaznowski, interview with the author, March 2006.
[35] Mike Seabrook, *Max: The Life and Music of Peter Maxwell Davies* (London: Victor Gollancz, 1994), 255. The McBurney reference is first discussed by Seabrook on page 170.

# 10 Peter Maxwell Davies at Dartington: the composer as teacher

*Philip Grange*

Peter Maxwell Davies's work with schoolchildren, both as composer and teacher, is well documented, but little has been written regarding his teaching of young composers often in their late teens or early twenties. This is in part because he himself has written extensively about his time at Cirencester Grammar School,[1] where between 1959 and 1962 his approach to musical pedagogy proved significant in motivating a whole generation of teachers. Furthermore, whenever Davies responds to questions about that period his comments tend to suggest an entirely positive experience from which he learnt much. For example, in an interview with Paul Griffiths in 1980, he recalled: 'I got the kids improvising and composing a lot, and watching them I learned a lot, too. It de-inhibited me, if you like.'[2]

However, although there are early articles by Davies addressing the issue of compositional technique,[3] he has only referred in passing to his work with emerging composers, and some of those comments, such as this one from the same interview with Griffiths, can suggest that the experience was disappointing:

> I had an experience of this last summer [1979] at Dartington, where I did a class on the first movement of [Beethoven's] *Eroica* Symphony. I thought that what I was going to say was frightfully obvious, but it turned out that it wasn't: the students had not heard the piece in the way that I had … if even those students hadn't heard the processes going on in that work, then that makes me realize that no matter how well the public knows and loves a particular piece, they probably don't know how it works.[4]

[1] See, for instance, 'In Classes Where They Sing and Play', *Times Educational Supplement*, 10 February 1961, 245; 'Composing Music for School Use', *Making Music*, 46 (Summer 1961), 7–8; 'Music Composition by Children', in *Music in Education*, ed. Willis Grant (London: Butterworths, 1963), 108–24; and 'Music in Schools', Presidential Address to the 1985 Schools Music Association's North of England Education Conference, transcript available at www.maxopus.com/essays/north.htm.

[2] In Paul Griffiths, *Peter Maxwell Davies* (London: Robson Books, 1982), 105.

[3] See 'The Young British Composer', *The Score*, 15 (1956), 84–5; 'Problems of a British Composer Today', *The Listener*, 62 (8 October 1959), 563–4; and 'Sets or Series', *The Listener*, 79 (22 February 1968), 250.

[4] Davies, in Griffiths, *Peter Maxwell Davies*, 115.

Yet Davies has been heavily involved in teaching young composers privately, at summer schools and institutions of higher education for most of his career, creating supportive and stimulating environments within which to learn and providing most students with an entirely positive experience.

Most notable among the summer schools have been the Wardour Castle Summer School of Music, a joint teaching venture that Davies, Harrison Birtwistle and Alexander Goehr undertook in 1964 and 1965;[5] Dartington Summer School of Music, where Davies taught between 1969 and 1984, and of which he was Director between 1979 and 1984; and the Hoy Young Composers' Summer Course that ran between 1989 and 1996. Davies is still committed to this work and currently teaches on the St Magnus Composers' Course and on the Advanced Composition Course at Dartington, a teaching role to which he returned in 2008 after an absence of twenty-four years. These courses were and continue to be significant (particularly that at Dartington, which Davies directed on his own for many years) because they reveal his attitude to the craft of composition, while also providing insights into his own way of working as a composer. The following draws extensively on my own experiences as a composition student at the Dartington Summer School, where I attended Davies's course every year from 1975 to 1981. It is supplemented by information supplied by other students, some of whom participated in courses both before and after those dates, and, to a certain extent, by the private composition lessons I had with Davies in 1977 and 1978 which maintained the same general ethos.

## Davies's teaching ethos

The overall outline of the two-week course at Dartington would now not appear particularly innovative, yet in the 1970s not even the most progressive institutions in Britain specializing in composition provided its integrated mixture of analysis, composition and workshop, combined with interaction with professional performers and a consistently high level of technical discussion. Today, any British university music department or music college that takes its commitment to composition seriously provides the opportunity for student compositions to be workshopped and performed by professional players, but in the 1970s this was not the case.[6] There were of course other

---

[5] The importance of the Wardour Castle Summer School in relation to Davies's later summer schools will be discussed towards the end of this chapter.

[6] In the 1970s, York University Music Department was certainly regarded as the most forward-looking in terms of its provision for student composers, having been founded on the basis that all members of staff would be composers themselves. However, while it did offer a platform for the performance of student work, the

organizations that offered young composers workshop and performance opportunities, most notably the Society for the Promotion of New Music (SPNM) and the BBC (in the form of the BBC Young Composers' Forum), but while young composers could thereby learn from the experience of hearing their works played, these events lacked the intense pedagogy of the Dartington course. For those who participated in this course it also became clear that its integration of analysis and creativity reflected Davies's own compositional process.

During the first week of the summer school the class would analyse two or three prescribed scores, sometimes writing short exercises in response to issues that arose from the analysis. The discussion that took place in week one also very often gave rise to the spontaneous setting of a task to be performed by the student composers themselves: 'write a monody which is not a monody'; 'compose a ritualistic piece to summon people to dinner'; 'write a passage to join these two chords together' (a cluster and a widely spaced B♭ major triad given as aural dictation, and only played once!); 'orchestrate this chord to make it sound as full as possible'; and so on. They would be completed either in class or over lunch and performed immediately.

Over the weekend, students would be expected to complete a short piece based on some aspect of the analytical work undertaken, and during the second week they would be joined by The Fires of London, the ensemble that Davies directed, for a series of morning workshops in which the short pieces would be played and discussed. In 1975, the assignment involved writing a short piece employing transformation processes, a technique employed by Davies in the *Second Fantasia on John Taverner's 'In Nomine'* (1964) which had been studied in the first week of the course.[7] In other years the assignment might be less obviously connected to the set works, but instead developed from tangential issues that had arisen. As is always best practice in the teaching of composition, the assignments were not stylistically prescriptive, and certainly the more a student's work literally sounded like Davies's the less interested he appeared to be in it. Furthermore, without the artificial necessity for the compositions to form part of an assessed course with strict assessment criteria (as is so often the case in academia), they could be discussed positively in terms of both how they diverted from the assignment brief and how much they might conform to it.

Unlike in SPNM workshops, the composers would be required to conduct their own music no matter how inexperienced they might be as conductors. Davies regarded this activity as a necessary part of the young composer's

performers involved were almost invariably fellow students, and it did not offer a systematic approach to the acquisition of compositional technique.

[7] The other set work that year was Sibelius's Seventh Symphony, with Davies drawing parallels between his and Sibelius's different approaches to a one-movement structure.

formative experience; it was also a strategy that ensured that the students had a more immediate understanding of what might be required to realize their own compositional intentions in practice. Response from the players as well as from Davies himself ranged from detailed analytical insight to specific issues of instrumental writing and notation, and was used to help inform revisions in time for the informal concert on the final Friday afternoon of the course at which the works were presented. As with the use of analysis as a starting point, the focus on conducting reflected Davies's own background, for he had been required to conduct his own work at Cirencester, with The Fires of London and on other occasions.

During the afternoons of the second week students had the opportunity to present recordings of their works written prior to the course. Davies did not always attend these sessions; having established the appropriate environment he could leave the students to learn from each other. If he did attend his remarks were almost invariably encouraging, but as with the workshops he might make fewer comments than was generally expected. Then at a later time on the course he might state something that left the students wondering if it applied to their music. It may appear an unusual strategy, but it had the effect of challenging the students to consider and evaluate for themselves what they did, a far more effective approach to learning than the spoon-feeding that has dogged certain aspects of British education since the 1980s.

While this general course outline remained for each year, there was also a fair degree of flexibility that allowed for a certain amount of spontaneity. Many students only attended one course, but others would return year after year, thereby serving something of an apprenticeship, a concept of which Davies approved. For a few lucky individuals Davies would offer private tuition throughout the year. This continued the same approach of analysis, practical exercises and composition, although it obviously could not involve workshops. However, it did tend to be intense, with a schedule of approximately ten pieces a month to analyse plus attendant exercises. These might well relate to the compositions a student wished to write. For example, appropriate preparation for the writing of a piano piece not only involved analysis of works from the canon, but also the reduction of entire orchestral movements for piano.

## Analysis, compositional technique, repertoire

In his first published article, which appeared in the March 1956 edition of *The Score*, Davies makes it clear that the acquisition of compositional technique through analysis is essential for any serious composer:

> His [the young composer's] technique should come from exhaustive analysis of the
> music of not only the greatest composers, but as many of the others as he can manage.
> Most young composers are familiar with at least the most superficial aspects of
> Schoenberg, Bartók, Stravinsky, etc., – perhaps even of Messiaen or Stockhausen –
> but they know surprisingly little about more ancient composers – their training has
> led them to take for granted that they know all there is to know about them.[8]

At Dartington, Davies's approach to the analysis of the prescribed scores was
never exhaustive, and although he often favoured the motivicism of Keller
and Réti, he did not espouse any particular analytical method.[9] Analysis
was undertaken very much from the point of view of a composer and not
from that of a music theorist. At times a considerable amount of attention
might be given to a detailed discussion of just one parameter – for example
the orchestration of the opening chord of 'Don' from Boulez's *Pli selon pli* –
while on other occasions there might be a thorough investigation of one
technique throughout an entire piece – the use of 'distorted mirrors' in
Beethoven's Piano Sonata in A♭, Op. 110, for example; both these works
will be discussed in due course.

It is notable that Davies's approach to analysis treated the composers
studied as colleagues who were part of a tradition to which we were all the
latest heirs. We were therefore all engaged in the same project, and by
studying how composers in the past had faced certain problems we could
learn from their solutions whether or not they were successful. This ethos
helped create a sense of camaraderie among the ten or so student composers.
Davies was also firmly against any competitive approach to the Arts and
stressed strongly at the beginning of each course that there were to be no
winners or losers among the group. This policy was always effective, even
though a sense of hierarchy might have emerged because some students on
the course were commissioned to write large-scale works for The Fires of
London. It is clear that Davies thoroughly appreciated that fostering a
supportive environment constitutes one of the most important foundations
for the teaching of composition, for not only does it enable composers to
flourish, but it also empowers them to discuss each other's work and ideas
in a constructive manner, and thereby learn from each other.[10]

---

[8] 'The Young British Composer', 85.
[9] For a useful summary of the analytical tradition to which both Keller and Réti belonged, see Jonathan Dunsby and Arnold Whittall, *Music Analysis in Theory and Practice* (London: Faber and Faber, 1988), 88–94 and 154–61.
[10] Davies has often noted how important his discussions were with fellow students at Manchester, particularly Goehr and Birtwistle – the more so since he gained so little from the composition teaching at Manchester University. See Mike Seabrook, *Max: The Life and Music of Peter Maxwell Davies* (London: Victor Gollancz, 1994), 33–50, and Alexander Goehr, 'Manchester Years', in *Finding the Key: Selected Writings of Alexander Goehr*, ed. Derrick Puffett (London: Faber and Faber, 1998), 27–41.

On several occasions Davies used his own scores to initiate an investigation of particular techniques, sometimes – as will be seen later in this chapter – offering information about the construction of a work that only the composer could reveal. Whenever possible works discussed on the course were also performed in one of the regular evening concerts.

There was often a direct link, too, between the works studied at Dartington and Davies's current interests as a composer. To understand this more fully, it is useful to trace Davies's association with Dartington back to his student days when he attended the summer school in 1957 in order to hear the premiere of *Alma Redemptoris Mater*, the commission for which funded his time there and his participation in the class directed by Aaron Copland. Between 1959 and 1961 he returned to act as translator for Luigi Nono and in 1960 he ran an analysis class featuring Byrd's Four-part Mass and works by Dunstable, Bull and Gesualdo. This repertoire was in marked contrast to that he used at Dartington in the 1970s, which focused almost exclusively on major, canonical works from the eighteenth to the twentieth century. This focus no doubt reflected Davies's own interests, which to a certain extent had shifted in the early 1970s, a shift that coincided with his new location in the Orkneys.

The works studied at Dartington, then, can be divided into five broad categories: (a) those that anticipated a relationship to something that Davies was currently composing or would be composing in the near future; (b) those that related to works that would be written in the distant future; (c) those by other composers that related to works Davies had written in the past; (d) those that were simply part of an ongoing interest; and (e) his own (then recent) already completed scores. As might be expected, some works studied would fulfil more than one of the above categories, and those works that acted as precursors and precedents have been returned to by Davies throughout his career.

## Beethoven's Op. 110

Within each of the above categories there could also be a significant differentiation in the scale of influence from past models on Davies's own work. For example, during the composition course in 1978, Beethoven's Piano Sonata in A♭, Op. 110, was subject to a thorough examination. The analysis dwelt for some considerable time on the evocation of clavichord writing to be found in the Recitativo that occurs during the opening of the third movement, in particular the spacing of the $B^7$ chord that begins the bar marked Adagio, where the seventh in the right hand is so placed that a vibrato effect will be produced because the naturally occurring seventh from the low B will be slightly lower

**Ex. 10.1** Beethoven, Piano Sonata in A♭, Op. 110, third movement, Recitativo

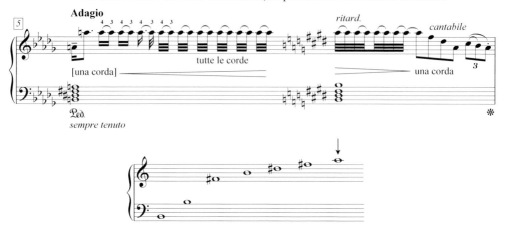

than the tempered tuning of the repeated A (Ex. 10.1).[11] This vibrato effect, which requires a certain degree of sensitivity in performance, was related by Davies to the expressive vibrato that a clavichord can produce,[12] and had, Davies maintained, sparked his interest in writing the Four Lessons for Two Keyboards (1978), which was premiered at Dartington on two clavichords that same year.

Beethoven's Op. 110 was also studied extensively in terms of its use of distorted mirror technique, whereby the motivic outline of an idea in the right hand would be reflected in the bass, but distorted, often because of the needs of tonality. The opening of the sonata provides a good example of this (Ex. 10.2).

This technique can also be noted in the inversional relationships between the two fugues in the third movement, and traced elsewhere in movements two and three (Exx. 10.3 and 10.4).

While such an understanding of this Beethoven sonata could be seen as providing the background technical thought for Davies's *Image, Reflection, Shadow* of 1982, Paul Griffiths also notes a more direct relationship between the last movement of the Beethoven and Davies's own Piano Sonata (1980–1):

> the particular attraction of Beethoven's Op.110 for Davies would seem to reside most obviously in its last movement, and its fusion there of two types, adagio and fugue, both repeated in altered forms to exacerbate one's worry about how the sonata will end.[13]

[11] Davies also discussed Chopin's Ballade No. 1, Op. 23, bar 172 in the same terms at the summer school course in 1977.

[12] Of course the vibrato on a clavichord is produced by other means.

[13] Paul Griffiths, 'Maxwell Davies's Piano Sonata', *Tempo*, 140 (1982), 6.

**Ex. 10.2** Beethoven, Piano Sonata in A♭, Op. 110, first movement, opening:
distorted mirror technique between the outer voices

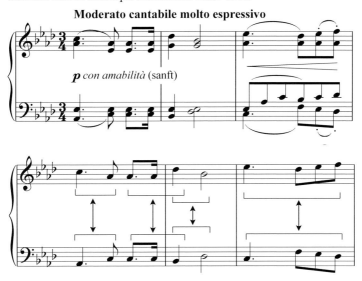

**Ex. 10.3** Beethoven, Piano Sonata in A♭, Op. 110, second movement, opening: distorted
mirror technique

Outlining the sections in the Beethoven movement he goes on to state:

> Davies's last movement is also multiple, to the extent that he divides it into four
> parts and calls it movements 4–7. It is also very clearly concerned about how it
> will end.[14]

[14] Ibid.

**Ex. 10.4** Beethoven, Piano Sonata in A♭, Op. 110, third movement: distorted mirror technique

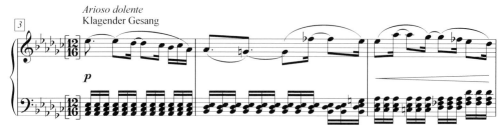

**Ex. 10.5** Direct allusion in Davies's Piano Sonata (Movement V, final bar) to Beethoven's Piano Sonata in A♭, Op. 110 (third movement, bar 127)

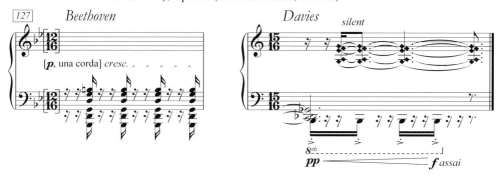

In tracing the relationship between the two works he even cites a direct allusion to the Beethoven example at the end of the fifth movement of the Davies Piano Sonata:

> a new passacaglia-like movement, Grave … ends with a direct recollection of the Beethoven sonata, the massive chords of G major having their echo here as a low B with aided resonances [Ex. 10.5].[15]

Already it is apparent that Davies's analytical engagement with other scores and the resultant influence on his own work is not at the level of the stylistic surface, but ranges widely from the inspiration a particular detail

---

[15] Ibid., 8.

might provide, through the adaptation and development of specific techniques to the use of structural and even detailed allusion. In asking students to study such works in this manner he was simultaneously demonstrating how he worked and how they could benefit from this approach, while also hoping to benefit from their insights.

A more generalized concern that arose from the analysis of Beethoven's Op. 110 sonata was also one that Davies demonstrated in his own *Ave Maris Stella* (1975), which was also a set work for the same 1978 Dartington course. This concern relates to the concept of establishing a musical idea so that its inclusion in the piece is deserved and justified. In the case of Beethoven's sonata, this was discussed in terms of the *arioso dolente*. Davies maintained that a lesser composer might well fail to integrate such music into the ongoing technical principles of the work and thereby reduce its effect to that of a superficial sentimental tune. However, its high degree of integration and placement in the third movement becomes a point of arrival that both justifies its inclusion and heightens its expressive power. In *Ave Maris Stella* this approach – almost redolent of a Protestant work ethic – relates to the final page of the score, which Davies indicated had been written first, with the rest of the piece composed to deserve and justify its inclusion.

## The 1976 and 1979 summer schools

Examples of works that were studied in retrospect are more numerous, and in 1976 included 'Don' from Boulez's *Pli selon pli* and Schumann's Symphony No. 2, both of which relate to Davies's First Symphony (1973–6). Given that the Davies work was completed in 1976 it must be presumed that the study of the other works effectively coincided with its completion. Indeed, the composer himself drew attention to this relationship in the programme note for the first performance of the First Symphony in 1978:

> The cross-phrasing and time-perspective devices in my third movement were developed from the opening of Schumann's Second Symphony, and the overall shape and some of the detailing of formal structure in the last movement came, on the surface level, from 'Don' in *Pli Selon Pli* of Boulez.[16]

The Dartington 1976 class discussion of 'Don' also focused on specific details in the orchestration and voicing of the opening chord, noting how its spacing alluded to the natural overtone series and, in terms of orchestration, the use of C and D trumpets using the same strong fingering to give different notes. The

---

[16] Davies, programme note to the First Symphony, in Griffiths, *Peter Maxwell Davies*, 159.

class also puzzled over the guitar B♭ octave, surely anathema to Boulez's compositional aesthetic at that time.

In addition to the Boulez example, Beethoven's String Quartet in C♯ minor, Op. 131, was discussed at the 1976 course. At that time Davies's own *Ave Maris Stella* was still being hailed as a technical and expressive breakthrough, but despite its indebtedness to Beethoven's Op. 131, the Beethoven was not discussed in these terms.[17] Rather, the analysis focused on the principles employed in order to establish unity in a manner reminiscent of Deryck Cooke's discussion of the late Beethoven string quartets in general.[18] However, the Op. 131 quartet is clearly a work to which Davies often returns, its influence on the formal structure of his own Piano Sonata of 1981 being noted by Stephen Pruslin (the work's dedicatee) in his programme note, which expands much further on Davies's indebtedness to late Beethoven than the relationship suggested by Griffiths:

> there is one aspect of the work it is difficult to reconcile with its otherwise demonstrable sonata ancestry. In the last Beethoven sonatas, the number of movements decreases from four to two. In the last quartets, however, the movements increase from four to seven. In this regard, the seven-movement Maxwell Davies sonata reminds us most strikingly not of a Beethoven sonata but of a quartet – the one in C-sharp minor, opus 131. And this is no accident: the last Beethoven quartets are written against a background of the Baroque suite and the classical serenade, which serve as an important second principle in the new sonata.
>
> The serenade in particular often exhibits a symmetrical grouping of movements around the centre, and this occurs explicitly in the Maxwell Davies.[19]

Beethoven's *Eroica* Symphony (which was discussed above in relationship to the 1979 course) provides another good example of a work to which Davies often returns. The analyses of this work undertaken at Dartington focused heavily on the relationship between the sonata form allusions of the musical surface and the overall structure, demonstrating a basic motivic connection between the first and second subjects of the first movement and a developmental approach to material that begins in bar five and continues until the coda, at which point the music becomes more regular in terms of phrasing, so that structurally the movement sounds like a developmental upbeat to the coda. The importance of Beethoven's Third Symphony for Davies may be seen in the reflection of this work in the overall shape of his

---

[17] The relationship between *Ave Maris Stella* and Beethoven's Opp. 130, 131 and 132 is discussed by Stephen Pruslin, in 'The Triangular Space: *Ave Maris Stella*', *Tempo*, 120 (1977), 16–22.

[18] See Deryck Cooke, 'The Unity of Beethoven's Late Quartets', in *Vindications: Essays on Romantic Music* (London: Faber and Faber, 1982), 143–70.

[19] Stephen Pruslin, liner notes to Davies's Piano Sonata (LP, Auracle: AUC 1005).

own *Worldes Blis* (1966–9), a reflection that is merely, if tantalizingly, alluded to in the published exchange between Davies and Griffiths.[20]

Interestingly, very few works analysed during the Dartington course did not in some way relate directly to Davies's own; these included 'Der Abschied' from Mahler's *Das Lied von der Erde* and the Impromptu, Op. 90 No. 1, by Schubert. The former was discussed at length in 1979 in terms of Mahler's expansion of musical expression (and as such could be said to relate to a whole host of Davies's works from the later part of the 1960s) and the manner in which a pulse is only gradually established at the start of the movement. If the main technical issue in the Mahler was metrical and rhythmic ambiguity, that in the Schubert was focused on the tonal ambiguity of the opening, although it is difficult to see how this could be emulated in a musical language that did not employ common practice tonality.

Examples of his own music that Davies discussed during the 1970s included, as already mentioned, the *Second Taverner Fantasia* and the first movement of the First Symphony – which were deliberately analysed in terms of their structural relationship to the repertoire works set for that year (Sibelius's Symphony No. 7 and the *Eroica* respectively) – and *Antechrist* (1967) and *Ave Maris Stella*, which were dealt with more in terms of their own technical processes of transformation and magic square manipulation respectively.

In the analysis of *Ave Maris Stella* Davies not only revealed and demonstrated his recently established use of magic squares,[21] but placed the resultant material within the context of the overall structure and some of his former compositional concerns. The right to deserve what might be described as the grand *telos* on the final page has already been mentioned, but he also sought to reveal that the point of greatest tension in the work (the beginning of the ninth section) was also the quietest. It could be argued that such moments exist in earlier works, as in the section before the megaphone scream in *Revelation and Fall* (1965–6), but he appeared to have discovered a new understanding of such stillness and introversion, inspired by the quietness of Hoy in Orkney where he had recently made his home. Another interesting issue related to the eighth movement, a regularly recurring theme in Davies's discussion of music, was the manner in which time passes, and the tendency to foreshorten repetitions in order that passages do not sound longer than they actually are.[22] For this he often cited the beginning

[20] See Griffiths, *Peter Maxwell Davies*, 116–17.

[21] This working can be seen in David Roberts's brief but incisive account of *Ave Maris Stella*, 'Review of Davies Scores', *Contact*, 19 (1978), 26–9. A more detailed account is given in Roberts's PhD thesis, 'Techniques of Composition in the Music of Peter Maxwell

Davies' (Birmingham University, 1985), 336–56.

[22] Having written a thesis on Indian music for his undergraduate degree Davies was also keen to point out different attitudes towards time in other cultures as well as the minimalists' adaptation of these.

of the first movement of Beethoven's Piano Sonata in F minor, Op. 2 No. 1, in which the harmonic rhythm halves with each successive phrase.[23] By analogy he noted that the overlapping of the magic square rows in the eighth section of *Ave Maris Stella* foreshortened in order to compensate for the manner in which a listener perceives something that has been previously heard. He also maintained that this was an important function of mensural canon, a technique used in the first section of *Ave Maris Stella* and the last section of *Antechrist*. Finally, on a number of occasions Davies mentioned the tendency of medieval music to form harmony outwards from a central tenor line, and the opening section of *Ave Maris Stella* is an excellent example of his development and adaptation of this approach; indeed, like a number of passages that were studied in depth, it is an innovatory amalgam of a whole range of compositional techniques, and a striking illustration of what Davies has always maintained is achievable if composers engage in the analysis of a whole range of music.

## The directorship at Dartington and beyond

1979 marked a considerable change in Davies's relationship with Dartington, as he took on the role of Director of the summer school following the retirement of Sir William Glock, who had held the position for twenty-seven years. In his biography of the composer, Mike Seabrook makes it clear that Davies had specific and visionary plans in taking on this responsibility, which involved increasing the intensity and standard of the whole venture so that its primary focus would be the training of professional musicians. Seabrook states:

> Max was unequivocal in his desire to turn Dartington into something much more like a serious musician's forcing house. Indeed, he more than once expressed the desire to restrict attendance to professional musicians seeking higher tuition.[24]

Such a desire is strongly reminiscent of another teaching venture that Davies undertook with Birtwistle and Goehr earlier, in 1964 and 1965, the Wardour Castle Summer School of Music, which can now, in retrospect, be seen as an important first indication of what were to become the defining characteristics of the Dartington experience. The idea for the Wardour Castle venture initially came from Birtwistle, who at the time had a position teaching woodwind at Cranborne Chase, a private school in Dorset which had the ruins of Wardour Castle in its grounds. Birtwistle invited his former colleagues from

[23] Davies demonstrates this process in 'Four Composition Questions Answered', *MaxOpus*, www.maxopus.com/essays/question.htm.
[24] Seabrook, *Max*, 182.

the so-called Manchester Group to help with the teaching, and resident professional performers including the Melos Ensemble were integrated into the programme and available to perform new works.[25] Seabrook states of Davies's own recollections of the Wardour Castle Summer School:

> It was, Max recalls, much like Dartington, but considerably more intense, because everyone there was planning in earnest to become a professional musician.[26]

While the Wardour Castle venture only lasted two years, Davies held the position of Director of Dartington Summer School for five. But Davies's educational aspirations for the position were never realized, thwarted by the Trustees of the Dartington Trust whose objective, Seabrook argues, 'was to make the concern as lucrative as possible'.[27] From the perspective of students on the composition course, however, Davies did introduce a number of significant changes. These included removing the class from its geographically isolated position in the Octagon to a more central site on the campus. This had a number of advantages, including the symbolic one of indicating that composition was central to the range of activities that took place at the summer school, but it also had the effect of diluting the all-important camaraderie that had hitherto existed. There was also an increasingly greater integration with other key activities, in particular the long-standing analysis course offered by Hans Keller, and a newly established conducting course directed by John Carewe. Both of these developments were a natural extension of important aspects of the composition course as Davies had structured it before 1980, but the interaction between the composers' and conductors' courses enabled the possibility of composers being able to write for larger forces.

Perhaps the most significant change in direction, however, was Davies's invitation to other composers to teach composition at the summer school.[28] It was rather a surprise, though, that the first composer he should invite in 1980 was Brian Ferneyhough. At that time Ferneyhough was only just emerging as a significant compositional voice, and although it was clear that Davies's musical priorities lay in a very different direction, he was genuinely intrigued by what Ferneyhough had to say. However, Ferneyhough, already a well-established teacher on the Continent, ran his composition course in a very independent manner, so from 1981 Davies returned to the well-tried team teaching of the Wardour Summer School, working alongside Anthony Payne in 1981 and Robert Saxton in subsequent years. In fact, since Davies left

---

[25] Among the new works premiered at Wardour Castle were Birtwistle's *Tragoedia*, a work which marked a significant breakthrough for the composer, and Davies's *In Illo Tempore* (1964–5), then known as *Ecce Manus Tradentis*.

[26] Seabrook, *Max*, 88.

[27] Ibid., 182.

[28] Although Elliott Carter had been present at the summer school in 1975, he was not there officially to teach.

Dartington in 1984 team teaching has been his preferred *modus operandi* on short courses, in which he has collaborated with younger, highly esteemed colleagues. For example, he ran the Hoy Composition Course between 1989 and 1996 with such composers as James MacMillan and Judith Weir, and is currently involved in the St Magnus Composers' Course with Alasdair Nicolson and Sally Beamish.

Seabrook paints a picture of Davies as frustrated and disappointed that he could not achieve his aspirations at Dartington, but although they are not located within a larger summer school, both the Hoy Young Composers' Summer Course and the St Magnus Composers' Course demonstrate an ongoing commitment to a particular vision of how composition should be taught.[29] The former grew out of his association with the Scottish Chamber Orchestra, who supplied support in the form both of professional performers with which the student composers could engage, and administrative expertise in raising funds. It too combined analysis with the practicalities of composing in a supportive and inspiring environment, where all concerned are engaged in a common creative task. The St Magnus course overlaps with the St Magnus Festival, which Davies founded in 1977, and with which he has always been strongly involved. It also interacts with the St Magnus Conducting Course, with student conductors conducting the composers' works, thereby building upon the approach taken at Dartington in the early 1980s, and in many respects it continues Davies's well-established combination of analysis and discussion of student works in relation to the practicalities of performance.

In discussing what he describes as 'Max's lifelong commitment to the education of the nation's future composers', Seabrook makes the point that 'while it is certain that his great gift to posterity internationally will undoubtedly be his compositions, it may well come to be adjudged that his greatest contribution to the musical life of his own country was his work in education'.[30] This most probably overstates the case, but Davies's contribution in this area has been significant, and while his involvement in music-making with young children has always been given due recognition, it is only more recently that his involvement in the training of young composers is beginning to receive the attention it deserves.

[29] Moreover, as explained above, in 2008 Davies returned to teach the Advanced Composition Course at the Dartington Summer School.
[30] Seabrook, *Max*, 243.

APPENDIX I

# Peter Maxwell Davies's articles, lectures, libretti, interviews and radio broadcasts

*Nicholas Jones*

The following list comprises the writings and spoken words of Peter Maxwell Davies that exist in printed form, published on the internet, or available at the British Library Sound Archive, the BBC Sound Archive and BBC Radio International. Programme notes and the composer's spoken introductions to some of his works on *MaxOpus* are not included.

The list is divided into the following sections: (1) Academic writings; (2) Articles (including letters to journals and newspapers); (3) Lectures and speeches; (4) Libretti and texts; (5) Interviews: (a) Books, journals, theses; (b) Newspapers; (c) Television and CD recordings; and (6) Radio broadcast talks and interviews: (a) British Library and BBC Sound Archives; (b) BBC Radio International; (c) Other.

The content of each category is arranged in chronological order.

## (1)  Academic writings

'An Introduction to Indian Music', 2 vols. (Mus.Bac. thesis, University of Manchester, 1956).

## (2)  Articles (including letters to journals and newspapers)

'The Young British Composer', *The Score*, 15 (1956), 84–5.
'News and Comments: Italy' [short note concerning musical life in Italy in the winter of 1957–8], *The Score*, 22 (1958), 65.
'Problems of a British Composer Today', *The Listener*, 62 (8 October 1959), 563–4.
'In Classes Where They Sing and Play', *Times Educational Supplement*, 10 February 1961, 245.
'Composing Music for School Use', *Making Music*, 46 (Summer 1961), 7–8 [reprinted from Cirencester Grammar School's *Music Magazine*, 1960].
'Sessions's Opera Stirs Berliners' [review of the premiere of Roger Sessions's *Montezuma*], *New York Times*, 21 April 1964, 43.
'A Letter', *Composer*, 15 (April 1965), 22–3.
'The Young Composer in America', *Tempo*, 72 (1965), 2–6 [reprinted from *The American Scholar*, 33/4 (1964)].
'Where Our Colleges Fail', *Times Educational Supplement*, 10 February 1967, 463.

*231*

'Sets or Series', *The Listener*, 79 (22 February 1968), 250.

'Peter Maxwell Davies on Some of His Recent Work', *The Listener*, 81 (23 January 1969), 121.

'Composer's Forum', *Musical Events*, 24 (January 1969), 23–4.

'The Orchestra Is Becoming a Museum', in 'The Symphony Orchestra – Has It a Future?', *Composer*, 37 (Autumn 1970), 6–8.

'*Taverner*: Synopsis and Documentation', *Tempo*, 101 (1972), 4–11.

'Pax Orcadiensis', *Tempo*, 119 (1976), 20–2.

'Benjamin Britten: Tributes and Memories', *Tempo*, 120 (1977), 4.

'Symphony', *Tempo*, 124 (1978), 2–5.

'Foreword', in *Michael Tippett OM: A Celebration*, ed. Geraint Lewis (Tunbridge Wells: Baton Press, 1985), 7.

'Art and Arts: The Arts Council and the Royal Philharmonic Orchestra' [letter], *The Times*, 5 December 1991, 17.

'London's Need for All Its Orchestras' [letter], *The Times*, 9 August 1993, 13.

'Notes from the Antarctic: Glacial Harmony', *The Observer*, 18 January 1998, 5.

'Music to Our Ears: Well Done DFEE' [letter], *Times Educational Supplement*, 21 January 2000, 24.

'Foreword', in *Perspectives on Peter Maxwell Davies*, ed. Richard McGregor (Aldershot: Ashgate, 2000), viii–ix.

'Notes from a Cold Climate: The Diary of Sir Peter Maxwell Davies', in Peter Maxwell Davies *et al.*, *Notes from a Cold Climate: Antarctic Symphony (Symphony No. 8)* (London: Browns, 2001), 13–48 [an extract from the diary was published in the *Sunday Telegraph*, 6 May 2001, 5].

'Studying with Petrassi', *Tempo*, 225 (2003), 7–8.

'Is Serious Music Doomed?', *Incorporated Society of Musicians Music Journal*, June 2005, 28–32 [abridged version of Davies's lecture 'Will Serious Music Become Extinct?' – see below, (3)].

'Four Composition Questions Answered', *MaxOpus*, www.maxopus.com/essays/question.htm.

'Influence of Aboriginal Music', *MaxOpus*, www.maxopus.com/essays/aborig.htm.

## (3)   Lectures and speeches

'Music Composition by Children', contribution to the fourteenth symposium of the Colston Research Society, Bristol University, 2–5 April 1962, in *Music in Education*, ed. Willis Grant (London: Butterworths, 1963), 108–24.

'Music by Schubert, Beethoven, Schoenberg and Maxwell Davies, Introduced and Played by Peter Maxwell Davies', an illustrated lecture given at the Bath Festival, Little Theatre, 23 June 1969; recording available at the BBC Sound Archive, T34065.

'Tradition and an Individual Talent', National Sound Archive lecture series, 13 March 1984; recording available at the British Library Sound Archive, T8585WR.

'Music in Schools', Presidential Address to the Schools Music Association's North of England Education Conference, Chester, 2–4 January 1985; transcript available on *MaxOpus*, www.maxopus.com/essays/north.htm.

'Is Anybody Listening? Reflections on the Composer's Relationship with Society Today', British Library Stefan Zweig Series lecture, 23 May 1995; recording available at the British Library Sound Archive: H4607; transcript available on *MaxOpus*, www.maxopus.com/essays/listen.htm.

'Will Serious Music Become Extinct?' The Royal Philharmonic Society Lecture, 24 April 2005; transcript published by the Royal Philharmonic Society (London, 2005).

'Religion and Politics: A Creative Involvement', speech given at the Bleddfa Centre, Knighton, Powys, 26 November 2005; transcript available on *MaxOpus*, www.maxopus.com/essays/religion.htm.

'A Case for Classical Music, Old and New', keynote speech given at the Incorporated Society of Musicians Annual Conference, 10 April 2007; transcript published in *Incorporated Society of Musicians Music Journal*, June 2007, 16–21.


## (4)  Libretti and texts

*I Can't Compose Today* (1966), two-part canon for mixed voices [unpublished].

*Notre Dame des Fleurs* (1966), music theatre work, text in French.

*Illuxit Leticia* (1966), for two unaccompanied voices [unpublished].

*Taverner* (1962–8, partly reconstructed 1970), opera in two acts, libretto after letters and documents of the sixteenth century.

*Blind Man's Buff* (1972), masque, text after nursery rhymes and Georg Büchner's satirical play *Leonce und Lena* (1836).

*Wedding Telegram (for Gary Kettel)* (1972), for soprano and instrumental ensemble [unpublished].

*A Puzzle-Canon for Gay News* (1972), for four unaccompanied male voices, text in Latin [published in *Gay News*, 13 (December 1972), 13].

*The Martyrdom of St Magnus* (1976), chamber opera in nine scenes, libretto based on the novel *Magnus* (1973) by George Mackay Brown, and his translation of a poem (in *An Orkney Tapestry*, 1969) from Njal's *Saga* (a thirteenth-century Icelandic saga).

*Le Jongleur de Notre Dame* (1977–8), masque, text based on medieval French legend as presented in Goutier de Coinci's miracle play in verse *Les Miracles de la Sainte Vierge* (c. 1220).

*The Two Fiddlers* (1978), opera in two acts for young people to play and sing, libretto based on George Mackay Brown's short story for children of the same name (1974).

*Kirkwall Shopping Songs* (1979), for young children.

*The Lighthouse* (1979), chamber opera in one act with a prologue, libretto based on *A Star for Seamen* by Craig Mair.

*Cinderella* (1979–80), pantomime opera in two acts for children to play and sing.

*The Yellow Cake Revue* (1980), comments in words and music on the threat of uranium mining in Orkney.

*The Medium* (1981), monodrama for solo mezzo-soprano.

*The Rainbow* (1981), music theatre work for young children to sing and play.

*Seven Songs Home* (1981), for a capella children's voices.

*Songs of Hoy* (1981), masque (for children).

*The No. 11 Bus* (1983–4), music theatre work.

*First Ferry to Hoy* (1985), for youth choir, instrumental ensemble, recorders and percussion group.

*The Peat Cutters* (1985), cantata (for brass band, youth choir and children's choir).
*A Grace* (1986), for unison voice(s) and instrument, text in Latin.
*Resurrection* (1986–7 [first commenced in 1963]), opera in one act with a prologue.
*Six Songs for St Andrew's* (1988), song cycle for very young children to play and sing.
*The Great Bank Robbery* (1988–9), music theatre work for children to play and sing.
*Hircus Quando Bibit* (1989), for voice and piano [unpublished].
*Jupiter Landing* (1989), music theatre work in one act for children to play and sing.
*Dinosaur at Large* (1989), music theatre work in one act for children to play and sing.
*Dangerous Errand* (1990), music theatre work for children to play and sing.
*The Spiders' Revenge* (1991), music theatre work for children to play and sing.
*A Selkie Tale* (1992), music theatre work for children to play and sing.
*The Turn of the Tide* (1992), for orchestra, children's chorus and young instrumentalists.
*Seven Summer Songs* (1993), for young children.
*Song for Roderick* (1999), for unaccompanied mixed voices [unpublished].
*Wedding Anthem* (1999), for unaccompanied mixed voices [unpublished].
*Grand Oratorio: The Meaning of Life* (2000), for male voices with castanets and tambourine [unpublished].
*Otter Island* (2003), cantata for children's voices, with piano accompaniment.

## (5)  Interviews

*(a)  Books, journals, theses*

'Peter Maxwell Davies', in Murray Schafer, *British Composers in Interview* (London: Faber and Faber, 1963), 173–82.
'The Origins of Vesalius: Peter Maxwell Davies Talks to Tom Sutcliffe', *Music and Musicians*, 18 (December 1969), 24 and 74.
'A Question of Identity: *Blind Man's Buff* and *Taverner*' [interview with Tom Sutcliffe], *Music and Musicians*, 20 (June 1972), 26–8.
'*Taverner*: Peter Maxwell Davies Talks to Stephen Walsh about His New Opera', *Musical Times*, 113 (July 1972), 653–5.
[Interview with Davies], in Brian Schlotel, 'A Study of Music Written for Use in Education by Some Modern British Composers' (PhD thesis, University of Reading, 1974).
'Safer Out Than In: Peter Maxwell Davies in Conversation [with Alison Hennegan]', *Gay News*, 168 (May–June 1979), 19–20.
'Ancient and Modern 3' [interview with Richard Bolley], *Early Music*, 8/4 (October 1980), 3 and 5.
'Conversations with the Composer', in Paul Griffiths, *Peter Maxwell Davies* (London: Robson Books, 1982), 101–31.
'Peter Maxwell Davies and The Fires of London' [interview with Dorle J. Soria], *HiFi/ Musical America*, 33 (September 1983), 6–8, 31–2 and 40.
'Interview mit Peter Maxwell Davies' [interview, in German, with Brunhilde Sonntag], *Zeitschrift für Musikpädagogik*, 8/21 (1983), 3–17.
'Peter Maxwell Davies and His Opera *The Martyrdom of St Magnus* – An Interview with the Composer [and Henning Lohner]', *Interface, Journal of New Music Research*, 13/4 (1984), 225–47.

'Peter Maxwell Davies', in Paul Griffiths, *New Sounds, New Personalities: British Composers of the 1980s* (London: Faber and Faber, 1985), 31–8.

'Peter Maxwell Davies' [interview with John Schneider], *Guitar Review*, 65 (Spring 1986), 1–7.

'Sir Peter Maxwell Davies in Conversation with Timothy Walker [Part 1]', *Classical Guitar*, 6/4 (December 1987), 11–12, 14, 16 and 18; and 'Part II', 6/5 (January 1988), 19–20 and 22.

'Sir Peter Maxwell Davies', in Richard Dufallo, *Trackings: Composers Speak with Richard Dufallo* (New York and London: Oxford University Press, 1989), 143–55.

'Peter Maxwell Davies's Symphony No. 4' [interview with Stephen Pruslin], *Musical Times*, 130 (September 1989), 520–1 and 523.

'Getting the MAX Habit' [interview with C. Main], *Music Teacher*, February 1990, 13.

[Various comments], in Mike Seabrook, *Max: The Life and Music of Peter Maxwell Davies* (London: Victor Gollancz, 1994).

'A Creature of Many Sounds: Sir Peter Maxwell Davies Gives His Views on the Horn [to Jonathan Stoneman]', *Horn Magazine*, 4/3 (1996), 18–19.

'Eighty Questions for a Sane Composer' [interview with Mark Alburger], *Twentieth Century Music Journal*, 5 (July 1998), 1–10.

'Modern British Composers and British Brass Playing: Interview [with Christopher Horn]', *Brass Bulletin*, 101 (1998), 106–9.

'Conversation with the Composer', in Nicholas Jones, 'Analytical Perspectives on the Third Symphony of Peter Maxwell Davies' (PhD thesis, Cardiff University, 1999), Vol. I, 259–80.

'Max Exposure: An Interview with Peter Maxwell Davies [and David Bündler]', *21st Century Music*, 7/7 (July 2000), 13–16.

'Maxwell Davies and the String Quartet: Paul Driver Talks to Sir Peter Maxwell Davies about the Role of the String Quartet throughout His Work', *Composition Today* [online], October 2002, www.compositiontoday.com/articles/max_string_driver.asp.

[Various comments], in *St Magnus Festival: A Celebration*, ed. Pamela Beasant (Kirkwall, Orkney: Orcadian Ltd, 2002).

'Max's Orkney Saga' [interview with Kenny Mathieson], *Northings – Highlands and Islands Arts Journal* [online], June 2003, www.hi-arts.co.uk/jun03_interview1.htm.

'Interview with Sir Peter Maxwell Davies, Master of the Queen's Music', *Royal Insight* [online], March 2005, www.royalinsight.gov.uk/OutPut/Page3933.asp.

'Charting a Creative Relationship' [Alistair Peebles discusses George Mackay Brown's life and work with Davies], *Northings – Highlands and Islands Arts Journal* [online], April 2006, www.hi-arts.co.uk/apr06_interview_max_on_gmb.html.


*(b) Newspapers*

'Out of the Labyrinth' [interview with Paul Griffiths], *The Times*, 5 September 1984.

'Peter Maxwell Davies: Interview [with James Wierzbicki] regarding *Eight Songs for a Mad King*', *St Louis Post-Dispatch*, 17 November 1985, available online, pages.sbcglobal.net/jameswierzbicki/davies.htm.

'Max Factory' [interview with Michael Church], *Independent*, 9 May 1997.

'The Island Is Full of Noises' [interview with Adam Sweeting], *Guardian*, 17 July 1998.

'The Composer with Some Remote Control: Sir Peter Maxwell Davies Talks to Christopher Morley', *Birmingham Post*, 17 February 1999.

'Seduced by the Sounds of Silence: Peter Maxwell Davies Tells Patricia Nicol Why
    Orkney Inspires Him', *Sunday Times*, 20 June 1999.
'A Lusty Horn and a Roman Carnival: Two Important New Works [*Roma Amor*
    and Concerto for Horn and Orchestra] by Sir Peter Maxwell Davies Bear Witness
    to His Still Abundant Creativity' [interview with Nick Kimberley], *Independent*,
    28 April 2000.
'Silent Harmonies from the Ice Field' [Davies talks to Hilary Finch about the *Antarctic*
    Symphony], *The Times*, 20 April 2001.
'Orcadian Rhythm' [interview with Gillian Bowditch], *Sunday Times*, 16 June 2002.
'Sir Peter Maxwell Davies: On Her Majesty's Service' [interview with Roderic
    Dunnett], *Independent*, 15 March 2004.
'Interview: Sir Peter Maxwell Davies: Airs to the Throne' [interview with Gillian
    Bowditch], *Scotsman*, 29 May 2004.
'Sounds and Silence' [interview with Stephen Moss], *Guardian*, 19 June 2004.
'The Max Factor' [interview with Hilary Finch], *The Times*, 9 July 2004.
'To the Very Ends of the Earth – Peter Maxwell Davies on Putting the Sounds of the
    Antarctic into Music' [interview with Michael Church], *Independent*, 11 February
    2005.
'Peter Maxwell Davies' [interview with Sue Fox], *Sunday Times*, 3 April 2005.
'Queen's Composer Sounds Note of Dissent' [interview with Charlotte Higgins],
    *Guardian*, 16 April 2005.
'Going to the Max' [Davies talks to Richard Morrison about the thirtieth anniversary
    of the St Magnus Festival], *The Times*, 28 April 2007.

*(c)  Television and CD recordings*
'Two Composers, Two Worlds: Dudley Moore and Peter Maxwell Davies' [30-minute
    BBC documentary], *Monitor*, directed by Humphrey Burton, edited by Huw
    Wheldon, broadcast BBC Television, 26 February 1961 [some of the footage is
    used in the *British Music Day* programme and the *Classic Britannia* series – see
    below].
*One Foot in Eden: A Film about Orkney and the Music of Peter Maxwell Davies*
    [50-minute Arts Council England film (ACE077)], directed by Barrie Gavin,
    produced by Platypus Films, broadcast 19 January 1978; available to view online
    (from ac.uk domain addresses only), artsonfilm.wmin.ac.uk/filmcollection.html.
'The Musical House that Max Built – A Profile of the Composer', *South Bank Show*
    (London Weekend Television), directed by Bryan Izzard, edited by Melvyn Bragg,
    broadcast ITV, 21 March 1982.
*British Music Day: Peter Maxwell Davies* [Davies talks to Charles Hazlewood about
    his life and music in this 30-minute programme], directed by Deborah May, BBC
    Classical Music Production, broadcast BBC Knowledge, 3 September 2000.
'Sir Peter Maxwell Davies in Conversation with Paul Driver [22 May 2004]' [CD
    recording], *Peter Maxwell Davies: Miss Donnithorne's Maggot and Eight Songs for a
    Mad King*, Psappha (Psappha Ltd, PSACD1001, 2004), track 17.
*Antarctic Symphony* [Davies discusses and conducts the *Antarctic* Symphony in this
    one-hour film], presented by Mary Ann Kennedy, produced by Mike Newman
    Productions for BBC Scotland, broadcast BBC4, 5 March 2005.
*The Culture Show* [10-minute segment in which Davies talks to Charles Hazlewood
    about his Royal Philharmonic Lecture (see above) and the role of the community
    composer], produced by the BBC, broadcast BBC2, 14 April 2005.

'Max Speaks: A Recorded Interview' [two-hour interview with Roderic Dunnett, CD recording], *Peter Maxwell Davies, A Portrait: His Works, His Life, His Words* (Naxos, 8.558191–92, 2006), CD 2.

'Sir Peter Maxwell Davies in Conversation with Paul Driver [17 July 2006]' [CD recording], *Peter Maxwell Davies: Mr Emmet Takes a Walk*, Psappha, cond. Etienne Siebens (Psappha Ltd, PSACD1002, 2007), track 19.

*Classic Britannia: Sixty Years of British Classical Music*, BBC television documentary series, broadcast BBC4, 22 June, 29 June and 5 July 2007; a specially recorded interview with Davies appears in episodes 1 ('The Landscape Changes: 1945–1962') and 2 ('Modernism and Minimalism: 1962–1980').

## (6) Radio broadcast talks and interviews

*(a) British Library and BBC Sound Archives*
*The following items are available to listen to at the British Library Sound Archive [BLSA] and the BBC Sound Archive [BBCSA]; the LP/tape/CD catalogue number is given for each item.*

'Has Modern Music Gone Too Far?' [Davies in discussion], BBC recording, 19 March 1960 (BBCSA, LP26416).

'Bath Festival' [Davies as conductor, harpsichordist and speaker], BBC recording, 16 June 1962 (BBCSA, T28376).

'Composer's Portrait' [Davies talks to Roger Smalley about his work and introduces some of his music], broadcast BBC Third Programme, 22 November 1965 (BLSA, NP946R; BBCSA, T30362).

'Composers Today No. 3: Innovation' [Davies in conversation with Alexander Goehr and Hans Werner Henze], broadcast BBC Third Programme, 25 June 1967 (BLSA, P210R; BBCSA, T31962).

'The Lively Arts' [Alan Blyth interviews Davies concerning *L'Homme Armé* and *Revelation and Fall*], broadcast BBC Radio 3, 28 February 1968 (BLSA, M1216W).

'Messiaen and the Music of Our Time' [Davies in discussion with Alexander Goehr and Charles Groves], broadcast BBC Radio 3, 12 March 1968 (BLSA, NP454W).

[John Amis interviews Davies regarding *Eight Songs for a Mad King* and *St Thomas Wake*], BBC recording, 30 June 1969 (BBCSA, LP32956).

'Meet the Composer' [Davies introduces music of his own choice and discusses its influence on his development], broadcast BBC Radio 3, 21 July 1969 (BLSA, NP1464W and NP1465W).

'Modern Music: Peter Maxwell Davies' [Davies talks to Stephen Walsh about *Revelation and Fall*], broadcast BBC Radio 3, 30 January 1970 (BLSA, NP1506R).

'A Word in Edgeways: The Artist in Contemporary Society' [Brian Redhead in discussion with Davies, V. S. Naipaul and Mitzi Cunliffe], broadcast BBC Radio 4, 16 October 1971 (BBCSA, T34250).

'Music Magazine' [Davies in interview with C. Ford], BBC recording, 8 July 1972 (BBCSA, T60642).

'Arts Commentary: The Making of an Opera' [Jeremy Noble talks to Davies and others concerned with the production of *Taverner*], broadcast BBC Radio 3, 15 July 1972 (BLSA, NP2005W; BBCSA, LP34683 f-b01).

'Today in Scotland' [Jameson Clark interviews Davies regarding *Stone Litany*], BBC recording, 20 September 1973 (BBCSA, LP35758 f02).

'Musica Nova' [Davies, Luciano Berio, György Ligeti and Martin Dalby in interview
   with Frederick Rimmer], broadcast BBC Radio 3, 22 September 1973 (BBCSA,
   LP35758 f01).
'Concert at Horsham' [Davies introduces *Hymn to St Magnus*], BBC recording,
   18 February 1975 (BBCSA, T37428).
'Conversation' [Davies introduces *Hymn to St Magnus* and talks with George Mackay
   Brown about his life on Orkney], broadcast BBC Radio 3, *c.* 1976 (BLSA,
   NP4380W).
'The Conductor and the Composer' [Davies in discussion with Sir Charles Groves],
   broadcast BBC Radio 3, 16 March 1977 (BLSA, M7027BW; BBCSA, LP37610).
'St Magnus Festival' [Davies talks to John Amis], broadcast BBC Radio 3, 24 June 1977
   (BLSA, T1539R).
'Not Now I'm Listening' [Davies talks about *Runes From a Holy Island*], BBC
   recording, 6 November 1977 (BBCSA, T38304 02).
'Music Weekly' [Davies talks to Michael Oliver about the First Symphony], broadcast
   BBC Radio 3, 5 March 1978 (BBCSA, T54277).
'Petrassi at Seventy-Five', broadcast BBC Radio 3, 14 July 1979 (BLSA, M8076BW;
   BBCSA, T054839).
'Profile: Peter Maxwell Davies' [interview with Ted Harrison], broadcast BBC Radio
   4, 20 June 1980 (BLSA, NP3943R; BBCSA, LP40046 f02).
'Kaleidoscope' [Davies talks to Michael Oliver about *The Lighthouse*], broadcast BBC
   Radio 4, 3 September 1980 (BLSA, NP4124BW).
'Edinburgh International Festival 1980: Festival Comment' [Davies talks to Elaine
   Padmore about *The Lighthouse*], broadcast BBC Radio 3, 5 September 1980 (BLSA,
   NP4130BW).
'An American Voice: The Life and Music of Aaron Copland' [David Wheeler talks to
   Davies and others], broadcast BBC Radio 3, 10 November 1980 (BLSA, T3487W;
   BBCSA, T054804).
'Music Weekly' [Davies talks to Michael Oliver about the Second Symphony], broadcast
   BBC Radio 3, 9 March 1981 (BLSA, NP4798BW; BBCSA, LP40087 b01-b02).
'St Magnus Festival, Orkney 1981' [Davies introduces the first broadcast of *The
   Rainbow*], BBC recording, 22 June 1981 (BBCSA, T049166).
'Desert Island Discs' [Davies in conversation with Roy Plomley], broadcast BBC
   Radio 4, 25 June (repeated 1 July) 1983 (BLSA, T5687BW).
'Prom Talk' [Jeremy Siepmann interviews Davies and Elgar Howarth], broadcast BBC
   Radio 3, 7 August 1983 (BLSA, NP7133BW).
'Big City' [Davies talks about *The No. 11 Bus*], broadcast BBC Radio London, 19
   March 1984 (BLSA, NP7779NW).
'Symphonies and Silence' [the programme follows Davies around various events in
   1984, including the St Magnus Festival], broadcast BBC Radio 3, 17 February 1985
   (BLSA, T7815BW).
[Untitled: Davies comments on the shape and structure of the Third Symphony], BBC
   recording, July 1985 (BBCSA, LP80932 b06).
'Any Questions?' [Davies is a panel member on the news and current affairs programme,
   chaired by John Timpson], broadcast BBC Radio 4, 12 July 1985 (BLSA, T8238R).
'A Word in Edgeways: Creativity and Interference' [Brian Redhead in discussion with
   Davies, Anne Devlin and Jeff Nuttall], broadcast BBC Radio 4, 3 August 1986
   (BLSA, B1100/2).

'Kaleidoscope: Works in Progress' [Michael Berkeley talks to Davies about composing and the importance of teaching music to children], broadcast BBC Radio 4, 4 September 1987 (BLSA, 1CDR0021066).

'St Magnus Festival' [Davies reflects on the first twelve years], broadcast BBC Radio 3, 21 July 1988 (BLSA, B3019/05).

'Proms 1988' [Davies talks to Nicholas Kenyon], broadcast BBC Radio 3, 11 September 1988 (BLSA, B3232/4).

'Kaleidoscope' [Davies talks to Paul Vaughan about *Resurrection*], broadcast BBC Radio 4, 21 September 1988 (BLSA, B3269/2).

'Richard Baker Compares Notes' [discussion with Davies], broadcast BBC Radio 4, 18 April 1989 (BLSA, B4169/2).

'Proms 1989' [Davies talks to Michael Berkeley about the Fourth Symphony and his close association with the Scottish Chamber Orchestra], broadcast BBC Radio 3, 10 September 1989 (BLSA, B4727/05).

'Kaleidoscope' [Davies talks to Paul Allen], broadcast BBC Radio 4, 1 November 1989 (BLSA, B4979/01).

'Music Weekly' [Davies talks to Michael Oliver about 'Maxfest' at the South Bank Centre], broadcast BBC Radio 3, 25 March 1990 (BLSA, B5689/2).

'Kaleidoscope' [Davies talks to Christopher Cook], broadcast BBC Radio 4, 3 April 1990 (BLSA, B5718/10).

'Music Weekly' [Davies and others talk to Michael Oliver about music education], broadcast BBC Radio 3, 15 July 1990 (BLSA, B7025/01).

'Mainly for Pleasure: Radio Goes to Town' [Davies talks to Chris De Souza at the Cheltenham International Festival of Music], broadcast BBC Radio 3, 12 July 1991 (BLSA, B8441/01).

'The Weaver of Time' [Davies and others talk to Kevin Crossley-Holland about George Mackay Brown], broadcast BBC Radio 4, 13 October 1991 (BLSA, B8716/2).

'Proms 1992: Interval Talk' [Davies talks to Anthony Burton about conducting his own and other composers' works], broadcast BBC Radio 3, 13 August 1992 (BLSA, H538/07).

'Peter Maxwell Davies' [Davies talks to Chris De Souza about his four decades of music-making], broadcast BBC Radio 3, 21 November 1994 (BLSA, H4291/2).

'Fairest Isle: Purcell, Our Contemporary?' [Michael Berkeley talks to Davies and other musicians about Purcell's place in the musical pantheon and his influence on composers today], broadcast BBC Radio 3, 8 January 1995 (BLSA, H4508/2).

'Night Waves' [Christopher Cook and Davies discuss the world premiere recording of *Resurrection*], broadcast BBC Radio 3, 4 July 1995 (BLSA, H7034/3).

'Music Matters' [Davies talks to Ivan Hewett about the influence of Sibelius on his work], broadcast BBC Radio 3, 18 November 1995 (BLSA, H6149/2).

'Proms News' [Davies talks to Stephen Johnson], broadcast BBC Radio 3, 4 August 1996 (BLSA, H7557/1).

'[Stewart] Collins and [Stuart] Maconie Live at the Mercury Music Prize' [interview with Davies concerning the nomination of the Collins Classics CD recording (14642) of *The Beltane Fire* and *Caroline Mathilde*], broadcast BBC Radio 1, 10 September 1996 (BLSA, H7767/2).

'The Third at 50' [Humphrey Carpenter introduces programmes celebrating the fiftieth anniversary of the Third Programme and Radio 3 with reminiscences from Davies and others], broadcast BBC Radio 3, 29 September 1996 (BLSA, H7839/2).

'The Envy of the World (1): No Fixed Points' [Humphrey Carpenter talks to Davies and others about the origins of the Third Programme in September 1946], broadcast BBC Radio 3, 29 September 1996 (BLSA, H7833/4).

'Clashing of Symbols' [Nicola Heywood Thomas looks at the symbolism and characters of *The Doctor of Myddfai* with help from Davies and David Pountney], broadcast BBC Radio 3, 5 October 1996 (BLSA, H7887/2).

'Music Machine: Equations and Creation' [Verity Sharp talks to Davies to find out the ways in which he uses numbers; they also discuss the use of mathematical patterns by other composers], broadcast BBC Radio 3, 22 July 1997 (BLSA, H9052/3).

'Music Matters' [Davies talks to Ivan Hewett about his visit to Antarctica], broadcast BBC Radio 3, 18 January 1998 (BLSA, H9630/1).

'Artists' Question Time' [Davies, Martyn Brabbins and Nicholas McGegan answer questions from a studio audience], broadcast BBC Radio 3, 17 October 1998 (BLSA, H10505/2).

'Desert Island Discs' [Davies in conversation with Sue Lawley], broadcast BBC Radio 4, 30 January 2005 (BLSA, 1CDR0022853).

> *The following items have not yet been added to the existing catalogues. However, the British Library Listening and Viewing Service can be contacted with details of the title and broadcast date of any BBC broadcast post-1992 and it will attempt to retrieve a copy for listening from the BBC.*

'Performance on 3' [Davies talks to Piers Burton-Page about *Worldes Blis*, *Eight Songs for a Mad King* and *St Thomas Wake* and introduces performances of these works by the BBC Symphony Orchestra], broadcast BBC Radio 3, 3 February 2004.

'Today' [Davies talks to Edward Stourton about his appointment as Master of the Queen's Music], broadcast BBC Radio 4, 8 March 2004; an audio clip of this four-minute interview is currently available through the BBC website, search.bbc.co.uk/cgi-bin/search/results.pl?q=peter+maxwell+davies&tab=av&scope=all.

'BBC Proms 2004' [Davies talks to Piers Burton-Page about the *Antarctic* Symphony], broadcast BBC Radio 3, 4 August 2004.

'BBC Proms Composer Portraits: Sir Peter Maxwell Davies' [Davies talks to Andrew McGregor about his music and introduces performances of his chamber works by the Artea Quartet], broadcast BBC Radio 3, 4 August 2004.

'Composer of the Week: Peter Maxwell Davies' [Davies in conversation with Donald Macleod – 1: Seascapes and Wave Types, 2: Early Music, 3: Community and Communication, 4: Orkney Stories, 5: Into the New Millennium], broadcast BBC Radio 3, 6–10 September 2004.

'Front Row' [on his 70th birthday, Davies talks to Mark Lawson about his career], broadcast BBC Radio 4, 8 September 2004.

'Music Matters' [Davies talks to Tom Service about the position he holds as the Master of the Queen's Music, the future of contemporary classical music, and the government's recently announced Music Manifesto], broadcast BBC Radio 3, 3 April 2005.

'Private Passions' [Davies in conversation with Michael Berkeley], broadcast BBC Radio 3, 16 April 2006.

'Music Matters: Radio 3 40th Anniversary Special' [Davies explains how his composing life has been enriched by Radio 3], broadcast BBC Radio 3, 6 October 2007.

'Music Matters' [Davies talks to Tom Service about writing the ten Naxos String Quartets], broadcast BBC Radio 3, 13 October 2007.

*(b)  BBC Radio International*

*The following radio programmes, available from BBC Radio International (formerly BBC Transcription Service), can be listened to at the BLSA. These discs were made for overseas broadcast and are not dated in the same way as conventional radio broadcasts. Each programme is supported by accompanying documentation.*

'Talking About Music 144: Peter Maxwell Davies [in discussion with John Amis]' (BLSA, 1LP0153900 S2 BD2, BBC Transcription side number 128690).
'Talking About Music 153: Roger Woodward and Peter Maxwell Davies [in discussion with John Amis]' (BLSA, 1LP0200129 S1 BD1, BBC Transcription side number 131588).
'Talking About Music 215: Peter Maxwell Davies [in discussion with Michael Berkeley]' (BLSA, 1LP0202427 S1 BD2, BBC Transcription side number 141952).
'Talking About Music 248: Peter Maxwell Davies [in discussion with Michael Oliver]' (BLSA, 1LP0203599 S2 BD2, BBC Transcription side number 146268).
'Talking About Music 281: Peter Maxwell Davies on Orkney' (BLSA, 1LP0204751 S1 BD2, BBC Transcription side number 151121).
'Talking About Music 305: Sir Michael Tippett – An 80th Birthday Tribute [from Davies and other musicians]' (BLSA, 1LP0205469 S1 BD1, BBC Transcription side number 154195).
'Talking About Music 367: Peter Maxwell Davies [in discussion with Nicholas Kenyon]' (BLSA, 1LP0207025 S1 BD2, BBC Transcription side number 160159).

*(c)  Other*

'Sir Peter Maxwell Davies: A Conversation with Bruce Duffie [Autumn 1985]', broadcast WNIB-FM, Classical 97, Chicago, 4 September 1994 and 4 September 1999; transcript lodged at the Archive of Contemporary Music at Northwestern University, USA, and available online, www.bruceduffie.com/pmd.html.
'Meer und Kathedral: Porträt Peter Maxwell Davies' [radio interview, in German, with Max Nyffeler], broadcast Bayerische Rundfunk, Munich, 28 September 1998; transcript available on *MaxOpus*, www.maxopus.com/essays/bayer.htm.
'Workshop Discussion: Naxos String Quartet No. 1', Canterbury Christ Church University Music Department, 17 October 2002, www.canterbury.ac.uk/arts-humanities/Music/SirPeter/NaxosStringQuartets/StringQuartetNo1/Workshop.aspx.
'Workshop Discussion: Naxos String Quartet No. 8', Canterbury Christ Church University Music Department, 10 March 2006, www.canterbury.ac.uk/arts-humanities/Music/SirPeter/NaxosStringQuartets/StringQuartetNo8/Workshop.aspx.
'Interview with Sir Peter Maxwell Davies' [Davies discusses his latest festival premieres with Sandy Burnett], July 2008, 22-minute recordable audio clip, www.intermusica.co.uk/audio.

# Source material used in the works
# of Peter Maxwell Davies, 1957–2006

*Richard McGregor*

This appendix presents a listing of Peter Maxwell Davies's works that have been identified as having acknowledged, or suggested, source material, such as plainchant. This information is presented through a chronological listing, with each work identified by year of completion, followed by the title of the work, the identification of source(s), the sets and magic squares derived from the source(s), and any relevant general comments. The identification of such sources is based on the following collections:

Willi Apel and Archibald T. Davidson, *Historical Anthology of Music, Vol. 1: Oriental, Medieval and Renaissance Music*, 2nd rev. edn (Cambridge, Mass.: Harvard University Press, 1949) [*HAM1*]

Benedictines of Solesmes (ed.), *Liber Usualis* (Tournai, Belgium: Desclée & Co., 1953) [*LU*]

John Stevens (ed.), *Musica Britannica, Vol. 4: Mediaeval Carols* (London: Stainer & Bell, 1952) [*MB4*]

Kenneth Elliot (ed.), *Musica Britannica, Vol. 15: Music of Scotland 1500–1700* (London: Stainer & Bell, 1957) [*MB15*]

| Year | Work | Source(s) | Sets and magic squares | General comments |
|---|---|---|---|---|
| 1957 | Alma Redemptoris Mater | Dum Compleréntur (LU, 884 and HAM1, 65), Alma Redemptoris Mater (LU, 277 (273) and HAM1, 65).[1] | 10-set derived from Alma chant. | |
| 1957 | St Michael | Dies Irae (LU, 1810 and HAM1, 14), Sanctus (LU, 1814), Agnus Dei (LU, 1815). | | Also possible references to Requiem Aeternam, Kyrie Eleison, Dona Eis Pacem. |
| 1959 | Ricercar and Doubles | 'Too Many a Well' (MB4). | | |
| 1959 | Five Motets | [unidentified] | | 'Alma Redemptoris' text included but derivation of the set from the chant is unlikely. |
| 1960 | O Magnum Mysterium | Puer Natus (LU, 408), Lux Fulgebit (LU, 403) (Nativity); see also O Magnum Mysterium (LU, 382). | | |
| 1960 | Quartet | Monteverdi: Sonata sopra Sancta Maria. | | |
| 1961 | Leopardi Fragments | Monteverdi: Vespers. | | |
| 1961 | Te Lucis Ante Terminum | Te Lucis Ante Terminum (LU, 266). | | |
| 1961 | 'Carol on St Steven' (from Four Carols) | Te Lucis Ante Terminum (LU, 266). | | Plus other plainchants? |
| 1962 | Sinfonia | Four movements from Monteverdi's Vespers. | | |
| 1962 | First Fantasia on an 'In Nomine' of John Taverner | Gloria Tibi Trinitas (LU, 914), Taverner: In Nomine. | | Gloria Tibi Trinitas is for Trinity Sunday. See also, possibly, Thomas Tomkins's In Nomine (HAM1, 176). |
| 1963 | Veni Sancte Spiritus | Veni Sancte Spiritus (LU, 880 and HAM1, 80), Dum Compleréntur (LU, 884 and HAM1, 80). | | |
| 1964 | Second Fantasia on John Taverner's 'In Nomine' | Gloria Tibi Trinitas (LU, 914), Taverner: In Nomine. | | See First Taverner Fantasia. |

| Year | Work | Source(s) | Sets and magic squares | General comments |
| --- | --- | --- | --- | --- |
| 1964 | Ecce Manus Tradentis [In Illo Tempore] | Good Friday plainchant; Tantum Ergo (LU, 1852), Gloria Tibi Trinitas (LU, 914), Taverner: In Nomine. | Extended transformation set. | See First Taverner Fantasia. This version of the Tantum Ergo chant, of Spanish origin, is for the Benediction of the Blessed Sacraments. Davies's motet In Illo Tempore was first performed in 1965 at the Wardour Castle Summer School of Music as Ecce Manus Tradentis. The instrumental introduction Eram Quasi Agnus was added in 1969 and the work as a whole goes under the title of Ecce Manus Tradentis. |
| (1969) | Eram Quasi Agnus [the introduction to Ecce Manus Tradentis] | Eram Quasi Agnus (LU, 644). | Extended transformation set. | Maundy Thursday. |
| 1965 | Seven In Nomine | Gloria Tibi Trinitas (LU, 914), Taverner: In Nomine, John Bull: keyboard piece from the Fitzwilliam Virginal Book, William Blitheman: organ piece from the Mulliner Book. | | David Roberts remarks that the original movements are based on the In Nomine cantus firmus (the Sarum antiphon Gloria Tibi Trinitas).[2] |
| 1965–6 | Revelation and Fall | Gloria Tibi Trinitas (LU, 914). | | |
| 1967 | Hymnos | [unidentified] | | 'The work is closely connected with the setting of a related text, "O lux quam non videt alia lux", which I used in my Five Motets of 1959.'[3] Hymnos is also related to Worldes Blis.[4] |
| 1967 | Antechrist | Haec Dies (LU, 783 and HAM1, 12), Deo Confitemini Domino (HAM1, 32a). | | Haec Dies is for Easter. Deo Confitemini Domino is a thirteenth-century motet. According to Paul Griffiths, Davies also uses the Gloria Tibi Trinitas plainchant.[5] |
| 1968 | Missa Super L'Homme Armé | L'Homme Armé (HAM1, 61?), Good Friday plainchant Victimae Paschali Laudes (HAM1, 16b)?; Crux Fidelis (LU, 709)? | | Plus Agnus Dei? |

| Year | Work | Source | Notes |
|---|---|---|---|
| 1969 | Worldes Blis | Nobilis Humilis (HAM1, 25b), Worldes Blis (HAM1, 23b), Victimae Paschali Laudes (LU, 780 and HAM1, 16b), Dies Irae (LU, 1810 and HAM1, 14), Ave, Plena Gracia. | Nobilis Humilis is a twelfth-century hymn; Ave, Plena Gracia is a carol by Davies (1964). |
| 1969 | Eight Songs for a Mad King | Handel: Messiah. | Plus other sources.[6] |
| 1969 | Vesalii Icones | Victimae Paschali Laudes (LU, 780 and HAM1, 16b). | Good Friday plainchant. This work also relates to Worldes Blis.[7] |
| 1969 | St Thomas Wake | John Bull: Parthenia (1611). | Uses 16–18 pitch sets. |
| 1970 | Taverner / Points and Dances from Taverner | Gloria Tibi Trinitas (LU, 914), Taverner: In Nomine. | See First Taverner Fantasia. |
| 1970 | Ut Re Mi | Quodcumque in Orbe (LU, 1334). | Hymn to St Peter (18/19 January). The use of Quodcumque in Orbe in this work is according to David Roberts.[8] In the volume of sketches at the British Library (Add. Ms. 71383) Ut Re Mi has been grouped with a plainchant for St Lucy, In Tua Patientia (LU, 1322; 13 December) – but it is not at present clear if it is associated with this work. |
| 1971 | From Stone to Thorn | Dies Irae (LU, 1810 and HAM1, 14), Victimae Paschali Laudes (LU, 780 and HAM1, 16b). | |
| 1972 | Hymn to St Magnus | Nobilis Humilis (HAM1, 25b). | Nobilis Humilis is a twelfth-century hymn. As Peter Owens has shown, this work relates to Worldes Blis.[9] |
| 1972 | Veni Sancte – Veni Creator Spiritus (Dunstable) | Veni Sancte Spiritus (LU, 880 and HAM1, 80), Veni Creator Spiritus (LU, 885 and HAM1, 80). | |
| 1972 | Tenebrae super Gesualdo | [source unidentified] | David Roberts and Peter Owens have identified links between this work and Hymn to St Magnus and Worldes Blis.[10] |
| 1974 | Dark Angels | A plainchant for the Feast of Pentecost.[11] | See Black Pentecost. |
| 1974 | Three Organ Voluntaries | 'Fethy O God Abuse' (anon.), 'All Sons of Adam' (MB15). | |

| Year | Work | Source(s) | Sets and magic squares | General comments |
|---|---|---|---|---|
| 1975 | *Ave Maris Stella* | *Ave Maris Stella* (*LU*, 1259). | Moon (9×9). | |
| 1975 | *Three Studies for Percussion* | *Ave Maris Stella* (*LU*, 1259). | | |
| 1976 | *Martyrdom of St Magnus* | *Ave Maris Stella* (*LU*, 1259). | Moon (9×9). | |
| 1976 | *Anakreontika* | *Ave Maris Stella* (*LU*, 1259). | | |
| 1976 | *Symphony No. 1* | *Sederunt Principes* (*LU*, 417), *Veni Sancte Spiritus* (*LU*, 880), *Veni Creator Spiritus* (*LU*, 885), *Ave Maris Stella* (*LU*, 1259); also uses Incipit from second part of *Dum Compleréntur* (*LU*, 884). | *Veni Creator Spiritus*: Moon (9×9; used in third movement); also a 7-transformation set. | *Ave Maris Stella* chant used in second movement. |
| 1977 | *A Mirror of Whitening Light* | *Sederunt Principes* (Feast of St Stephen, 26 December: *LU*, 416), *Veni Sancte Spiritus* (*LU*, 1837). | *Veni Sancte Spiritus*: Mercury (8×8). *Sederunt Principes*: Sun (6×6)? | The title refers to alchemy but also refers to the spirit Mercurius, or Quicksilver. According to David Roberts, the antiphon *Ad Invocandum Spiritum Sanctum* (*LU*, 1837) is also used.[12] |
| 1977 | *Westerlings* | *Veni Sancte Spiritus* (*LU*, 1837). | Mercury (8×8). | The use of *Veni Sancte Spiritus* in this work is according to David Roberts.[13] |
| 1978 | *Le Jongleur de Notre Dame* | *Gloriosae Virginis* (*LU*, 1623F). | | This plainchant (for The Nativity of the Blessed Virgin Mary), is for 8 September – Davies's birthday. |
| 1978 | *Salome* | *Joannes Vocabitur* (*LU*, 1504). | Venus (7×7). | Plainchant for John the Baptist (24 June). |
| 1979 | *Black Pentecost* | A plainchant for the Feast of Pentecost. | Venus (7×7), Sun (6×6), Mars (5×5). Mars square found in sketches; Davies sketch says: 'superpose magic squ and twelve set throughout' (Add. Ms. 71331). | See *Dark Angels*. |
| 1979 | *The Lighthouse* | [unidentified] | Venus (7×7). | |

| Year | Work | Chant (LU) | Charts / squares | Notes |
|---|---|---|---|---|
| 1980 | Symphony No. 2 | Panem di Caelo (LU, 1035), Nativitas Tua (LU, 1627). | Panem di Caelo: Mars (5×5). Nativitas Tua: Sun (6×6). More complex multiple charts. | Panem di Caelo is for the thirteenth Sunday after Pentecost. Nativitas Tua is for 8 September – Davies's birthday. |
| 1981 | Piano Sonata | Panem di Caelo (LU, 1035), Nativitas Tua (LU, 1627). | | |
| 1981 | Brass Quintet | Lux Aeterna (LU, 1815)? | Probably shares sets with Image, Reflection, Shadow. | |
| 1981 | The Medium | | | |
| 1982 | Image, Reflection, Shadow | 'Hymn to St Ignatius' (LU, 1354?). Lux Aeterna (LU, 1815). | Sun (6×6). Moon (9×9) for this chant? Contains more extended charts, possibly derived from Sun and Venus squares; also has four charts, and extended compound transformation set(s). | |
| 1982 | Organ Sonata | 'Lamentations of Jeremiah' (LU, 626 [+ 669, 715?]), Ego Vir Videns (LU, 673). | Moon (9×9). | Plainchant for Maundy Thursday, First Nocturn (see MS Mus. 1405). |
| 1983 | Into the Labyrinth | Victimae Paschali Laudes (LU, 780), Dies Irae (LU, 1810), Sancte Michael Archangele (LU, 1655). | Victimae: Moon (9×9)? | Victimae is for Easter Sunday, Sancte Michael is for 29 September (the Feast Day of St Michael). Both Victimae and Dies Irae chants are referred to in sketches (Add. Ms. 71339). |
| 1983 | Sinfonietta Accademica | Victimae Paschali Laudes (LU, 780), Dies Irae (LU, 1810), Sancte Michael Archangele (LU, 1655). | | See Into the Labyrinth. |
| 1984 | Symphony No. 3 | Sancte Michael Archangele (LU, 1655). | Mercury (8×8). Also uses Sun (6×6, which Davies labels 'Metin' square) and Venus (7×7). Has various extended multiple charts. | See Nicholas Jones's articles in Tempo and Music & Letters.[14] |

| Year | Work | Source(s) | Sets and magic squares | General comments |
| --- | --- | --- | --- | --- |
| 1986 | Violin Concerto | *Mor Fea.* | | Highland bagpipe tune composed by Davies. |
| 1986 | *Winterfold* | *Hodie nobis* (*LU*, 375) but in 'a more interesting Portugese variant from a manuscript source',[15] | | |
| 1987 | Strathclyde Concerto No. 1 | *Dum Compleréntur* (*LU*, 884), *Veni Creator Spiritus* (*LU*, 885). | | Davies labels *Dum Compleréntur* chant 'Your tune' (Add. Ms. 71351). Possibly also uses *Veni Sancte Spiritus* (*LU*, 880). |
| 1987 | *Resurrection* | *Laetentur Caeli* (*LU*, 408), *Puer Natus* (*LU*, 408), *Herodes Iratus Occidit* (*LU*, 427), *Victimae Paschali Laudes* (*LU*, 780), *Cor Meum* (*LU*, 1474). (Alternative version of *Laetentur Caeli* is at *LU*, 394 but set suggests use of *LU*, 387.) | | *Laetentur Caeli* and *Puer Natus* are for the Nativity; *Herodes* chant is for 27 December (Massacre of the Innocents), and *Victimae* for the Resurrection. Davies's programme note for the opera confirms use of all four of these chants.[16] Sketches also have a reference to *Worldes Blis* (Add. Ms. 71284). |
| 1988 | Strathclyde Concerto No. 2 | *Franciscus Pauper et Humilis* (*LU*, 1644), *Dum Compleréntur* (*LU*, 884), *Ego Sum Pauper* (*LU*, 1647). | Moon (9×9) is implied for *Ego Sum Pauper* (derivation in sketches; Add. Ms. 71353). | *Franciscus Pauper* is for 17 September; *Ego Sum Pauper* is for 18 September. |
| 1988 | Trumpet Concerto | *Franciscus Pauper et Humilis* (*LU*, 1644), *Ego Sum Pauper* (*LU*, 1647). | Moon (9×9) for *Franciscus Pauper* chant? (Appears in sketches (Add. Ms. 71356), but not clear whether it applies to the work.) | *Laetentur Coeli* (*LU*, 387), *Puer Natus* (*LU*, 408), *Herodes Iratus Occidit* (*LU*, 427) and *Cor Meum* (*LU*, 1474 – see below): these four chants are probably not for the concerto – possibly misfiled? |
| 1989 | *Threnody on a Plainsong for Michael Vyner* | *Cor Meum* (*LU*, 1474) [or *Aquae Multae* (*LU*, 1690)?]. | | There appears to be some confusion over which chant is used in this work. *Cor Meum* is for 26 May. *Aquae Multae* is for 17 October but has the line 'Defecit caro mea et cor meum'. |

| | | | | |
|---|---|---|---|---|
| 1989 | Strathclyde Concerto No. 3 | Dum Compleréntur (LU, 884)? | Mercury (8×8): has Strathclyde Concerto No. 1 chart repeated, changed, compound set(s)); Moon (9×9: set partitioning here is more complicated); 12×12 square. | |
| 1989 | Symphony No. 4 | Adorna Thalalmum (LU, 1359), Dum Compleréntur (LU, 884). | Adorna Thalalmum: Moon (9×9) or Uranus (10×10). Dum Compleréntur has a 20-note compound set transformation. | Adorna Thalalmum is for 2 February. |
| 1990 | Strathclyde Concerto No. 4 | Cumha craobh nan teud. | Uranus (10×10)? | Classical pipe tune. |
| 1991 | Strathclyde Concerto No. 5 | Haydn: Overture to L'isola disabitata, Jan Albert Ban: Vanitas. | L'isola disabitata: Moon (9×9), set lines called 'modes' – see Symphony No. 6. | |
| 1991 | Strathclyde Concerto No. 6 | Third Sunday of Advent (LU, 334ff)? | See Naxos Quartet No. 6: here, 8- or 12-set? | |
| 1992 | The Turn of the Tide | [unidentified] | According to Davies, this piece has a magic square.[17] | |
| 1992 | Strathclyde Concerto No. 7 | [unidentified] | Moon (9×9); Mars (5×5). | See MS Mus. 1417. |
| 1993 | Strathclyde Concerto No. 8 | [unidentified] | Moon (9×9) and extended transformation squares; Mars (5×5). | See MS Mus. 1417. |
| 1993 | Chat Moss | Haec Dies (LU, 778, 801), Domine Audivi (LU, 695). (Canticle for Habbakuk is at LU, 692.) | | Haec Dies is for Easter; Domine Audivi (Habakkuk's Prayer) is for Good Friday. |

| Year | Work | Source(s) | Sets and magic squares | General comments |
|---|---|---|---|---|
| 1993 | Symphony No. 5 | Haec Dies (LU, 778, 801), Domine Audivi (LU, 695). (Canticle for Habbakuk is at LU, 692.) Also uses Chat Moss. | Mercury (8×8) for both chants. Haec Dies chant is reduced through Venus (7×7), Sun (6×6), Mars (5×5), Jupiter (4×4) to Saturn (3×3) – see Naxos Quartet No. 3. | |
| 1994 | Strathclyde Concerto No. 9 | Veni Sancte Spiritus (LU, 880)? – see also Veni Sancte Spiritus (LU, 1837). | Mercury (8×8). | LU, 880 version is for Whit Sunday; LU, 1837 is an Invocation to the Holy Ghost – see A Mirror of Whitening Light. See also MS Mus. 1423. |
| 1995 | Time and the Raven | Immolabit Hedum Multitudo (LU, 926), 'Améwara Inatäija Verses', 'Die Gesang der gelben Blume', Parade. | | Immolabit is for Corpus Christi; 'Améwara' is an aboriginal song; 'Die Gesang' is a melody by Hans Henny Jahnn from his Perrudja (1929); Parade is an early piano piece (1949) by Davies. |
| 1995 | The Doctor of Myddfai | [unidentified] | | May use Symphony No. 5 charts. |
| 1996 | Symphony No. 6 | Immolabit Hedum Multitudo (LU, 926), 'Améwara Inatäija Verses', 'Die Gesang der gelben Blume', Parade. | Immolabit: Moon (9×9); 'Die Gesang': Uranus (10×10) and Venus (7×7); 'Améwara': additional sets from Symphony No. 5? Parade: Mercury (8×8). | See Time and the Raven. |
| 1997 | Job | Nudus Egressus Utero (from Job 1:21). Not a Liber Usualis chant.[18] | Venus (7×7). | See initial sketches for Symphony No. 6 (MS Mus. 1429–31). |
| 1997 | The Jacobite Rising | [unidentified] | Mars (5×5). | 'Crux square' (see MS Mus. 1438). |
| 1997 | Orkney Saga II | 'Hymn to St Magnus' (probably Nobilis Humilis; HAM1, 25b), fourteenth-century Icelandic plainchant. | | See Worldes Blis, Hymn to St Magnus and Orkney Saga III. |

| Year | Title | Source | Magic square | Notes |
|---|---|---|---|---|
| 1998 | A Reel for Seven Fishermen | Crux Fidelis (LU, 709). | | Crux Fidelis is for Good Friday. |
| 1998 | Roma Amor | Dies Irae (LU, 1810 and HAM1, 14), Sanctus (LU, 1814). | | See St Michael. Sanctus plainchant is used in the middle, slow movement of Roma. |
| 1999 | Orkney Saga III | 'Hymn to St Magnus' (probably Nobilis Humilis; HAM1, 25b), fourteenth-century Icelandic plainchant. | | See Worldes Blis, Hymn to St Magnus and Orkney Saga II. |
| 1999 | Mr Emmet Takes a Walk | J.S. Bach: Prelude in F minor (Das Wohltemperirte Clavier, Book 2), Andrea Gabrieli: Edipo Tiranno, Mozart: 'Come furia disperata' (Don Giovanni), Schumann: Symphony No. 2. | Moon (9×9). | |
| 1999 | Spinning Jenny | [unidentified] | 'I have based its construction, for the first time, on a magic square of twelve.'[119] | |
| 2000 | Symphony No. 7 | Haydn: [one of the] Op. 20 String Quartets (in the symphony's second movement). | Mars (5×5), Sun (6×6); Mercury (8×8); Moon (9×9). | Fourth movement: connection to Symphony No. 1? See MS Mus. 1449. |
| 2000 | Symphony No. 8 | Dum Compleréntur (LU, 884). | Moon (9×9) and extended transformation set. | 'These two sounds – the ice-break and the avalanche – determined there and then that I use a Pentecost plainsong, associated with the descent of the Holy Spirit upon the Apostles, in this palpably most un-Christian symphony.'[20] See MS Mus. 1452. |
| 2001 | Crossing King's Reach | Nudus Egressus Utero.[21] | Venus and Mars squares. | See Job. |
| 2001 | Dove, Star-Folded | Greek Byzantine Hymn. | | |
| 2001 | De Assumptione Beatae Mariae Virginis | Quae Est Ista (LU, 1600). | | The chant is for 15 August (the Feast of the Assumption of the Blessed Virgin Mary). |
| 2002 | Veni Creator Spiritus (for flute and bass clarinet) | Dum Compleréntur (LU, 884), Veni Creator Spiritus (LU, 885). | Veni: Moon (9×9). | |

| Year | Work | Source(s) | Sets and magic squares | General comments |
|------|------|-----------|------------------------|------------------|
| 2002 | Veni Creator Spiritus (for organ) | Veni Creator Spiritus (LU, 885)? | | |
| 2002 | Linguae Ignis | Dum Compleréntur (LU, 884), Veni Creator Spiritus (LU, 885). | | |
| 2002 | Mass | Dum Compleréntur (LU, 884), Veni Creator Spiritus (LU, 885). | | |
| 2002 | Piano Trio | 'Chant for September 8th'[22] (Nativitas Tua: LU, 1627?). | | See Symphony No. 2? 8 September is Davies's birthday. |
| 2002 | Naxos Quartet No. 1 | Dum Compleréntur (LU, 884). | Material also drawn from the middle, slow section of the Strathclyde Concerto No. 3: 'This material was subjected to a process of transformation through a twelve-unit "most perfect pandiagonal magic square".'[23] | |
| 2003 | Seven Skies of Winter | Dum Compleréntur (LU, 884). | | |
| 2003 | Naxos Quartet No. 3 | Audi Filia et Vide (LU, 1755), In Nomine melody. | Audi Filia: 'magic square of Saturn (3×3) within one of Mars (5×5) within one of Venus (7×7) – all this alongside an independent square of the Moon (9×9).'[24] Compare this technique with Symphony No. 5. | Audi Filia chant is for 22 November (St Cecilia). See Rodney Lister's chapter in this present volume. |

| 2003 | *Dum Complêrentur* | *Dum Complêrentur* (*LU*, 884). | |
| 2004 | *Michael Archangelus* | *Sancte Michael Archangele* (*LU*, 1655).[25] | |
| 2004 | *The Fall of the Leafe* | Martin Peerson: *The Fall of the Leafe* (keyboard piece from the *Fitzwilliam Virginal Book*). | 'Out of the thematic material of the Peerson I have fashioned, by permutation and a magic square filter, a theme of my own which appears at the outset.'[26] |
| 2005 | Naxos Quartet No. 6 | Advent plainchant: *Dominica Tertia Adventus* (*LU*, 340ff?), Christmas plainchant: *Haec Dies* (*LU*, 403ff)? | |
| 2005 | *O Verbum Patris* | *Verbum Caro* (*LU*, 469) (or at *LU* 390), *Dominica Tertia Adventus*? (*LU*, 340ff?), Christmas plainchant: *Haec Dies* (*LU*, 403ff)? | *Verbum Caro* is for Epiphany (*LU*, 469) or the Nativity (*LU*, 390). See Naxos Quartet No. 7. |
| 2005 | Naxos Quartet No. 7 | *Quae Est Ista* (*LU*, 1600), *Vidimus Stellam* (*LU*, 462), *O Verbum Patris*. | *Verbum Caro*: Mercury (8×8)? |
| 2005 | *St Bartholomew's Prayer* | *Te Gloriosus* (*LU*, 1613) or *Vos Qui* (*LU*, 1614). | *Vidimus Stellam*: Sun (6×6). *O Verbum Patris*: Mercury (8×8). |
| 2006 | Naxos Quartet No. 8 | *Quae Est Ista*? (*LU*, 1600 or 1679), John Dowland: *Queen Elizabeth Galliard*. | *Quae Est Ista* is for 15 August. *O Verbum Patris* is Davies's own setting (2005) of the poem by Hildegard von Bingen. |
| | | | *Te Gloriosus* is for 24 August, *Vos Qui* for 25 August. |

1. Please note that *Dum Complêrentur* is also at *LU*, 903 (for the Saturday in Whitsun Week).
2. See David Roberts, 'Techniques of Composition in the Music of Peter Maxwell Davies' (PhD thesis, Birmingham University, 1985), 282.
3. Peter Maxwell Davies, programme note for *Hymnos*, *MaxOpus*, www.maxopus.com/works/hymnos.htm.
4. See Peter Owens, '*Worldes Blis* and Its Satellites', in *Perspectives on Peter Maxwell Davies*, ed. Richard McGregor (Aldershot: Ashgate, 2000), 43.
5. Paul Griffiths, *Peter Maxwell Davies* (London: Robson Books, 1982), 60.
6. 'I have, however, quoted far more than the *Messiah* – if not the notes at least aspects of the styles of many composers are referred to, from Handel to Birtwistle' (Davies, programme note for *Eight Songs for a Mad King*, in Griffiths, *Peter Maxwell Davies*, 148).

7. See Owens, 'Worldes Blis', 43.

8. See Roberts, review of Griffiths, *Peter Maxwell Davies*, in *Contact*, 24 (1982), 23–5.

9. Owens, 'Worldes Blis', 43.

10. See Roberts, 'Techniques of Composition', 274; and Owens, 'Worldes Blis', 43.

11. See Roderic Dunnett, 'Introduction to Peter Maxwell Davies's Mass, *Missa Parvula* and Other Sacred Works', reprinted from Hyperion Records, *MaxOpus*, www.maxopus.com/essays/sacred.htm.

12. Roberts, review of Davies's scores, in *Contact*, 23 (1981), 28.

13. Ibid., 26–9.

14. Nicholas Jones, '"Preliminary Workings": The Precompositional Process in Maxwell Davies's Third Symphony', *Tempo*, 204 (1998), 14–22, and 'Peter Maxwell Davies's "Submerged Cathedral": Architectural Perspectives on the Third Symphony', *Music & Letters*, 81/3 (2000), 402–32.

15. See Davies's programme note for *Winterfold*, Chester Music Ltd, www.chesternovello.com/Default.aspx?TabId=2432&State_3041=2&worldId_3041=11094.

16. Davies, programme note for *Resurrection*, *MaxOpus*, www.maxopus.com/works/resurrec.htm.

17. Davies, programme note for *The Turn of the Tide*, *MaxOpus*, www.maxopus.com/works/turntide.htm.

18. A possible version of the chant used by Davies can be found at the La Trobe University Medieval Music Database, www.lib.latrobe.edu.au/MMDB/Alist/AfileN19.htm.

19. Davies, programme note for *Spinning Jenny*, *MaxOpus*, www.maxopus.com/works/spinning.htm.

20. Davies, programme note for Symphony No. 8, *MaxOpus*, www.maxopus.com/works/symph_8.htm.

21. Davies, programme note for *Crossing King's Reach*, *MaxOpus*, www.maxopus.com/works/crossing.htm.

22. Davies, programme note for Piano Trio, *MaxOpus*, www.maxopus.com/works/pianotri.htm.

23. Davies, liner notes for the First Naxos String Quartet (CD, Naxos: 8.557396, 2004).

24. Davies, liner notes for the Third Naxos String Quartet (CD, Naxos: 8.557397, 2005).

25. 'The plainsong is taken from the *Liber Usualis*, and is for the Feast of the Archangel St Michael' (Davies, programme note for *Michael Archangelus*, score (London: Chester Music, 2004)).

26. Davies, programme note for *The Fall of the Leafe*, *MaxOpus*, www.maxopus.com/works/fall.htm.

# Index

255